STUDY PLANNER

CHAPTER 01 문장의 구조	학습일	
UNIT 01	월	일
UNIT 02	월	일
Review Test	월	일

	학습일	
UNIT 13	월	일
UNIT 14	월	일
UNIT 15	월	일
Review Test	월	일

CHAPTER 02 to부정사	학습일	
UNIT 03	월	일
UNIT 04	월	일
Review Test	월	일

CHAPTER 08 비교 구문	학습일	
UNIT 16	월	일
UNIT 17	월	일
Review Test	월	일

CHAPTER 03 동명사	학습일	
UNIT 05	월	일
UNIT 06	월	일
Review Test	월	일

CHAPTER 09 분사	학습일	
UNIT 18	월	일
UNIT 19	월	일
Review Test	월	일

CHAPTER 04 시제	학습일	
UNIT 07	월	일
UNIT 08	월	일
Review Test	월	일

CHAPTER 10 접속사	학습일	
UNIT 20	월	일
UNIT 21	월	일
Review Test	월	일

CHAPTER 05 조동사	학습일	
UNIT 09	월	일
UNIT 10	월	일
Review Test	월	일

CHAPTER 11 가정법	학습일	
UNIT 22	월	일
UNIT 23	월	일
Review Test	월	일

CHAPTER 06 수동태	학습일	
UNIT 11	월	일
UNIT 12	월	일
Review Test	월	일

CHAPTER 12 특수 구문	학습일	
UNIT 24	월	일
UNIT 25	월	일
Review Test	월	일

SCORECARD

PASS 기준: Level 2 → 25점 이상, Level 3 → 41점 이상, Review Test → 60점 이상

CHAPTER 01 문장의 구조	Level 2	Level 3
UNIT 01	/ 30점	/ 50점
UNIT 02	/ 30점	/ 50점
Review Test		/ 70점

CHAPTER 07 관계사	Level 2	Level 3
UNIT 13	/ 30점	/ 50점
UNIT 14	/ 30점	/ 50점
UNIT 15	/ 30점	/ 50점
Review Test		/ 70점

CHAPTER 02 to부정사	Level 2	Level 3
UNIT 03	/ 30점	/ 50점
UNIT 04	/ 30점	/ 50점
Review Test		/ 70점

CHAPTER 08 비교 구문	Level 2	Level 3
UNIT 16	/ 30점	/ 50점
UNIT 17	/ 30점	/ 50점
Review Test		/ 70점

CHAPTER 03 동명사	Level 2	Level 3
UNIT 05	/ 30점	/ 50점
UNIT 06	/ 30점	/ 50점
Review Test		/ 70점

CHAPTER 09 분사	Level 2	Level 3
UNIT 18	/ 30점	/ 50점
UNIT 19	/ 30점	/ 50점
Review Test		/ 70점

CHAPTER 04 시제	Level 2	Level 3
UNIT 07	/ 30점	/ 50점
UNIT 08	/ 30점	/ 50점
Review Test		/ 70점

CHAPTER 10 접속사	Level 2	Level 3
UNIT 20	/ 30점	/ 50점
UNIT 21	/ 30점	/ 50점
Review Test		/ 70점

CHAPTER 05 조동사	Level 2	Level 3
UNIT 09	/ 30점	/ 50점
UNIT 10	/ 30점	/ 50점
Review Test		/ 70점

CHAPTER 11 가정법	Level 2	Level 3
UNIT 22	/ 30점	/ 50점
UNIT 23	/ 30점	/ 50점
Review Test		/ 70점

CHAPTER 06 수동태	Level 2	Level 3
UNIT 11	/ 30점	/ 50점
UNIT 12	/ 30점	/ 50점
Review Test		/ 70점

CHAPTER 12 특수 구문	Level 2	Level 3
UNIT 24	/ 30점	/ 50점
UNIT 25	/ 30점	/ 50점
Review Test		/ 70점

내신공략
중학영문법

문제풀이책
3

내신공략 중학영문법의 구성 및 특징

시리즈 구성

내신공략 중학영문법 시리즈는 중학교 영어 교과과정의 문법 사항을 3레벨로 나누어 수록하고 있으며, 각각의 레벨은 **개념이해책**과 **문제풀이책**으로 구성됩니다. 두 책을 병행하여 학습하는 것이 가장 이상적인 학습법이지만, 교사와 학생의 필요에 따라 둘 중 하나만을 독립적으로도 사용할 수 있도록 구성했습니다.

개념이해책은 문법 개념에 대한 핵심적인 설명과 필수 연습문제로 이루어져 있습니다.

문제풀이책은 각 문법 개념에 대해 총 3단계의 테스트를 통해 체계적으로 문제를 풀어볼 수 있도록 구성되어 있습니다.

특징

❶ 최신 내신 출제 경향 100% 반영

– 신유형과 고난도 서술형 문제 비중 강화

점점 어려워지는 내신 문제의 최신 경향을 철저히 분석·반영하여 고난도 서술형과 신유형 문제의 비중을 더욱 높였습니다. 이 책으로 학습한 학생들은 어떤 유형의 문제에도 대처할 수 있습니다.

– 영어 지시문 문제 제시

영어로 문제가 출제되는 최신 경향을 반영하여, 일부 문제를 영어 지시문으로 제시했습니다. 문제풀이책의 Level 3 Test는 모두 영어 지시문으로만 제시됩니다.

– 독해 지문 어법 문제 수록(문제풀이책)

독해 지문에서 어법 문제가 출제되는 내신 문제 스타일에 익숙해지도록, 독해 지문과 함께 다양한 어법 문제를 풀어볼 수 있습니다.

❷ 개념이해책과 문제풀이책의 연계 학습

문법 개념 설명과 필수 문제로 구성된 개념이해책으로 문법 개념을 학습한 후, 다양한 문제를 3단계로 풀어보는 문제풀이책으로 복습하며 확실한 학습 효과를 거둘 수 있습니다.

❸ 성취도 평가와 수준별 맞춤형 학습 제안

문제를 풀어보고 나서 점수 기준에 따라 학생의 성취도를 평가할 수 있습니다. 개념이해책에서 Let's Check It Out과 Ready for Exams 점수를 합산한 결과에 따라 문제풀이책의 어느 레벨부터 학습하면 되는지 가이드가 제시됩니다. Review Test에서는 일정 점수 이상을 받아야 다음 챕터로 넘어갈 수 있습니다.

❹ 추가 학습을 위한 다양한 학습자료 제공

다양하게 수업에 활용할 수 있는 교사용 자료가 제공됩니다. 다락원 홈페이지(www.darakwon.co.kr)에서 무료로 다운받으실 수 있습니다.

개념이해책과 문제풀이책 연계 학습법

개념이해책으로 문법 개념 학습

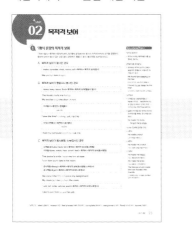

문제풀이책으로 문법 개념을 복습

QR코드를 찍으면 개념이해책 문법 설명이 보여요!

개념이해책 Let's Check It Out과 Ready for Exams 풀고 점수 합산

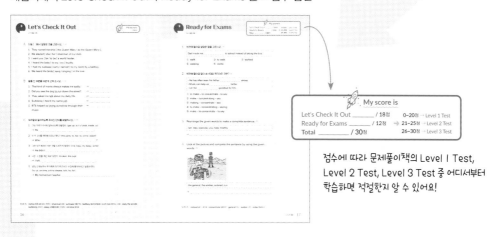

My score is

Let's Check It Out	/ 18점	0~20점 → Level 1 Test
Ready for Exams	/ 12점	21~25점 → Level 2 Test
Total	/ 30점	26~30점 → Level 3 Test

점수에 따라 문제풀이책의 Level 1 Test, Level 2 Test, Level 3 Test 중 어디서부터 학습하면 적절한지 알 수 있어요!

챕터 내용을 모두 학습한 후 Review Test 풀기

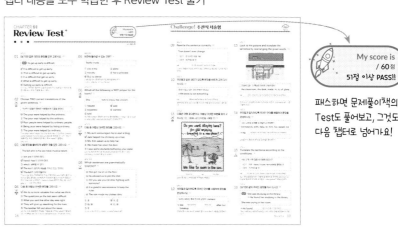

My score is

/ 60점

51점 이상 PASS!!

패스하면 문제풀이책의 Review Test도 풀어보고, 그것도 패스하면 다음 챕터로 넘어가요!

문제풀이책의 구성

문법 개념 요약

개념이해책에서 학습한 문법 개념이 표로 더욱 간결하게 요약 제시됩니다. 핵심 용어가 빈칸으로 처리되어 있어서 학생들이 직접 내용을 채워 넣으며 개념을 복습할 수 있습니다.

● **개념이해책 연계 학습용 QR코드**

QR코드를 찍으면 개념이해책 문법 개념 설명 페이지로 연결되어 내용을 즉시 확인할 수 있습니다.

Level 1 Test

학습한 문법 사항을 간단히 확인할 수 있는 드릴형 연습 문제입니다.

● **VOCA**

문제에 쓰인 주요 단어가 정리되어 편리하며, 문법과 단어 공부를 같이 할 수 있습니다.

Level 2 Test

중간 난이도의 문제를 풀면서 앞에서 배운 문법 사항을 실제 문제 풀이에 적용하는 연습을 합니다. 객관식과 주관식 서술형이 50% 정도로 섞인 내신 유형 문제로 구성되어 있습니다. 지시문은 한글로 제시됩니다.

● **My score is**

30점 만점으로 25점 이상일 때 PASS할 수 있어 학생들의 성취 욕구를 자극할 수 있으며, PASS 기준에 미달했을 때는 다시 앞부분을 복습하도록 합니다.

Level 3 Test

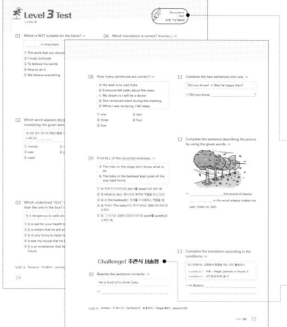

높은 난이도의 다양한 내신 유형 문제로 구성되어 있으며, 문제가 모두 영어 지시문으로 제시됩니다. 최신 유형도 포함되어 있어 내신 시험에 철저히 대비할 수 있습니다.

• My score is
50점 만점으로 41점 이상일 때 PASS할 수 있습니다.

• Challenge! 주관식 서술형
주관식 서술형 문제의 비중이 30퍼센트 정도로 구성되어 있습니다.

Review Test

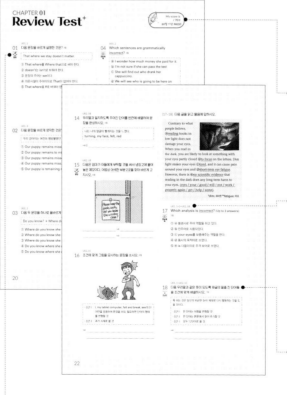

각 챕터의 내용을 통합적으로 다룬 문제들을 통해 응용력과 실전 감각을 키울 수 있습니다. 객관식과 주관식 서술형이 50% 정도로 구성되어 있습니다.

• My score is
70점 만점으로 60점 이상일 때 PASS할 수 있습니다. Review Test를 PASS하면 해당 문법 개념을 마스터했다는 성취감과 자신감을 가지고 다음 챕터로 넘어갑니다.

• 인덱스 번호
문제에 대한 문법 개념이 어디에 나왔는지 알려주는 번호입니다. 인덱스 번호는 개념이해 책 기준입니다.

U01_1+3+GP
유닛 번호 개념번호 Grammar Point

• 독해형 어법 문제
독해 지문에서 어법 문제가 출제되는 내신 시험에 대비할 수 있도록, Review Test의 마지막 2문제는 독해형으로 제시됩니다.

| 고난도 | 특히 어렵거나 최신 유형이라 익숙하지 않은 문제 | 한눈에 쏙 | 여러 문법 개념이 한 문제 속에 들어가 있는 문제 | ✓ 함정 | 학생들이 잘 헷갈리는 문법 항목이거나 부주의하면 틀릴 수 있는 문제 |

차례

내공 중학영문법을 써본
독자들의 추천!

최고의 수업은 학생들이 최고로 쉽게 이해하고 기억하는 수업이듯 최고의 책도 결국은 이해하고 기억하기 쉬운 책이 아닐까 싶다. 내공 중학영문법은 개념 설명이 간결하여 이해하기 쉽고 실제 시험에 출제되는 신유형의 문제들로 구성되어 학생들의 실전 시험에 직접적인 도움이 된다는 꾸준한 호평을 받고 있는 책이다.

대치동 학원 원장 **유니스 리**

유명 출판사의 여러 문법 교재 제작에 참여했지만 지루하고 어려운 영문법을 어떻게 맛깔나게 구현할 것인가가 늘 품었던 난제였다. 재치가 번뜩이는 예문, 간결하고 깔끔한 설명, 학습자에게 가장 효율적인 동선을 제시해 타 교재는 그냥 평범하게 만들어 버리는 내공 중학영문법만의 마법을 부리고 있는 듯하다.

파주 너희가별이다 원장 **최현진**

교재를 선택하는 데 있어서 '티칭' 입장과 '학생' 입장을 모두 고려했을 때 편한 책을 선택하는데요, 어려워 보이거나 문제가 많거나 했을 때는 쉽게 포기할 수도 있는 부분이 있어서 매번 책을 볼 때는 중점적으로 보는 편입니다. 내공 중학영문법은 문법 학습과 필수 기출 유형은 개념이해책을 통해서 학습하고, 이러한 개념을 문제풀이 책에서 다시 한 번 되새길 수 있어서 매우 좋습니다. 고등학교 가기 전, 필수 잇템 교재로 생각됩니다.

태안 박쌤영어 강사 **박희진**

개념이해책에서 문법을 배우며 수업 중에 함께 문제를 풀고, 워크북 개념의 문제풀이책에서 문제들뿐만 아니라 표 형식의 문법 정리 내용 역시 암기하도록 구성되어서, 학생들이 문법 내용을 덩어리로 익힐 수 있다. 저자들의 창의성이 돋보이는 풍부한 양의 학교 시험 대비 up-to-date한 신유형 문제들과 영어 몰입 교육이 가능한 영어로 출제되는 문제들 역시 이 책의 장점이다.

마포 껌학원 원장 **김현우**

내공 중학영문법으로 공부를 한 후, 37점이었던 처참한 점수가 90점 가량으로 많이 올라갔습니다. 이 책에서는 문법에 대해 상세하고 정확하게 알려주고 있으니 저처럼 기초가 없이 영어 공부를 시작하는 중학생이라면 이 책을 써보는 걸 추천합니다.

경성중학교 3학년 05년생 **신경○**

이 책으로 강의를 하면서 문법은 무조건 많이 풀어야 한다는 기존의 생각을 완전히 버리게 되었다. 개념 정리부터 기본 문제, 심화 문제까지 알차게 구성되어 있어 아이들이 어느 부분에서 이해가 부족한지 정확하게 찾아낼 수 있다. 특히 문제풀이책은 난이도별로 문제를 단순하게 모아둔 문제은행의 개념이 아니라, 이전 단계의 핵심 문제를 적절히 업그레이드해서 어느 유형에서도 응용이 가능하게 했다. 수록된 문제의 유형 역시 흔하지 않은 구성으로 되어 있어 대충 풀고 넘어가기에는 함정이 많다. 그래서 이 책을 선택하는 아이들은 정말 '제대로' 된 영어 공부를 하게 된다. 개념을 단계별로 정리하는 것부터 문제의 양과 질, 그리고 부가자료까지 버릴 게 하나도 없는 주옥 같은 책이다.

여의도/마포 강사 **김경민**

- -

개념이해책과 문제풀이책이 같이 있어 문제의 양이 부족하지 않았고 난이도가 잘 나눠져 있어서 내가 어느 위치에 있는지 파악하며 쉽게 문법을 배울 수 있었다. 문법 문제를 항상 어설프게 느낌으로만 풀던 내가 이 책으로 공부를 하고 나서는 이 문제가 어떤 개념을 물어보는 것인지, 정답의 근거가 무엇인지 잘 설명할 수 있게 되었다.

여의도중학교 **최민준**

누가 봐도 알기 쉽고 접근하기 쉽게 책이 구성되어 있다. 그리고 요즘 학생들의 관심사를 배려한 모든 예문과 답문의 단어가 정성스럽게 선택되어 있는 점에 감탄했다. 힘든 영어 공부를 하는 학생을 최고로 배려해 만들어진 교재임을 한눈에 알 수 있다.

미국 국공립 학교 교사 20년차 Reena Han

고난도 문제도 쉽게 풀 수 있도록 다양한 난이도의 풍부한 문제 수와 고퀄리티의 문제들이 가득해서 문법을 확실하게 익힐 수 있는, 엄청난 내공이 담긴 교재!♡

중계 Amy English 원장 **장여주**

영문법에 예외가 많아서 항상 한계에 도달하는 느낌을 받았었는데 신영주 선생님과 이 책으로 공부하면서 내가 정확히 알지 못해서 예외라고 느끼고 외우려고 했다는 점을 깨달을 수 있었습니다. 그 동안 수많은 문제집을 풀면서 가졌던 크고 작은 질문에 대해서도 명쾌한 답을 제시해주었고 이러한 성취의 경험을 통해 사소한 의문도 지나치지 않는 공부 습관을 잡을 수 있었습니다. 교재를 접하는 학생의 수준과 상관없이 실력을 향상시키는 데 반드시 도움이 되는 책이라고 생각합니다.

외대부고 13기 **배현진**

CHAPTER 01
문장의 구조

UNIT 01 주어, 목적어, 주격 보어

개념이해책
12쪽 함께 보기

■ 아래 표의 빈칸에 알맞은 내용을 써 넣으세요. >>> 정답 2쪽

CONCEPT 1 주어와 목적어의 이해

명사류	주어	목적어
1)_____	A puppy is under the table.	We admire Yi Sun-sin.
2)_____ : to부정사구, 동명사구	To blame others is easy.	We enjoy riding our bikes.
3)_____ (= 복수 명사)	The rich grow richer, and the poor grow poorer.	The volunteers helped the homeless.
4)_____	How to study is more important than what to study.	I don't know how to stop playing the game.
5)_____ : that절, if/whether절, 의문사절, what절	Where we will stay hasn't been decided yet. What we want is peace.	Columbus believed (that) the Earth is round.

CONCEPT 2 주격 보어의 이해

6)_____	He is a professor.	
7)_____ : 형용사, 분사	He always looks neat. She stayed smiling.	

Level 1 Test

>>> 정답 2쪽

A 밑줄 친 부분을 바르게 고쳐 쓰시오.

1 Play golf is not expensive in California.

→ _____

2 Lazy will spoil your life.

→ _____

3 It is important keep your body clean.

→ _____

4 The cake smells well.

→ _____

5 My plan is listen to English news every day.

→ _____

B 주어진 단어를 사용하여 문장을 완성하시오.

1 나는 어디에서 공부해야 할지 모르겠다. (where, study)

→ I don't know _____ _____

_____ .

2 김 선생님은 나에게 질문이 있는지 물으셨다. (if)

→ Ms. Kim asked me _____

_____ _____ any questions.

3 나는 그녀가 사실대로 말했다고 생각한다.
(that, tell the truth)

→ I think _____ _____

_____ _____ _____ .

VOCA spoil 망치다 | tell the truth 사실대로 말하다

12

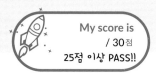
[01~02] 빈칸에 알맞지 않은 것을 고르시오. 각 2점

01
I like _____.

① to meet you
② comfortable
③ living on my own
④ what you like
⑤ men that cook

02
That is _____.

① interesting
② mine
③ sleep deeply
④ what she thinks
⑤ what you can't do by yourself

03 다음 중 어법상 어색한 문장을 고른 것은? 3점

ⓐ Kind is an important factor to success.
ⓑ The strong endures longer than the weak.
ⓒ It is hard to believe everything.
ⓓ That he said was wrong.

① ⓐ, ⓑ
② ⓐ, ⓑ, ⓒ
③ ⓐ, ⓑ, ⓓ
④ ⓑ, ⓓ
⑤ ⓓ

04 밑줄 친 'that'이 나머지와 다르게 사용된 것은? 2점

① Mt. Seorak is a mountain that many people visit during fall.
② That he can't attend the party is a pity.
③ It's wonderful that she won the prize.
④ She thought that her mother was angry.
⑤ The problem is that you spend too much time playing games.

05 어법상 어색한 부분을 고쳐 문장을 다시 쓰시오. 4점

서술형

The fruit has turned hardly.

→ _____

06 두 문장을 [보기]와 같이 한 문장으로 고쳐 쓰시오. 5점

서술형

보기 I don't know. + Does he like soccer?
→ I don't know if he likes soccer.

Do you know? + Where does she live?

→ Do you know _____?

07 주어진 단어를 이용하여 우리말을 영작하시오. 6점

서술형

나는 그녀가 거짓말을 했다고 생각하지 않는다.
think, that, tell a lie

→ _____
_____

08 우리말과 일치하도록 조건에 맞게 문장을 완성하시오. 6점

서술형

네가 거리에서 주운 지갑이 그가 찾고 있는 것이다.

·조건 1 어휘 – look for
·조건 2 현재 진행형으로 쓸 것
·조건 3 빈칸에 5단어로 쓸 것

→ The wallet you picked up on the street is
_____.

VOCA comfortable 편안한 | factor 요인, 요소 | success 성공 | endure 참다 | during ~ 동안 | a pity 유감스러운 일 | prize 상 | wallet 지갑

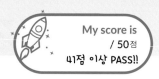

01 Which is NOT suitable for the blank? 2점

> _____ is important.

① The work that you should focus on
② I must conclude
③ To believe his words
④ How to do it
⑤ We believe everything

02 Which word appears third in the blank when translating the given sentence? 3점

> 내 모든 돈이 언니의 생일선물을 사는 데 사용되었다.
> = All of _____.

① money   ② my
③ was   ④ present
⑤ used

03 Which underlined "It[it]" is used differently than the one in the box? (2 answers) 3점

> It is dangerous to walk alone at night.

① It is bad for your health to eat late at night.
② It is certain that he will arrive on time.
③ Is it very funny to listen to their show?
④ It was my house that he bought last week.
⑤ It is an entertainer that he wants to be in the future.

04 Which translation is correct? (Find ALL.) 2점

> 무지개를 보는 것은 행운이다.

① To see a rainbow is good luck.
② It is good luck to see a rainbow.
③ Seeing a rainbow is good luck.
④ It is good luck you see a rainbow.
⑤ That see a rainbow is good luck.

05 Who finds the error and corrects it properly? 3점

> That the film that you watched was too violent.

① 수영: 문장 앞의 That을 It으로 바꾸어야 한다.
② 경욱: was는 were가 되어야 한다.
③ 성원: the film 뒤의 that은 what이 되어야 한다.
④ 효리: 문장 맨 앞의 That은 삭제해야 한다.
⑤ 수지: 문장 맨 앞의 That은 What이 되어야 한다.

06 Which sentences are incorrect? (Find ALL.) 2점

① They are enjoying themselves.
② I don't mind to help you.
③ I want eating some fruits and vegetables.
④ They will give up to look for the secret.
⑤ We decided to follow his advice.

07 Which of the underlined words is used differently than the others? 3점

① She thought that her mother was angry.
② I hope that she will tell me a better way.
③ It's sad that some people are sad.
④ Texan is the company that my sister works for.
⑤ Do you think that you are right?

VOCA focus on ~에 집중하다 | conclude 결론을 내리다 | certain 확실한 | on time 제시간에 | entertainer 연예인 | violent 폭력적인 | secret 비밀

08 How many sentences are correct? 4점

> ⓐ His wish is to visit India.
> ⓑ Everyone felt sadly about the news.
> ⓒ My dream is I will be a doctor.
> ⓓ She remained silent during the meeting.
> ⓔ While I was studying, I fell sleep.

① one   ② two
③ three   ④ four
⑤ five

09 Find ALL of the <u>incorrect</u> analyses. 4점

> ⓐ The men on the stage don't know what to do.
> ⓑ The baby in the backseat kept quiet all the way back home.

① ⓐ 주어가 단수이므로 don't를 doesn't로 써야 해.
② ⓐ what to do는 명사구로 목적어 역할을 하고 있어.
③ ⓑ in the backseat는 주어를 수식해주는 역할을 해.
④ ⓑ 주어는 The baby이고 주격 보어는 형용사로 바르게 쓰였어.
⑤ ⓑ '그 아기는 조용히 있었다'이므로 quiet를 quietly로 고쳐야 해.

Challenge! 주관식 서술형

10 Rewrite the sentence correctly. 5점

> He is fond of to drink Coke.

→ _____

11 Combine the two sentences into one. 5점

> Did you know? + Was he happy then?

→ Did you know _____ ?

12 Complete the sentence describing the picture by using the given words. 6점

→ _____ the sound of leaves

_____ in the wind always makes me

sad. (listen to, fall)

13 Complete the translation according to the conditions. 8점

> 보스턴에서는 교회에서 땅콩을 먹는 것이 불법이다.
>
> · Condition 1   어휘 – illegal, peanuts, in church, it
> · Condition 2   빈칸에 8단어로 쓸 것

→ In Boston, _____

_____ .

VOCA   remain ~한 채로 있다 | be fond of ~을 좋아하다 | illegal 불법의 | peanut 땅콩

목적격 보어

■ 아래 표의 빈칸에 알맞은 내용을 써 넣으세요. >>> 정답 2쪽

개념이해책
15쪽 함께 보기

① 5형식 문장의 목적격 보어

목적격 보어	자주 사용되는 동사
명사	1) m_____, consider, 2) e_____, 3) n_____, call
형용사, 분사	make, 4) k_____, leave, 5) f_____
6)_____	지각동사
과거분사	사역동사: 7) m_____, 8) h_____, 9) l_____ 지각동사: 10) s_____, watch, 11) h_____, smell, feel
동사원형	사역동사, 지각동사, help
12)_____	준사역동사: 13) h_____, get ask, tell, order, advise, want

② 목적어 보어가 분사인 경우

지각동사 + 목적어 + 현재분사 └───┘ 14)_____ 관계	지각/사역동사 + 목적어 + 과거분사 └───┘ 15)_____ 관계

 Level 1 Test

>>> 정답 2쪽

A [ ]에서 알맞은 것을 고르시오.

1 This dress makes me [look / to look] fat.

2 Mom calls me [as Chatterbox / Chatterbox].

3 The music made me [sleepily / sleepy].

4 He asked me [go out / to go out] with him.

B 어법상 어색한 곳을 찾아 바르게 고치시오.

1 I saw she study at the café.

_____ → _____

2 I watched the sun to rise above the mountain.

_____ → _____

3 She is going to have her watch repair.

_____ → _____

4 You should help the baby standing up.

_____ → _____

C 주어진 단어를 빈칸에 배열하여 문장을 완성하시오.

1 선생님들은 그를 말썽꾸러기라고 불렀다.
(him, a troublemaker, called)

→ The teachers _____.

2 그는 종종 문을 열어놓는다. (leaves, open, the door)

→ He often _____.

3 나는 금고가 비어 있는 것을 발견했다.
(the safe, found, empty)

→ I _____.

4 이리 와서 내가 돈 세는 것 좀 도와줘.
(the, me, count, money, help)

→ Come and _____.

VOCA chatterbox 수다쟁이 | go out with ~와 사귀다[데이트하다] | repair 수선하다 | troublemaker 말썽꾸러기 | safe 금고

 **Level 2 Test**

>>> 정답 3쪽

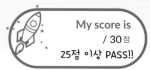
[01~02] 빈칸에 알맞지 <u>않은</u> 것을 고르시오. 각 2점

01

My son makes me _____.

① sadly
② happy
③ angry
④ proud
⑤ tired

02

I _____ him put up the tent.

① had
② let
③ helped
④ got
⑤ made

03 다음 문장을 바르게 설명한 학생을 <u>모두</u> 고르시오. 3점

The doctor advised the patient not smoke.

① 하얀: the patient는 목적격 보어이다.
② 미소: 환자가 흡연하지 않도록 의사가 충고하는 것이다.
③ 한우: not smoke는 not to smoke가 되어야 한다.
④ 지나: the patient 다음에 not을 쓸 수 없다.
⑤ 준호: advise 동사는 목적격 보어로 동사원형을 취한다.

04 다음 문장들 중에서 어법상 어색한 부분을 바르게 고친 것을 <u>모두</u> 고르시오. 4점

ⓐ My mom asked me doing the laundry.
ⓑ I have never seen anyone to sing like that.
ⓒ Can anybody help me changing the bulb?

① ⓐ doing → do
② ⓐ doing → to do
③ ⓑ to sing → sing
④ ⓑ to sing → singing
⑤ ⓒ 고칠 곳이 없다.

05 다음 우리말 문장을 영어로 옮길 때, 빈칸에 들어갈 알맞은 말을 각각 1단어로 쓰시오. 4점 | 서술형

그의 부모님의 기대가 그로 하여금 책임감을 느끼게 했다.

→ His parents' expectations _____ him _____ responsible.

06 다음은 선우의 부모님이 선우에게 허락하거나 허락하지 않는 것들이다. 말이 자연스럽게 이어지도록 빈칸에 공통으로 들어갈 단어를 쓰시오. 4점 | 서술형

• They don't _____ me stay out late.
• They _____ me have parties.
• They don't _____ me listen to loud music.

→ _____

07 조건에 맞게 우리말 문장을 영작하시오. 6점 | 서술형

그 남자는 그의 새 집이 지어지도록 했다.

· 조건 1   어휘 – have, build
· 조건 2   7단어로 쓸 것

→ _____

08 주어진 단어들을 배열하여 그림을 묘사하시오. 5점 | 서술형

the girl, the blind man, helped, cross the road

→ _____

VOCA put up a tent 텐트를 치다 | advise 충고하다 | patient 환자 | do the laundry 빨래하다 | bulb 전구 | expectation 기대 | responsible 책임감이 있는 | stay out late 늦게까지 외출하다 | blind 눈이 먼 | cross 가로지르다, 건너다

 **Level 3 Test**

>>> 정답 3쪽

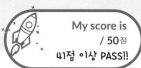
01 Which is the common word for the blanks? 2점

> • My goldfish _____ me happy.
> • Can you _____ him agree with my plan?

① get
② make
③ keep
④ come
⑤ let

02 Which is suitable for the blank?
(Up to 3 answers) 2점

> The king _____ the knight kneel in front of the crowd.

① asked
② made
③ helped
④ wanted
⑤ had

03 Which sentence needs a <u>different</u> word for the blank? 3점

① He heard someone _____ out of the room.
② They told us to _____ to the park.
③ The doctor allowed us _____ swimming.
④ I saw Ms. Kim _____ to school.
⑤ She made me _____ along with my sister.

04 Choose ALL of the correct words for the blank. 3점

> Did you see anyone _____ you?

① follow
② followed
③ following
④ to follow
⑤ follows

05 Whose translation is correct? 3점

> 너 어디서 머리 했니?

① 용찬: Where did you have your hair done?
② 민국: Where did you your hair have done?
③ 향아: Where did you have your hair do?
④ 유빈: Where did you have your hair doing?
⑤ 지우: Where did you have your hair to do?

06 Which correction is right? 3점

> I saw the dog barked at a stranger.

① barked → barking
② barked → to bark
③ barked → barks
④ the dog barked → barked the dog
⑤ the dog barked → barking the dog

07 Which underlined word is grammatically <u>incorrect</u>? 2점

① My mom's car broke down, so she had it <u>fixed</u>.
② I must have my coat <u>cleaned</u>.
③ I had my house <u>painted</u> yesterday.
④ I don't like having my picture <u>taken</u>.
⑤ I lost my key, so I had another one <u>make</u>.

VOCA goldfish 금붕어 | agree with ~에 동의하다 | knight 기사 | kneel 무릎 꿇다 | in front of ~ 앞에 | crowd 군중 | allow 허락하다 | ollow 따라가다 | bark 짖다 | stranger 낯선 사람 | fix 수리하다

18

08 Which sentences are <u>incorrect</u>? 3점

> ⓐ I felt someone walking toward me.
> ⓑ She will have her car wash later.
> ⓒ Did you tell him to stay back?
> ⓓ He has seen me walking down the street.
> ⓔ They made us wait for their son.

① ⓐ, ⓑ, ⓒ   ② ⓑ
③ ⓑ, ⓓ   ④ ⓒ, ⓓ, ⓔ
⑤ ⓒ, ⓔ

09 Which CANNOT make a grammatically correct sentence? 4점

① make / . / helped / me / She / the / bed
② last / stolen / watch / . / night / his / had / He
③ keep / . / You / must / your / password / safe
④ London / . / leave / her / to / advised / Sam
⑤ to / made / ? / What / you / specially / the / so / day

10 How many are NOT suitable for the blank? 4점

> They made him _____.
>
> ⓐ so sadly
> ⓑ king of England
> ⓒ felt happy
> ⓓ going there alone
> ⓔ look like a little girl
> ⓕ to tell them everything

① one   ② two
③ three   ④ four
⑤ five

Challenge! 주관식 서술형

11 Translate the sentence by using the given words. 4점

> 우리는 그 방을 따뜻하게 유지했다.
> the room, warm, keep

→ _____

12 Fill in blank (A) by using the given words to complete the dialog as shown in the example. 4점

> **보기**   A: I can't see things well.
>   B: Why don't you <u>have your eyes tested</u>? (test, eyes)
> - - - - - - - - - -
> A: I have a cavity.
> B: Why don't you ____(A)____ ? (fill, cavity)

(A) _____

13 Combine the two sentences into one. (9 words) 6점

> We saw John yesterday. He was smiling at a tall girl.

→ _____
_____

14 Translate the sentence according to the conditions. 7점

> 엄마는 나에게 어떤 돈도 낭비하지 말라고 말씀하셨다.
>
> · Condition 1   Words – waste, any money, to, tell
> · Condition 2   빈칸에 7단어로 쓸 것

→ Mom _____
_____.

VOCA   toward ~ 쪽으로 | stay back 물러서다 | cavity 충치 | fill 채우다

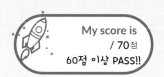

My score is
/ 70점
60점 이상 PASS!!

U01_1

01 다음 문장을 바르게 설명한 것은? 3점

함정

> That where we stay doesn't matter.

① That where를 Where that으로 써야 한다.
② doesn't는 isn't로 바꿔야 한다.
③ 문장의 주어는 we이다.
④ 의문사절이 주어이므로 That이 없어야 한다.
⑤ That where을 If로 바꿔야 한다.

U01_3

02 다음 문장을 바르게 영작한 것은? 2점

> 우리 강아지는 여전히 행방불명인 상태이다.

① Our puppy remains missing.
② Our puppy remains to miss.
③ Our puppy remains missed.
④ Our puppy remains miss.
⑤ Our puppy is remaining missing.

U01_2

03 다음 두 문장을 하나로 올바르게 연결한 것은? 2점

> Do you know? + Where did she meet him?

① Where do you know she meet him?
② Where do you know she meets him?
③ Where do you know she met him?
④ Do you know where she meets him?
⑤ Do you know where she met him?

U01_2

04 Which sentences are grammatically underline{incorrect}? 3점

한눈에 쏙

> ⓐ I wonder how much money she paid for it.
> ⓑ I'm not sure if she can pass the test.
> ⓒ She will find out who drank her cappuccino.
> ⓓ We will see who is going to be here on time.
> ⓔ We finally found out what she had enough money.

① ⓐ, ⓒ
② ⓑ, ⓔ
③ ⓑ, ⓓ, ⓔ
④ ⓒ, ⓓ
⑤ ⓔ

U01_2+U02_1B+1C

05 Which CANNOT make a grammatically correct sentence? 4점

고난도

① enjoyed / motor / riding / kickboard. / a / I
② start. / I / when / to / know / don't
③ angrily. / me / She / made
④ separate / dad / got / My / trash. / me / to / the
⑤ me / the / Jane / assignment. / complete / to / helped

U02_1B

06 다음 문장을 영작할 때 2번째와 5번째 올 단어가 알맞게 짝지어진 것은? 4점

고난도

> 나는 나의 이름이 불려지는 것을 들었다.

① heard – call
② heard – calling
③ heard – called
④ hearing – called
⑤ hear – to call

U02_1C

07 Which of the underlined words is grammatically incorrect? 2점

My teacher ⓐ let ⓑ us ⓒ going ⓓ home ⓔ early.

① ⓐ   ② ⓑ
③ ⓒ   ④ ⓓ
⑤ ⓔ

U01_3+GP

08 다음 문장들 중에서 어법상 어색한 부분을 모두 바르게 고친 것은? 3점

한눈에 쏙

ⓐ Did the kids keep silently?
ⓑ I asked him where he would go.
ⓒ She returned the gift what he sent.
ⓓ Jack helped me climb up a tree.
ⓔ I saw my brother go out.

① ⓐ silently → silent   ⓒ what → that
② ⓐ silently → silent
③ ⓑ he would → would he   ⓒ what → that
④ ⓒ what → that
⑤ ⓓ climb → to climb   ⓔ go → gone

U01_2

09 우리말과 일치하도록 주어진 단어를 사용하여 문장을 완성하시오. 4점

숙제가 너무 많아서 어디에서 시작해야 할지 모르겠다.
(where, start)

→ I don't know ＿＿＿＿＿ ＿＿＿＿＿
＿＿＿＿＿ because I have too much
homework.

U01_3

10 Rewrite the sentence correctly. 4점

The party is getting noise.
(파티가 시끄러워지고 있다.)

→ ＿＿＿＿＿＿＿＿＿＿＿＿＿＿＿

U01_2

11 Combine the two sentences into one. 5점

I wonder. + Does she really like me?

→ I wonder ＿＿＿＿＿＿＿＿＿＿ .

U01_GP

12 조건에 맞게 우리말을 영작하시오. 6점

★
고난도

그가 자메이카에서 태어난 것은 사실이다.

· 조건 1   어휘 – true, he, be born, Jamaica
· 조건 2   9단어로 쓸 것
· 조건 3   가주어 It을 쓸 것

→ ＿＿＿＿＿＿＿＿＿＿＿＿＿＿
＿＿＿＿＿＿＿＿＿＿＿＿＿＿＿

U02_1C

13 우리말과 일치하도록 주어진 단어를 빈칸에 배열하여 문장을 완성하시오. 4점

그 야구 경기는 아빠의 기분이 더 좋아지게 만들었다.
feel, made, better, my dad

→ The baseball game ＿＿＿＿＿＿＿＿
＿＿＿＿＿＿＿＿＿＿ .

14 U02_1B

우리말과 일치하도록 주어진 단어를 빈칸에 배열하여 문장을 완성하시오. 4점

> 나는 나의 얼굴이 빨개지는 것을 느꼈다.
> turning, my face, felt, red

→ I _____.

15 U02_1B

함정

다음은 엄마가 아들에게 부탁할 것을 써서 냉장고에 붙여 놓은 메모이다. 어법상 어색한 부분 2곳을 찾아 바르게 고치시오. 4점

Please keep the drinks coolly. Did you leave the window close?

_____ → _____

_____ → _____

16 U02_1C

조건에 맞게 그림을 묘사하는 문장을 쓰시오. 6점

> ·조건1 I, my tablet computer, fall and break, see의 단어만을 응용하여 문장을 쓰되, 필요하면 단어의 형태를 변형할 것
> ·조건2 과거 시제로 쓸 것

→ _____

[17~18] 다음 글을 읽고 물음에 답하시오.

　Contrary to what people believe, ⓐreading books in low light does not damage your eyes. When you read in the dark, you are likely to look at something with your eyes partly closed ⓑto focus on the letters. Dim light makes your eyes ⓒtired, and it can cause pain around your eyes and ⓓshort-term eye fatigue. However, there is ⓔno scientific evidence that reading in the dark does any long-term harm to your eyes. (eyes / your / good / will / rest / work / properly again / get / help / some).

*dim: 희미한 **fatigue: 피로

17 U01_1+2+U02_1B

한눈에 쏙

Which analysis is incorrect? (Up to 3 answers) 3점

① ⓐ 동명사로 주어 역할을 하고 있다.
② ⓑ 진주어로 사용되었다.
③ ⓒ your eyes를 보충해주는 역할을 한다.
④ ⓓ 동사의 목적어로 쓰였다.
⑤ ⓔ is 다음이므로 주격 보어로 쓰였다.

18 U01_1+U02_1C

★ 고난도

다음 우리말과 같은 뜻이 되도록 윗글의 밑줄 친 단어들을 조건에 맞게 배열하시오. 7점

> 푹 쉬는 것은 당신의 피곤한 눈이 제대로 다시 활동하는 것을 도울 것이다.
> ·조건1 한 단어는 어형을 변화할 것
> ·조건2 한 단어는 본문에서 찾아 추가할 것
> ·조건3 모두 12단어로 쓸 것

→ _____

CHAPTER 02
to부정사

03 용법, 의미상의 주어, 부정

■ 아래 표의 빈칸에 알맞은 내용을 써 넣으세요. >>> 정답 4쪽

개념이해책
22쪽 함께 보기

CONCEPT 1 to부정사의 용법

1)_____ 용법	2)_____ 역할	To hide our true feelings is not easy.	
	3)_____ 역할	When do you expect to see him back?	
	4)_____ 역할	My mom's dream was to be a firefighter.	
5)_____ 용법	6)_____ 수식	They needed a smart leader to lead their team.	
	7)_____ 수식	My sister has been looking for somebody to marry.	
8)_____ 용법	9)_____	I drink coffee (in order[so as]) to keep awake.	
	감정의 10)_____	The hacker was pleased to figure out the password.	
	판단의 11)_____	He must be foolish to buy the used phone.	
	12)_____	The witch lived to be 999 years old.	
	13)_____ 수식	The machine is complicated to use.	

CONCEPT 2 to부정사의 의미상의 주어

14)_____ 형용사	easy, difficult, hard, necessary, possible, impossible 등	15)_____ +목적격
16)_____ 형용사	kind, nice, foolish, stupid, polite, rude, careful, wise 등	17)_____ +목적격

CONCEPT 3 to부정사의 부정

18)_____[19)_____] to+동사원형

Level 1 Test

>>> 정답 4쪽

A 밑줄 친 to부정사의 용법을 구분하시오.

1 I hope to see penguins in South Africa.

→ _____

2 They ran toward him to get his autograph.

→ _____

3 Let me buy something cold to drink.

→ _____

B [ ]에서 알맞은 것을 고르시오.

1 It is easy [for / of] me to speak Korean.

2 It was foolish [for / of] them to make the same mistake.

C 밑줄 친 부분이 어색하면 바르게 고치시오.

1 I asked him not play the online game.

→ _____

2 He studied hard not to fail the test.

→ _____

3 They told her never take off the mask.

→ _____

4 We should try to not pollute the river.

→ _____

VOCA autograph (유명인의) 사인 | take off 벗다 | pollute 오염시키다

24

>>> 정답 4쪽

01 밑줄 친 부분의 쓰임이 [보기]와 같은 것은? 2점

> [보기] I was glad to hear that he didn't come.

① My brother wants to be a fashion designer.
② It wasn't easy to talk about my feelings.
③ They plan to play soccer after school.
④ My dream is to travel around the world.
⑤ She was pleased to get the present.

02 빈칸에 공통으로 들어갈 말은? 2점

> · It is impossible _____ me to do that alone.
> · It is unlikely _____ him to pass the exam.

① at
② from
③ for
④ of
⑤ by

03 다음 문장을 바르게 이해한 학생은? 3점

> Lucy told Gyuri not to climb the tree.

① 성현: Lucy는 규리에게 아무 말도 하지 않았어.
② 한솔: Lucy는 규리랑 말하는 걸 싫어해.
③ 혁진: Lucy는 규리에게 나무에 오르지 말라고 말했어.
④ 경민: 규리는 원래 나무에 오르지 못해.
⑤ 윤아: 규리는 Lucy에게서 나무에 오르라는 말을 들었어.

04 다음 우리말을 영작할 때 앞에서 4번째 올 단어는? 3점

> 내가 문을 잠그지 않은 것은 부주의했다.

① careless
② for
③ of
④ to
⑤ not

05 밑줄 친 우리말에 해당하는 문장을 8단어로 영작하시오.

서술형 6점

> I was late for school today. I felt bad.
> 내일은 늦지 않으려고 노력할 것이다.

→ _____

_____

06 조건에 맞게 그림을 묘사하는 문장을 완성하시오. 5점

서술형

> · 조건 1   to부정사의 의미상의 주어를 쓸 것
> · 조건 2   대명사를 사용할 것
> · 조건 3   어휘 – stop, cry

→ It looks hard _____.

07 괄호 안의 단어를 이용하여 빈칸을 채우시오. 각 2점

서술형

(1) It was mean _____ _____ to say that. (Andy)

(2) It's not easy _____ _____ to break our bad habits. (we)

08 주어진 단어들을 빈칸에 알맞게 재배열하시오. 5점

서술형

> A: Did you see the pyramids?
> B: _____, but _____
> _____.
>
> enough, I, time, I, wanted, didn't, to, have

VOCA feeling 감정 | pleased 기쁜 | unlikely 일어날 것 같지 않은 | careless 부주의한 | mean 야비한 | break (습관을) 고치다 | pyramid 피라미드

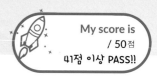
01 Which underlined part is used in the same way as in the given sentence? (2 answers) 3점

> Miguel searched the Internet to find his old friends.

① Mom turned the TV on to watch a soap opera.
② I got up early to get ready for the game.
③ He bought a cap to wear in the sun.
④ I would like to have lunch with you.
⑤ His purpose in life is to become an actor.

02 Which CANNOT be used for any of the blanks? (Find ALL.) 3점

> • It was very kind _____ you to help the foreigner.
> • Eating healthy food is important _____ you _____ live a long life.

① of   ② to
③ for   ④ with
⑤ by

03 Which words appear second and fourth when translating the given sentence? 4점

> 그녀는 나에게 자기 아이스크림을 먹지 말라고 말했다.

① me – to   ② did – not
③ told – not   ④ didn't – not
⑤ told – to

04 Which correction is right? 3점

> Will you give me two pieces of paper to write?

① me → to me   ② pieces → piece
③ of → for   ④ paper → papers
⑤ write → write on

05 Which sentence needs a different word for the blank? 2점

① It is difficult _____ me to write a letter.
② It was hard _____ them to stand the situation.
③ It is quite normal _____ him to skip breakfast.
④ It is nice _____ your son to apologize to his friend first.
⑤ It won't be easy _____ me to win the boxing title.

06 Which translation is correct? 3점

> 그 배우는 우리에게 자신의 사진을 찍지 말라고 요청했다.

① The actor asked us not take pictures of him.
② The actor not asked us not to take pictures of him.
③ The actor didn't ask us to take pictures of him.
④ The actor didn't ask us not to take pictures of him.
⑤ The actor asked us not to take pictures of him.

VOCA soap opera 드라마 | purpose 목적 | foreigner 외국인 | healthy 몸에 좋은 | piece 조각 | stand 견디다 | situation 상황 | normal 보통의 | skip 거르다 | apologize 사과하다

07 How many of the given words in ⓐ~ⓕ are NOT suitable for the blank? 3점

> It was _____ for you to make such a decision.
>
> ⓐ necessary   ⓑ important
> ⓒ not easy   ⓓ careful
> ⓔ wise   ⓕ impossible

① one   ② two
③ three   ④ four
⑤ five

08 Which CANNOT make a grammatically correct sentence? 4점

① water / drink / . / It's / not / the / to / safe
② her / not / asked / snacks / eat / . / He / his
③ us / to / It's / . / for / important / others / help
④ anything / . / write / to / didn't / have / She / with
⑤ want / me / to / you / ? / did / Why / here / meet

Challenge! 주관식 서술형

09 Choose the <u>necessary</u> words and rearrange them correctly to complete the translation. 5점

> 북극고래(bowhead whale)들은 200살까지 살 수 있다.
> order, live, years, 200, to, old, be, in, can

→ Bowhead whales _____.

10 Look at the picture and describe the situation by using the given words. 6점

→ It looks hard _____

all of the bricks on his bike. (he, carry)

11 Complete the sentence according to the conditions. 7점

> 그녀가 그런 말을 하다니 화가 났음에 틀림없어.
>
> · Condition 1 확실한 추측을 나타내는 조동사를 쓸 것
> · Condition 2 to부정사를 이용해서 '~하다니'를 표현할 것
> · Condition 3 어휘 – angry, to say
> · Condition 4 주어진 어휘를 변형하지 말고 그대로 쓸 것

→ She _____

such a thing.

12 Find the sentence that describes the picture and translate it into Korean. 7점

> ⓐ Mom told me not to open the basement door.
> ⓑ Mom didn't tell me to open the basement door.

(   ) → _____

VOCA decision 결정 ┃ necessary 필요한 ┃ careful 주의 깊은 ┃ brick 벽돌 ┃ basement 지하실

UNIT 04 시제, 독립부정사, 대부정사

■ 아래 표의 빈칸에 알맞은 내용을 써 넣으세요. >>> 정답 5쪽

개념이해책
25쪽 함께 보기

CONCEPT 1 부정사의 시제

종류	형태	의미
단순부정사	1)_____	본동사와 같거나 앞으로 다가올 시제
완료부정사	2)_____	본동사보다 앞선 시제

CONCEPT 2 독립부정사

3)_____	확실히	8)_____	설상가상으로
4)_____	우선	9)_____	슬픈 이야기지만
5)_____	사실을 말하자면	10)_____	이상한 말이지만
6)_____	솔직히 말하면	11)_____	말하자면
7)_____	간단히 말하면	12)_____	~은 말할 것도 없이

CONCEPT 3 대부정사

동사의 중복을 피하기 위해 'to + 동사원형'에서 13)_____ 를 생략하고 14)_____ 만 쓰는 형태

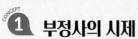 Level 1 Test

>>> 정답 5쪽

A 빈칸에 들어갈 말을 [보기]에서 골라 쓰시오. (중복 가능)

보기	to	frank	tell	be
	mention	truth	not	the

1 솔직히 말해, 난 그것을 이해할 수가 없어.

→ _____ _____ _____,

I can't understand that.

2 사실을 말하자면, 그 사고는 우연이 아니었어.

→ _____ _____ _____

_____, the accident was not

accidental.

3 그는 춤을 잘 춰. 노래는 말할 것도 없지.

→ He is good at dancing, _____

_____ _____ singing.

B 문장 전환에 알맞도록 빈칸을 채우시오.

1 She seems to be interested in me.

→ It _____ that _____

_____ _____ in me.

2 It appeared that the coach was satisfied.

→ The coach _____ _____

_____ satisfied.

C to 이하에 생략된 말을 쓰시오.

1 She couldn't stand up though she wanted to.

→ _____

2 You can wear my dress if you want to.

→ _____

VOCA accident 사고 | accidental 우연의 | satisfied 만족한

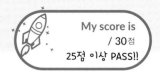

>>> 정답 5쪽

01 다음 우리말을 영어로 바르게 옮긴 것은? (답 2개) 3점

그들은 그 결정에 실망하고 있는 것처럼 보인다.

① They seem to be disappointed with the decision.
② They seem that they are disappointed with the decision.
③ It seems to have been disappointed with the decision.
④ It seems that they are disappointed with the decision.
⑤ It seems that they have been disappointed with the decision.

02 밑줄 친 우리말을 영어로 바르게 나타낸 것은? 2점

<u>간단히 말하면</u>, you have to make a decision by tomorrow.

① To begin with   ② Strange to say
③ So to speak   ④ To be brief
⑤ To be frank

03 다음 문장에서 생략 가능한 부분은? 3점

You may use my photo if you want to use it.

① use   ② want to
③ to use   ④ it
⑤ use it

04 다음 영작에서 어법상 어색한 부분을 찾아 바르게 고친 것은? 3점

그는 길을 잃어버린 것처럼 보였다.
= He seemed that he has lost his way.

① He → It
② seemed → seems
③ has lost → lost
④ He → It, has lost → had lost
⑤ He → It, has lost → lost

05 두 문장의 뜻이 같도록 빈칸에 알맞은 말을 쓰시오. 5점

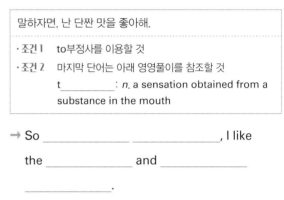

It seems that Dr. Baek finished writing the novel.

→ Dr. Baek seems _____

_____.

06 우리말과 같은 의미가 되도록 조건에 맞게 영작을 완성하시오. 6점

말하자면, 난 단짠 맛을 좋아해.

· 조건 1   to부정사를 이용할 것
· 조건 2   마지막 단어는 아래 영영풀이를 참조할 것
      t_____ : *n.* a sensation obtained from a substance in the mouth

→ So _____ _____, I like

the _____ and _____

_____.

07 대화의 밑줄 친 우리말에 해당하는 표현을 조건에 맞게 영어로 쓰시오. 4점

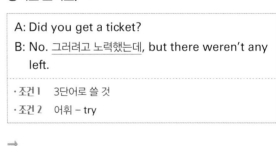

A: Did you get a ticket?
B: No. <u>그러려고 노력했는데</u>, but there weren't any left.

· 조건 1   3단어로 쓸 것
· 조건 2   어휘 – try

→ _____

08 다음 문장 전환에서 어법상 어색한 부분을 찾아 바르게 고치시오. 4점

It appears that the boy detective caught the thief.
= The boy detective appears to caught the thief.

_____ → _____

VOCA disappointed 실망한 | decision 결정 | lose one's way 길을 잃다 | novel 소설 | sensation 감각 | obtain 얻다 | substance 물질 |
detective 탐정 | thief 도둑

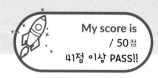

Level 3 Test

01 Which pair is correct for the blanks? 3점

> The cats seemed to be hungry.
> = It _____ that the cats _____ hungry.

① seems – are ② seems – were
③ seemed – will be ④ seemed – were
⑤ seemed – are

02 Which translation is incorrect? 2점

① To tell the truth, she wanted to go there.
(사실대로 말하면)

② The dog is, to be sure, a family member.
(확실히)

③ To begin with, we will do some warm-ups.
(함께 시작하기 위해서)

④ To be frank with you, I'm fond of your sister.
(솔직히 말하자면)

⑤ To make matters worse, it started to snow.
(설상가상으로)

03 Which underlined word "to" is used differently than the others? 2점

① She is planning to go to Montego Bay.
② Who is that girl Malcolm is speaking to?
③ I threw the ball away because I wanted to.
④ He is going to Thailand for winter vacation.
⑤ We're looking forward to hearing from you soon.

04 Which correction is right? 3점

> ⓐ He seems to be greatly shocked.
> ⓑ She seemed that she has gone to Paris.

① ⓐ be → is
② ⓐ seems → seem
③ ⓑ She → It, gone → been
④ ⓑ She → It, has gone → had gone
⑤ ⓑ She → It, has gone → went

05 Who analyzes the sentence correctly? 4점

> To be honest with you, I don't think that shirt looks good on you.

① 민호: To be honest with you는 문장 전체를 수식하는 거야.
② 승표: honest가 아니라 honesty로 써야 해.
③ 명진: 'I'는 셔츠가 'you'한테 어울린다고 생각해.
④ 제영: that은 주격 관계대명사로 쓰인 거야.
⑤ 성실: 문장에서 to부정사는 주어 역할을 해.

06 Among the underlined parts, which can be omitted? 3점

① Well, it's really hard to say.
② I haven't decided what to buy yet.
③ Please give me something cold to drink.
④ You may go to the party if you want to go.
⑤ What I want is to clean out my closet.

07 Each of the following sentences has an error. Which correction is right? 4점

> ⓐ She seems to be popular when young.
> ⓑ Your cat appears to has been very well loved and cared for.

① ⓐ be → had been, ⓑ has → had
② ⓐ be → have been, ⓑ appears → appear
③ ⓐ be → was, ⓑ has been → was
④ ⓐ be → have been, ⓑ has → have
⑤ ⓐ She → It, ⓑ Your cat → It

VOCA warm-up 준비 운동 | be fond of ~을 좋아하다 | look good on ~에게 어울리다 | closet 벽장 | care for 돌보다

08 Which sentences are grammatically underline{incorrect}? (2 answers) 3점

① Call me anytime you want to.
② She seems that she has been lucky.
③ Sad to say, I'm leaving tomorrow.
④ I can't go to the beach though I'd love to.
⑤ He seemed to had grown up in a wealthy family.

Challenge! 주관식 서술형

09 Find the one who marks the sentence underline{incorrectly} and correct the error. 각 2점

> 미라: ⓐ Strange to say, the bird cannot fly. (○)
> 정성: ⓑ To making matters worse, he didn't apologize. (✕)
> 기태: ⓒ We cannot accept such behavior, to be briefly. (○)

(1) 잘못 채점한 사람: _____

(2) 그 문장에서 틀린 곳: _____

(3) 바르게 고친 것: _____

10 Write the omitted words at the end of the sentence. 5점

> I didn't want to attend the meeting, but I had to.

→ _____

11 Fill in the blanks to make the two sentences have the same meaning. 5점

> The employee doesn't seem to work hard.

→ It _____ _____
  that _____ _____
  _____ _____ .

12 Choose the underline{necessary} words and rearrange them to translate the sentence. 5점

> 두말할 나위 없이, 우리는 많은 관심을 끌었다.
> attracted, we, mention, say, attention, needless, a lot of, to

→ _____
  _____

13 This is your friend's notebook. Find TWO errors and correct them. 5점

> 1. S seems to V
> → It seems that S+V
> e.g. "Sorry" seems to be the hardest word to say.
> → "Sorry" seems that it is the hardest word to say.
> 2. S seemed to have p.p.
> → It seemed that S had p.p.
> e.g. The boys seemed to have lost their map.
> → It seems that the boys lost their map.

_____ → _____

_____ → _____

VOCA   wealthy 부유한 | behavior 행동 | attend ~에 참석하다 | employee 직원 | attract 끌다 | attention 관심

Review Test

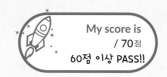

My score is
/ 70점
60점 이상 PASS!!

---

01 U03_1+GP
밑줄 친 부분의 쓰임이 [보기]와 같은 것은? 2점

> 보기   It is difficult <u>to exercise</u> every morning.

① We need a mentor <u>to depend</u> on.
② It's a good idea <u>to get</u> a part-time job.
③ The old lady has no one <u>to talk</u> with.
④ She grew up <u>to be</u> a famous painter.
⑤ I would be glad <u>to visit</u> the village again.

---

02 U03_2

How many words are NOT suitable for the blank? 2점

> Was it _____ of him to wait for her for so long?
>
> | hard | stupid | polite |
> |------|--------|--------|
> | necessary | silly | foolish |
> | important | possible | patient |

① 0개   ② 1개
③ 2개   ④ 3개
⑤ 4개

---

03 U03_3
다음 문장을 영어로 바르게 옮긴 학생은? 2점

> 그의 아버지는 그에게 복수하려고 하지 말라고 말했다.

① 유미: His father told him doesn't seek revenge.
② 소정: His father told him to not seek revenge.
③ 현주: His father told not him to seek revenge.
④ 아리: His father told him not to seek revenge.
⑤ 민주: His father didn't tell him to seek revenge.

---

04 U04_3
다음 대화에서 어법상 어색한 부분은? 2점

> A: Would you like ① <u>to have</u> ② <u>dinner</u> with me tonight?
> B: ③ <u>I'd</u> ④ <u>like</u>, but I ⑤ <u>have</u> a previous engagement.

---

05 U03_1B+GP
다음 문장들을 완성할 때 빈칸에 들어갈 수 없는 것은? 2점
함정

> ⓐ Can you give me a pen to _____ ?
> ⓑ I'd like some milk to _____ .
> ⓒ They borrowed two chairs to _____ .
> ⓓ She brought a sports magazine to _____ .
> ⓔ What clothes do you want to _____ ?

① drink   ② wear
③ sit on   ④ read
⑤ write on

---

06 U03_1A+GP
Which correction is right? 2점

> I decided for me not to study abroad.

① for → of   ② for me → 삭제
③ me → my   ④ not to → to not
⑤ to study → studying

---

07 U04_1
다음 문장 전환에서 빈칸에 알맞은 것으로 짝지어진 것은? 2점
함정

> He doesn't seem to have had a plan then.
> → It _____ that he _____ a plan then.

① seems – has   ② seems – has had
③ seems – had   ④ doesn't seem – has
⑤ doesn't seem – had

---

08 U04_2
빈칸에 알맞은 것을 고르면? 2점

> My daughter speaks Chinese, _____ English.

① to be honest   ② to begin with
③ so to speak   ④ not to mention
⑤ strange to say

---

09 _{U03_1C}
다음 문장의 빈칸에 알맞은 것은? 2점

> Your handwriting is hard _____.

① read
② to read
③ reading
④ for read
⑤ be read

10 ★ 고난도
_{U03_2+U04_1}
How many of ⓐ~ⓔ are grammatically incorrect? 3점

> ⓐ A: Will you join me?
>   B: Sure. I'd love to.
> ⓑ It was so rude for your friend to do that.
> ⓒ The girl seems to have been shocked.
> ⓓ How many times have I told you not to hang out with them?
> ⓔ It seems that your dad has been handsome when young.

① one
② two
③ three
④ four
⑤ five

11 _{U03_1C}
Rearrange the given words to translate the sentence. 4점

> 그 배우는 일어나서 자신이 슈퍼스타가 된 것을 알았다.
>
> find, to, a, the, superstar, woke up, actor, himself

→ _____

_____

12 _{U04_3}
밑줄 친 문장에서 생략할 수 있는 부분에 괄호로 표시하시오. 3점

> I'm sorry that I yelled at you. I didn't mean to yell at you.

13 _{U04_3}
주어진 단어 중 4개를 골라 빈칸에 배열하여 문장을 완성하시오. 4점

> have, to, want, you, don't, that

→ You don't have to wear that windbreaker if

_____.

14 _{U03_3}
대화의 빈칸에 알맞은 표현을 조건에 맞게 쓰시오. 4점

> · 조건 1   엄마가 사용한 단어를 변형하여 3단어로 쓸 것
> · 조건 2   각 단어는 3글자, 2글자, 5글자로 쓸 것

→ _____ _____ _____

15 _{U04_1+GP}
다음 문장과 같은 의미가 되도록 문장을 전환할 때 빈칸에 알맞은 말을 쓰시오. 4점

> The kids appeared to have gotten lost in the forest.

→ It _____ that _____

_____ in the forest.

16 _{U04_1+GP}
Find the sentence that has an error and correct it. 4점

> ⓐ Max seems to be sick yesterday.
> ⓑ The answer appears to be incorrect.

(   ) _____ → _____

17 조건에 맞게 빈칸에 알맞은 말을 쓰시오. 4점 U04_2

> · 조건 I   to부정사를 사용할 것
> · 조건 2   3단어로 쓸 것
> · 조건 3   유의어 – certainly, definitely, no doubt

→ She is, _____, a great

singer.

---

18 밑줄 친 표현의 용법이 같은 문장들의 첫 글자를 이용하여 단어를 완성하시오. 4점 U03_1B+1C

> ⓐ Grandma will go to Japan <u>to meet</u> Ozima.
> ⓑ Susie has something important <u>to tell</u> you.
> ⓒ Nancy called him <u>to ask</u> a question.
> ⓓ Oh, she finally came here <u>to study</u> Korean.
> ⓔ Will went to the store <u>to buy</u> some milk.

→ Your answer is □R□□□.

---

19 주어진 문장을 [보기]와 같이 전환하시오. 4점 U03_2

> 보기   He lost a sock. He was careless.
> → It was careless of him to have lost a sock.

My sister deleted my secret folder. It was cruel.

→ _____

_____

---

20 괄호 안의 단어를 이용하여 우리말을 영작하시오. 각 2점 U04_1

> 어젯밤에 비가 온 것 같아. (seem, rain)

(1) _____ _____ to

_____ last night.

(2) _____ that

_____ last night.

[21~22] 다음 글을 읽고 물음에 답하시오.

Lindsay had an awful weekend. Her parents went to Ottawa to visit her aunt, but she stayed home. Last Saturday, she went down to the basement to do the laundry. She went back upstairs, but the door ⓐwas locked! Lindsay, fortunately, found some food to eat. There were extra groceries in the basement. She ⓑlay some clothes from the laundry on the floor and slept on them. Early Sunday morning, her parents came home and found her ⓒslept in the basement. Her father said, "Last night, we called you ⓓto have seen if everything was okay, but you didn't answer the phone. We have come back as soon as possible. We're just relieved ⓔthat you're all right."

---

21 윗글의 밑줄 친 부분 ⓐ~ⓔ 중 어법상 어색한 것으로 짝지어진 것은? 4점 U02_1B+U04_1 ★고난도

① ⓐ, ⓔ   ② ⓒ, ⓓ

③ ⓑ, ⓒ, ⓓ   ④ ⓑ, ⓓ, ⓔ

⑤ ⓒ, ⓓ, ⓔ

---

22 윗글의 내용을 다음과 같이 요약하고자 할 때 빈칸 (A)와 (B)에 각각 들어갈 적절한 말을 쓰시오. 각 3점 U03_1C ★고난도

> Lindsay was locked in the basement when she went downstairs ___(A)___ the laundry. Her parents came back home next day because she didn't ___(B)___ the phone.

(A) _____

(B) _____

CHAPTER 03

동명사

개념이해책
32쪽 함께 보기

■ 아래 표의 빈칸에 알맞은 내용을 써 넣으세요. >>> 정답 7쪽

CONCEPT 1 동명사의 용법

1)_____ 역할	Taking pictures here **is not allowed.**
2)_____ 역할	What I hate the most is **repeating myself.**
3)_____의 목적어 역할	My girlfriend likes **going to the movies with me.**
4)_____의 목적어 역할	Can you sneeze without **closing your eyes?**

CONCEPT 2 동명사의 의미상의 주어

| 사람, 생물 | 5)_____ 격 [6)_____ 격]+-ing |
| 부정대명사, 무생물 | 7)_____ 격+-ing |

CONCEPT 3 동명사의 부정

| 8)_____ [9)_____]+-ing |

Level 1 Test

>>> 정답 7쪽

A 우리말과 일치하도록 밑줄 친 부분을 바르게 고치시오.

1 건강한 것은 모든 이에게 정말로 중요하다.

= <u>Be</u> healthy is really important to everyone.

→ _____

2 저를 집까지 안전하게 태워다 주셔서 감사합니다.

= Thank you for <u>to drive</u> me home safely.

→ _____

3 너는 오늘 그 보고서 쓰는 것을 끝마쳐야 한다.

= You have to finish <u>write</u> the report today.

→ _____

4 그는 방과 후에 말 타기를 즐긴다.

= He enjoys <u>to ride</u> his horse after school.

→ _____

B 밑줄 친 부분이 어색하면 고치시오.

1 The teacher is upset about <u>he</u> being late.

→ _____

2 They didn't mind <u>Beth's</u> going there.

→ _____

3 <u>Me</u> forgetting her name was embarrassing.

→ _____

C 괄호 안에 주어진 단어를 이용하여 문장을 완성하시오.

1 I regret _____ _____ to snowboard. (not, learn)

2 I appreciate your _____ _____ anything to him. (not, say)

VOCA upset 화난 | embarrassing 당황스러운 | regret 후회하다 | appreciate 감사하다

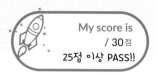

01 빈칸에 들어갈 말로 적절한 것은? 2점

_____ a movie takes a long time in Italy.

① Download
② Downloading
③ Downloads
④ Downloaded
⑤ To downloading

02 빈칸에 들어갈 말이 바르게 짝지어진 것은? 3점

My son drove my car to Miami. _____ driving to the city was easier than _____ had expected.

① He – I
② His – Me
③ His – I
④ Him – I
⑤ Him – Me

03 다음 우리말을 바르게 영작한 것은? 3점

그는 시험을 통과하지 못할 것을 두려워한다.

① He is not afraid of passing the test.
② He is not afraid of not passing the test.
③ He is afraid of not passing the test.
④ He is afraid of passing not the test.
⑤ He is afraid not of passing the test.

04 밑줄 친 단어의 역할이 주어진 문장과 다른 예문을 쓴 학생은? 2점

The wind was perfect for sailing a yacht.

① 건희: I'm poor at remembering names.
② 혜련: He hates going outside when it is raining.
③ 광숙: She was fond of walking dogs in the snow.
④ 혜진: Waiting for lunchtime is hard for me.
⑤ 선숙: We like going on field trips on Fridays.

05 문장에서 어법상 어색한 것을 찾아 고치시오. 4점

서술형

My grandmother enjoys swimming in the summer and skate in the winter.

_____ → _____

06 그림을 보고, 주어진 단어들 중 필요한 것만 골라 문장을 완성하시오. 5점

서술형

don't, they, like, having, she, them, didn't

→ _____

a party at her house.

07 주어진 단어들을 우리말에 맞도록 배열하시오. 5점

서술형

그는 공부할 시간이 없다고 늘 불평한다.
not, about, study, time, always, complains, having, he, to

→ _____

08 조건에 맞도록 우리말을 영작하시오. 6점

서술형

많이 웃는 것은 우리의 건강에 좋다.

· 조건 1   동명사를 사용할 것
· 조건 2   동명사의 의미상의 주어가 꼭 필요하면 쓸 것
· 조건 3   어휘 – laugh a lot, be good for

→ _____

VOCA expect 예상하다 | sail 항해하다 | yacht 요트 | be fond of ~을 좋아하다 | go on a field trip 현장 학습을 가다 | complain 불평하다

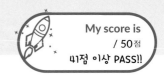
01 Which underlined word is used in the same way as in the given sentence? 2점

> What I hate the most is waiting in line.

① Dancing on the stage made her famous.
② She enjoys cooking for her friends.
③ Making fun of fat people is not right.
④ Is your favorite pastime playing baseball?
⑤ I am interested in making a study group.

02 Who analyzes the sentence correctly? 3점

> She was proud of her son's winning a gold medal.

① 수은: 시제가 과거니까 winning을 won으로 써도 돼.
② 지민: her son's는 '그녀의 아들의'라고 해석해야 해.
③ 정민: of는 전치사이고 her son은 문장의 목적어야.
④ 꽃별: 전치사 뒤에는 명사도 쓰니까 win으로 써도 돼.
⑤ 현정: her son's는 winning의 의미상의 주어야.

03 Which correction is right? 3점

> Swimming with the children all day have made the coach exhausted.

① Swimming → Swim
② children → childs
③ have → has
④ coach → coach's
⑤ exhausted → exhausting

04 Which TWO of the underlined words are used differently than the others? 3점

① Dorothy, are you good at finding things?
② Translating Korean into English is difficult.
③ Answering very easy questions is boring.
④ You should give up smoking very soon.
⑤ She's worried about entering the competition.

05 Which words come third and fourth when translating the sentence? 3점

> 그녀는 자전거를 타고 그 산을 오르지 않을 것을 고려했다.
> (cycle up)

① considered cycling   ② considered to
③ not to   ④ not cycling
⑤ cycling up

06 Among the underlined parts, which is grammatically correct? (Find ALL.) 3점

① I appreciate your inviting me to your house.
② She couldn't stand my friend's saying that.
③ Do you mind me turning off the fan?
④ She likes Mickey working at her office.
⑤ They denied anybody's entering the house.

07 Which sentence is incorrect? (2 answers) 3점

① She surely remembered he saying that.
② I don't like the idea of your going camping.
③ I'm sorry about her failing the entrance exam.
④ Not having anything to do on a holiday is boring.
⑤ Forgive me for not to send an email sooner.

VOCA wait in line 줄 서서 기다리다 | pastime 취미, 여가 활동 | win a gold medal 금메달을 따다 | exhausted 녹초가 된 | translate 번역하다 | entrance exam 입학 시험

08 The following show whether the given sentences are grammatically correct (C) or incorrect (I). How many are marked right? 4점

> ⓐ She denied losing my bag. → C
> ⓑ He is ashamed of having not a car. → C
> ⓒ Sharing your things with your friends are nice. → C
> ⓓ I'm thinking about not go there. → I

① one　　　　　　② two
③ three　　　　　④ four
⑤ none

09 Which sentence has the most errors? 4점

① Do you mind calling back later?
② I am used to you not to be around.
③ Thank you for not to give up on me.
④ There is few chance of the bus to be lately.
⑤ Everybody dislike Jason to keep the ball.

Challenge! 주관식 서술형

10 Rearrange the given words to translate the sentence. 6점

> 손을 씻기 전에 음식을 먹지 마라.
> hands, food, your, don't, before, washing, eat

→ _____

11 Translate the sentence according to the conditions. 7점

> 엄마는 내가 사실을 말하지 않은 것에 대해 화를 내셨다.
> ┈┈┈┈┈┈┈┈┈┈┈┈┈┈┈┈┈┈┈┈┈┈┈┈┈┈┈┈┈┈┈
> · Condition 1　동명사의 의미상의 주어를 쓸 것
> · Condition 2　소유격을 두 번 사용할 것
> · Condition 3　be angry about ~에 대해 화를 내다

→ _____
　_____

12 Find the sentence that has an error and correct it. 4점

> ⓐ Walking dogs is a great way to get exercise.
> ⓑ I kept thinking about to go to that college.

(　　) _____ → _____

13 This is a conversation between Gyumin and Hyerim about the use of gerunds(동명사). Based on what Hyerim says, correct the error in the underlined sentence. 4점

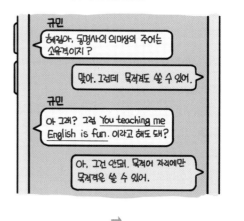

→ _____ → _____

VOCA　deny 부인하다 ｜ ashamed of ~을 부끄러워하는 ｜ share 나누다 ｜ give up on ~을 포기하다 ｜ walk 산책시키다 ｜ get exercise 운동하다

06 동명사, 현재분사, to부정사

개념이해책
35쪽 함께 보기

■ 아래 표의 빈칸에 알맞은 내용을 써 넣으세요. ›››› 정답 7쪽

① 동명사와 현재분사

	기능	표현
동명사	1)_____ : 주어, 목적어, 보어	2)_____, 목적
현재분사	형용사, 3)_____	4)_____, 상태

② 동명사와 to부정사

동사	목적어
dislike, finish, enjoy, mind, give up, avoid, deny, delay, keep (on), postpone 등	5)_____
want, hope, wish, plan, agree, decide, choose, refuse, expect, would like 등	6)_____
like, love, hate, begin, start, continue	7)_____

③ 동명사의 관용적 표현

- on+-ing: 8)_____
- go on+-ing: 10)_____
- look forward to+-ing: 12)_____
- be used[accustomed] to+-ing: 14)_____
- be far from+-ing: 16)_____
- be busy+-ing: 18)_____
- It's no use[good]+-ing: 20)_____
- be tired of+-ing: 22)_____
- have difficulty[trouble, a hard time]+-ing: 23)_____

- cannot help+-ing: 9)_____
- go+-ing: 11)_____
- How[What] about+-ing ~?: 13)_____
- be worth+-ing: 15)_____
- There is no+-ing: 17)_____
- feel like+-ing: 19)_____
- spend[waste] 시간[돈]+-ing: 21)_____

Level 1 Test

›››› 정답 8쪽

A 동명사나 현재분사에 밑줄을 치고 구분하시오.

1 My kid is great at solving jigsaw puzzles.

→ _____

2 Do you know the woman singing alone?

→ _____

B [ ]에서 알맞은 것을 고르시오.

1 He [failed / finished] printing the document.

2 I won't [want / give up] writing this book.

3 Did you [promise / enjoy] flying a kite?

C 밑줄 친 부분이 어색하면 고치시오.

1 I cannot help but <u>laughing</u>.

→ _____

2 She felt like <u>to walk</u> in the rain.

→ _____

3 Are you having a hard time <u>to follow</u> me?

→ _____

4 Computers are far from <u>replacing</u> people.

→ _____

VOCA jigsaw puzzle 직소 퍼즐 | document 서류 | replace 대체하다

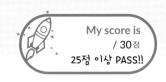

01 밑줄 친 부분의 쓰임이 나머지와 <u>다른</u> 하나는? 2점

① I need two <u>sleeping</u> bags for camping.
② She often goes to a <u>swimming</u> pool near her house.
③ <u>Telling</u> a lie can be helpful sometimes.
④ Their house has a very large <u>living</u> room.
⑤ She saw a <u>jogging</u> couple every morning.

02 빈칸에 알맞지 <u>않은</u> 것의 개수는? 3점

> She _____ watching bullfighting.
>
> ⓐ enjoys   ⓑ gave up   ⓒ doesn't mind
> ⓓ finished   ⓔ planned   ⓕ failed
> ⓖ loves   ⓗ hates   ⓘ considered

① one
② two
③ three
④ four
⑤ five

03 두 문장 중 <u>어색한</u> 것을 찾아 바르게 고친 학생은? 3점

> ⓐ This book is definitely worth to read twice.
> ⓑ On coming back home, she started preparing dinner.

① 이고은: ⓐ read → reading
② 박철용: ⓐ to read → reading
③ 김경민: ⓑ coming → came
④ 김정은: ⓑ coming → to come
⑤ 김낙연: ⓑ preparing → to prepare

04 다음 중 어법상 <u>어색한</u> 것은? 2점

① Please remember to come on time.
② I hope to see you in person this time.
③ He learned to read at the age of three.
④ Would you mind calling back later?
⑤ You must stop to smoke for your health.

05 주어진 단어 중 필요한 <u>6단어</u>를 골라 배열하여 영작을 완성하시오. 5점 [서술형]

> 그는 잠이 오지 않아 시험 삼아 따뜻한 우유를 마셔 보았다.
> some, any, to drink, he, warm, tried, milk, drinking

→ He couldn't sleep, so _____

_____.

06 다음 두 문장 중 <u>어색한</u> 것을 찾아 바르게 고치시오. 4점 [서술형]

> ⓐ I don't remember to meet him before.
> ⓑ Everyone in my family agreed to build a treehouse.

(   ) _____ → _____

07 조건에 맞도록 영작을 완성하시오. 5점 [서술형]

> 나는 밤에 공부하는 데 어려움이 있어서 주로 이른 아침에 공부한다.
>
> ·조건 1   빈칸에 관사를 쓰지 말 것
> ·조건 2   3단어로 완성할 것

→ I _____ at

night, so I usually study early in the morning.

08 그림을 보고 조건에 맞게 문장을 완성하시오. 6점 [서술형]

> ·조건 1   어휘 – spend, buy
> ·조건 2   과거 시제로 쓸 것

→ Mrs. Seo _____ 50,000 won

_____ a hat for her baby.

VOCA   bullfighting 투우 | definitely 확실히 | in person 직접 | call back 다시 전화하다 | agree 동의하다 | treehouse 나무 위의 집

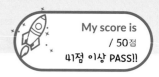
01 Which sentence does NOT have a gerund (동명사)? 2점

① Playing computer games is my hobby.
② Is he still reading a comic book in his room?
③ I hardly enjoy listening to classical music.
④ What is your reason for being late?
⑤ Becoming a soccer player is her dream.

02 Which word CANNOT be used when translating the sentence? 3점

> Rob은 젓가락을 사용하는 데 익숙하지 않다.

① not   ② used
③ accustomed   ④ to
⑤ use

03 How many sentences are grammatically incorrect? 3점

> ⓐ I look forward to see you soon.
> ⓑ Don't you remember seeing me before?
> ⓒ He's having a hard time looking for an exit.
> ⓓ I don't think being rich is the most important thing.
> ⓔ She spent her whole life try to make her country rich.

① one   ② two
③ three   ④ four
⑤ five

04 Which words are suitable for the blank? 3점

> A: Look! Those fish are about _____ in the river.
> B: Unless we stop _____ trash there, all the fish will die.

① to die – to throw   ② to die – throwing
③ die – to throw   ④ dying – throwing
⑤ dying – to throw

05 Which correction is right? 2점

> Many people think that be healthy is the most important thing of all.

① many → much   ② that → if
③ be → being   ④ is → are
⑤ thing → things

06 Who understands the underlined words correctly? 3점

> Roger is ⓐ changing his clothes in the ⓑ changing room.

① 보나: ⓐ는 동명사이고 ⓑ는 현재분사야.
② 성광: ⓐ는 진행이고 ⓑ는 능동의 현재분사야.
③ 명기: ⓐ는 현재분사이고 ⓑ는 동명사야.
④ 종욱: ⓐ와 ⓑ 둘 다 동명사야.
⑤ 상우: ⓐ는 용도를 나타내고 ⓑ는 목적을 나타내.

07 Which of the underlined parts is grammatically incorrect? (Find ALL.) 3점

① We will go to fish this weekend.
② That is absolutely far from being true.
③ Mary is busy to write her report.
④ CN Tower is worth to visit at least once.
⑤ It is no use complaining about it.

08 How many of the underlined words are used differently than in the given sentence? 3점

> What I like the most is learning a foreign language.
>
> ⓐ Who is that crying man?
> ⓑ Look at the boys playing hockey.
> ⓒ What are you learning these days?
> ⓓ My hobby is taking pictures of clouds.

① none   ② one
③ two   ④ three
⑤ all

VOCA reason 이유 | exit 출구 | trash 쓰레기 | changing room 탈의실 | complain 불평하다

09 How many of the following CANNOT make a grammatically correct sentence? 4점

> ⓐ expect / you / here / seeing / I / . / didn't
> ⓑ questions / She / to / . / avoided / my / answer
> ⓒ continued / snow / The / . / until / falling / dark
> ⓓ a / donation / you / like / Would / ? / making
> ⓔ tickets / . / They / agreed / for / to / reserve / us / two

① one
② two
③ three
④ four
⑤ none

10 Which words are correct for the blanks? 3점

> It has _____ all day and _____ for another day or two.

① rained – rained
② raining – will rain
③ snowing – will
④ snowed – won't stop
⑤ snowed – snows

Challenge! 주관식 서술형

11 Translate the sentence by using the given words. 6점

> 그는 계속해서 필라테스(Pilates)를 배우기로 결심했다.
> decide, keep, learn

→ _____

12 Fill in each blank by using the word "sleep." 각 2점

(1) He likes _____ in a hammock.

(2) She dislikes _____ in unfamiliar places.

(3) I would like _____ in my mom's arms again.

13 Complete the sentence describing the picture by using the words from the picture. Change the form if necessary. 5점

I shouldn't have climbed up here without Simba.

→ The cat regrets _____

_____ _____ Simba.

14 Find the sentence that has an error and correct it. 4점

> ⓐ I am tired of Mr. Jackson being selfish.
> ⓑ Micky couldn't help be worried about his pets at home.

( ) _____ → _____

VOCA make a donation 기부하다 | reserve 예약하다 | hammock 그물 침대 | unfamiliar 낯선, 생소한 | selfish 이기적인

Review Test

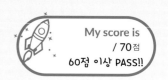

U06_1

01 밑줄 친 부분에 대해 바르게 이해하고 있는 학생은? 2점

> ⓐ Ben sometimes takes a sleeping pill.
> ⓑ Diego was sleeping on the sofa.

① 정윤: ⓐ sleeping은 진행을 나타내는 현재분사야.
② 애리: ⓐ '잠을 위한 약'이므로 sleeping은 동명사야.
③ 덕준: ⓑ sleeping은 보어 자리니까 동명사야.
④ 은미: ⓑ sleeping은 목적을 나타내는 현재분사야.
⑤ 희정: ⓐ ⓑ sleeping 둘 다 -ing니까 동명사야.

U05_1+2

02 Whose analysis of the given sentence is <u>incorrect</u>? (3 answers) 3점

> They insisted on his becoming the leader of the club.

① 승화: insist on은 '~을 고집하다'의 뜻이야.
② 연흥: his는 동명사의 의미상의 주어인데 him으로는 쓸 수 없어.
③ 재교: becoming은 on의 목적어로 쓰인 동명사야.
④ 서희: becoming은 to become으로도 쓸 수 있어.
⑤ 상미: his를 빼도 전혀 의미상의 차이가 없어.

U05_1

03 Which underlined word is used in the same way as in the given sentence? 2점

> My second bad habit is not <u>putting</u> things back.

① <u>Taking</u> a hot bath makes me relaxed.
② Brush your teeth before <u>going</u> to bed.
③ His favorite activity is <u>shopping</u> online at night.
④ Excuse me. Would you mind my <u>sitting</u> next to you?
⑤ I haven't finished <u>watching</u> the movie yet.

U05_1+3

04 한눈에 쏙 다음을 영작할 때 문장 맨 앞에서부터 4번째와 7번째 올 단어로 바르게 짝지어진 것은? 3점

> 미우는 오늘 학교에 가지 않는 것에 대해 행복해하는 것처럼 보인다.
> = Miu _____ to _____ today.

① not – happy　　② not – about
③ be – about　　④ be – going
⑤ be – not

U05_3

05 밑줄 친 부분 중 어법상 <u>어색한</u> 것은? 2점

> The coach ① <u>suggested</u> ② <u>didn't</u> ③ <u>staying</u> up ④ <u>late</u> at night ⑤ <u>before</u> a game.

U06_GP

06 다음 영작에서 <u>어색한</u> 것을 찾아 바르게 고친 것은? 3점

> 내 이마에 한번 손 좀 대봐.
> =Try to put your hands on my forehead.

① Try → Tried　　② Try → Trying
③ to put → putting　　④ to put → put
⑤ on → at

U06_GP

07 다음 우리말과 뜻이 같도록 할 때, 빈칸에 알맞은 것은? 2점

> 아빠는 도시락 가져가는 것을 잊으셨다.
> = Dad forgot _____ his lunchbox.

① bring　　② brought
③ bringing　　④ to bring
⑤ to have brought

U06_3

08 Which is the common word for the blanks? 2점

- There is no use _____ the harbor tomorrow.
- The port in Pohang is worth _____ twice.

① to visit   ② visit

③ visits   ④ visiting

⑤ to visiting

U06_3

09 How many sentences are grammatically correct? 4점

ⓐ He had difficulty to find a new job.
ⓑ The boy is far from being stupid.
ⓒ She felt blue, so she couldn't help cry.
ⓓ Everybody was tired of his lying.
ⓔ I'm planning to go to skiing this winter.

① one   ② two

③ three   ④ four

⑤ five

U06_3

10 우리말과 일치하도록 주어진 단어를 빈칸에 배열하여 문장을 완성하시오. (한 단어는 반드시 어형 변화할 것) 5점

내 여동생은 그 게임에서 10만 점을 넘기는 데 어려움을 겪었다.

a, hard, over, points, get, my, time, sister, 100,000, had

→ _____

_____ in

the game.

U05_2+3+GP

11 Find the sentence that has an error and correct it. 4점

ⓐ I can't imagine not your knowing how to do it.
ⓑ My father was upset about not catching a single fish.

(   ) _____ → _____

U05_2+3+GP

12 [보기]와 같이 동명사를 이용하여 두 문장을 한 문장으로 다시 쓰시오. 5점

보기   Kelly won a scholarship.
       I am so excited about that fact.

       → I am so excited about Kelly winning a scholarship.

He didn't join the team.
I couldn't understand that fact.

→ _____

_____

U05_3+GP

13 그림을 보고 주어진 단어를 빈칸에 바르게 배열하여 문장을 완성하시오. 5점

smoking, of, ashamed, not, he, is

→ _____ at

the bus stop.

U05_3

14 Find the error and correct it. 4점

Having not a friend to play with made him feel lonely.

_____ → _____

15 ^{U06_3} 우리말과 일치하도록 괄호 안의 단어를 이용하여 빈칸에 알맞은 표현을 쓰시오. 4점

> 아버지가 돌아가셨다는 소식을 듣자마자 Luke는 큰 소리로 울기 시작했다. (hear, pass away)

→ _____ _____ the news of

his _____ _____

_____, Luke began to cry out loud.

16 ^{U06_1} 다음 중 동명사가 쓰인 문장들의 첫 글자를 골라 넣어 아래의 단어를 완성하시오. 4점

> ⓐ Aawut is dreaming of being a K-pop singer.
> ⓑ Eating only what you want is not good for your health.
> ⓒ Paying attention in class is important.
> ⓓ Is your brother having fun at the party?
> ⓔ I'm saving money for a new computer.
> ⓕ Sending an email to him is a better choice.

→ ☐ L ☐ ☐ ☐ E

17 ^{U06_GP} 다음은 다이아몬드에 관한 Q&A이다. 어법상 어색한 부분을 모두 찾아 바르게 고치시오. 6점

함정

> Q: What material is used to cut diamonds?
> A: A diamond is used to cutting another diamond. Because this stone is so hard, one of the only things that can be used to cutting it is another diamond.

→ _____

_____

[18~19] 다음 글을 읽고 물음에 답하시오.

There are many things ⓐfor teenagers to do outside home. Home is not ⓑconsidering the center of entertainment anymore. However, teens have to keep in mind that ⓒhave an exciting life outside home doesn't mean that family relationships are unimportant. When there are some problems to solve, (A)부모님이나 형제자매에게 조언을 요청하는 것 is something that they need to do. Teenagers who have close relationships with their family members ⓓis lucky. The reason is that they do not have to go too far ⓔto get some advice.

18 ^{U03_2+U11_1+U05_1+U01_1+U03_1C} 윗글의 밑줄 친 ⓐ~ⓔ 중 어법상 어색한 것을 찾아 바르게 고친 것은? (정답 최대 3개) 4점

★ 고난도

① ⓐ for → of
② ⓑ considering → considered
③ ⓒ have → having
④ ⓓ is → are
⑤ ⓔ to get → gotten

19 ^{U05_1} 윗글의 밑줄 친 (A)와 같은 뜻이 되도록 주어진 단어를 배열하시오. 6점

★ 고난도

> a / sibling / advice / a / for / or / asking / parent

→ _____

CHAPTER 04
시제

개념이해책
42쪽 함께 보기

 아래 표의 빈칸에 알맞은 내용을 써 넣으세요. >>> 정답 9쪽

❶ 단순 시제

종류	내용
현재 시제	① 현재의 동작, 상태 ② 현재의 1)_____, 반복적 행위 ③ 불변의 2)_____, 사실, 격언
과거 시제	① 과거의 동작, 상태 ② 역사적 3)_____
미래 시제	① 미래에 일어날 동작, 상태 ② 주어의 4)_____ 표현 ③ 계획, 예정

❷ 현재 시제가 미래를 나타내는 경우

5)_____의 부사절	when, before, after절	When he arrives home, I'll call you.
	6)_____절	If the weather is fine, I will go out.
7)_____ 동사 + 미래 부사구	go, come	He comes[is coming] back home tomorrow.
	leave, arrive	She leaves[is leaving] L.A. next week.

❸ 현재완료 시제

용법	의미	자주 함께 쓰이는 표현
완료	8)_____	9) j_____, 10) a_____, 11) y_____
경험	12)_____	13) e_____, never, before, once
계속	14)_____	15) f_____, 16) s_____, how long
결과	17)_____	go, come, leave, lose, buy

Level 1 Test

>>> 정답 9쪽

A [ ]에서 알맞은 것을 고르시오.

1 My mom [does / is doing] yoga every day.

2 If you [do / will do] your best, you will achieve your goal.

3 I will see you when you [will get / get] there.

4 He [read / has read] the cartoon more than 20 times so far.

5 When [did you leave / have you left] Mokpo?

6 They have [been / gone] to Hong Kong many times.

B 어법상 어색한 부분이 있으면 찾아 고치시오.

1 He has seen the exhibition last week.

_____ → _____

2 Tina has been to the bank. She'll be back soon.

_____ → _____

3 He has been driving for two hours ago.

_____ → _____

4 I'll stay home until I will get over the flu.

_____ → _____

VOCA do one's best 최선을 다하다 | achieve 달성하다, 이루다 | goal 목표 | exhibition 전시(회) | get over 극복하다 | flu 독감

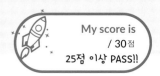
01 밑줄 친 부분의 용법이 나머지와 <u>다른</u> 하나는? 2점

① <u>Have</u> you ever <u>tried</u> windsurfing?
② Three years <u>have passed</u> since you entered middle school.
③ I <u>have been</u> to Africa before.
④ <u>Have</u> you ever <u>done</u> anything special for your parents?
⑤ I <u>have</u> never <u>seen</u> Ted furious like that.

02 다음 대화의 빈칸에 가장 알맞은 것은? 2점

> A: Have you done your homework?
> B: Actually, I _____.
> A: Can you tell me why?
> B: I lost my book.

① am   ② do
③ have   ④ haven't
⑤ am not

03 다음 중 어법상 <u>어색한</u> 문장의 개수는? 3점

> ⓐ When have you started doing chin-ups?
> ⓑ He has been ill two weeks ago.
> ⓒ She has been to Guam before.
> ⓓ We have found this machine in 2016.
> ⓔ Have you gotten the letter yesterday?

① 1개   ② 2개
③ 3개   ④ 4개
⑤ 5개

04 다음 문장에서 어법상 <u>어색한</u> 부분을 올바르게 고친 것을 <u>모두</u> 고르시오. 3점

> I have been to my uncle's house the other day.

① have been → have gone
② have been → went
③ have been → go
④ the other day → then
⑤ the other day → before

05 'ride'를 각 빈칸에 알맞은 형태로 쓰시오. 4점

 서술형

> A: Have you ever _____ a horse before?
> B: Yes, I have. When I visited Jeju-do, I _____ one.

06 괄호 안의 단어를 활용하여 빈칸에 알맞은 말을 쓰시오. 4점

 서술형

> I'm Jane. My father is a computer programmer. I've been interested in computers ever since I was very young. In fact, I have already _____ some programs. (write)

07 다음 대화의 빈칸에 알맞은 말을 쓰시오. 5점

서술형

> A: How long have you been here?
> B: I have been here _____ noon.

08 오늘은 목요일이다. 이번 주의 날씨 그림을 보고 최근 4일 동안의 날씨를 묘사하는 문장을 조건에 맞게 영작하시오. 7점

서술형

MON	TUE	WED	THU

· 조건 1   어휘 – the weather, sunny, for, days
· 조건 2   8단어로 쓸 것

→ _____

_____

VOCA windsurfing 윈드서핑 | furious 몹시 화가 난 | chin-up 턱걸이 | the other day 지난번에, 일전에

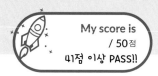
01 Which is proper for the blank? 2점

> My brother leaves for Africa _____. He is going to volunteer at an NGO.

① two days ago   ② before

③ last year   ④ soon

⑤ yesterday

02 Which set has suitable words for the blanks? 3점

> • I have _____ delivered the package.
> • She hasn't met her ideal type _____.

① just – already   ② yet – already

③ yet – just   ④ just – yet

⑤ already – just

03 Which underlined verb represents a different time than the others? 3점

① He <u>works</u> at the National Assembly.

② My dad never <u>skips</u> breakfast.

③ I won't climb the mountain if it <u>snows</u> tomorrow.

④ She always <u>takes</u> a shower in the morning.

⑤ She <u>goes</u> to school with her friend every day.

04 Which of the underlined parts has the same usage as in the given sentence? 3점

> I've never <u>heard</u> such a ridiculous story.

① <u>Have</u> you ever <u>tried</u> it before?

② He <u>has</u> just <u>come</u> back home.

③ <u>Have</u> you <u>decided</u> what to eat for lunch?

④ She <u>has studied</u> politics for seven years.

⑤ He <u>has lost</u> his puppy.

05 Which correction is right? 3점

> I'm not sure when he announce his retirement.

① when → if

② when → that

③ announce → announces

④ announce → will announce

⑤ he → does he

06 Which is suitable for the blank? 3점

> Maria _____ German, but she can communicate in it a little.

① masters

② mastered

③ wasn't mastering

④ hasn't mastered

⑤ will master

VOCA NGO (= nongovernmental organization) 비정부기구, 엔지오 | deliver 배달하다 | package 소포, 택배 | ideal type 이상형 | National Assembly 국회 | ridiculous 웃기는, 터무니없는 | politics 정치(학) | announce 발표하다 | retirement 은퇴, 퇴직 | master 완전히 익히다 | communicate 의사소통하다

50

07 How many sentences are <u>incorrect</u>? 4점

> ⓐ Where did my glasses gone?
> ⓑ Mike has to paint the door before it will rain.
> ⓒ He has lived in the town for 2002.
> ⓓ Do you know that she is coming back tomorrow?
> ⓔ I have just made a cake for you.

① 1개   ② 2개
③ 3개   ④ 4개
⑤ 5개

08 Which CANNOT make a grammatically correct sentence? (2 answers) 4점

① prison / ? / has / he / When / of / gotten / out
② yesterday / I / him / since / . / haven't / seen
③ ever / used / app / this / you / before / Have / ?
④ 2018, / house / In / to / they / a / moved / have / . / new
⑤ family / . / to / support / hard / worked / She / her / has

Challenge! 주관식 서술형

09 Find the error in the dialog and correct it. 4점

©doamama

> Cathy: Have you ever heard of Nelson Mandela?
> Minsu: Nelson Mandela? No. Who's that?
> Cathy: He has fought for equality for blacks in South Africa. He died in 2013.

_____ → _____

10 Fill in the blanks to combine the two sentences into one. 5점

> Tommy was interested in art when he was a kid. He is still interested in art.

→ Tommy _____

art _____ he was a kid.

11 Translate the sentences according to the conditions. 6점

> 우리는 아직 택배를 받지 못했다.
>
> • Condition 1   어휘 – the parcel, receive, yet
> • Condition 2   6단어로 쓸 것
> • Condition 3   현재완료로 쓸 것

→ _____

12 Look at Yuki's wish list and make two complete sentences as in the example. 각 5점

Yuki's wishes	*Did* or *Didn't*
To try kimchi	Done
To meet Lee Minho	Not done
To go to Gyeongju	Done

> 보기   Yuki has tried kimchi.

(1) To meet Lee Minho

→ _____

(2) To go to Gyeongju

→ _____

VOCA   support 부양하다, 지지하다 | equality 평등 | blacks 흑인

UNIT 08 과거완료 시제, 진행 시제

■ 아래 표의 빈칸에 알맞은 내용을 써 넣으세요. >>> 정답 10쪽

개념이해책
45쪽 함께 보기

CONCEPT 1 과거완료 시제

종류	의미	예문
1)_____	2)_____	He had just finished the work when I arrived.
3)_____	4)_____	I had never seen a dolphin before I came here.
5)_____	6)_____	How long had you waited there until you met him?
7)_____	8)_____	I had lost my wallet, so I couldn't pay for the meal.

CONCEPT 2 진행 시제

종류	형태	종류	형태
현재 진행형	9)_____	현재완료 진행형	11)_____
과거 진행형	10)_____	과거완료 진행형	12)_____

CONCEPT 3 동사의 12 시제

현재	기본	She writes a poem.	완료	She 18)_____ a poem.	
	진행	She 13)_____ a poem.	완료 진행	She 19)_____ a poem.	
과거	기본	She 14)_____ a poem.	완료	She 20)_____ a poem.	
	진행	She 15)_____ a poem.	완료 진행	She 21)_____ a poem.	
미래	기본	She 16)_____ a poem.	완료	She 22)_____ a poem.	
	진행	She 17)_____ a poem.	완료 진행	She 23)_____ a poem.	

Level 1 Test

>>> 정답 10쪽

A 다음 [ ]에서 알맞은 것을 고르시오.

1 Before she was 20 years old, she [has been / had been] to America three times.

2 I [have had / had had] a lot of money before I lent it to him.

3 He has to give up on buying a car because he [has spent / had spent] all his money.

4 A movie was on TV which I [have seen / had seen] before.

5 I found out that my sister [have worn / had worn] my sweater without telling me.

B 밑줄 친 부분을 바르게 고치시오. (단, 모두 진행 시제로 쓸 것)

1 He has been having dinner at 7 yesterday.

→ _____

2 We have chatted for about an hour when Molly turned up.

→ _____

3 She talked on the phone since she came home.

→ _____

VOCA lend (-lent-lent) 빌려주다 | give up on ~을 포기하다 | find out 알아내다 | chat 수다 떨다 | turn up 나타나다

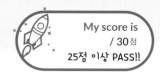
[01~02] 빈칸에 들어갈 말로 알맞은 것을 고르시오. 각 2점

01

> She wanted to go out but found that someone
> _____ the door.

① locked   ② has locked

③ has been locking   ④ is locking

⑤ had locked

02

> Mina couldn't see anything well because she
> _____ her glasses.

① break   ② broke

③ was broken   ④ breaking

⑤ had broken

03 밑줄 친 동사의 올바른 형태로 알맞은 것은? 3점

> A: What's this?
> B: It's a book about American history. I <u>read</u> it
>   since last month.

① have been reading   ② read

③ will read   ④ am reading

⑤ was reading

04 어법상 어색한 부분을 바르게 고친 학생은? 3점

> ⓐ She has been waiting for him for 2 hours.
> ⓑ We ate the cake she had made for us.
> ⓒ It had snowed a lot during the night, so the
>   bus didn't come this morning.
> ⓓ My father has been in the Army since 2011.
> ⓔ Jane has been taking piano lessons since
>   three months.

① 용준: ⓐ been을 없앤다.

② 지현: ⓑ had made → has made

③ 해수: ⓒ didn't come → hadn't come

④ 수지: ⓓ has been → was

⑤ 정재: ⓔ since → for

05 빈칸에 알맞은 말을 올바른 시제로 쓰시오. 5점

서술형

> Tom은 가진 돈을 전부 써버렸기 때문에 그 책을 살 수가
> 없었다.

→ Tom couldn't buy the book because he

_____ _____ all his money.

06 괄호 안의 단어를 사용하여 빈칸을 채우시오. 5점

서술형

> Yesterday, it started to rain, and it rained all
> day. Today, it is still raining. In this situation,
> what would you say?

→ It _____ _____

_____ since yesterday. (rain)

07 괄호 안에 주어진 단어를 사용하여 표의 내용과 일치하도
록 빈칸 (A)와 (B)에 알맞은 말을 쓰시오. 각 5점

서술형

What Justin Should Do	Done
Do his math homework	○
Write a diary entry	×

> When Justin's mother went out at 7 p.m., she
> said to Justin, "Do what you should do before
> I come back." Justin ____(A)____ (already) when
> his mother came back at 9 p.m. However, he
> ____(B)____ (not) by the time she came back.

(A) _____

(B) _____

VOCA lock 잠그다 | glasses 안경 | history 역사 | Army 군대, 육군 | take a lesson 수업을 듣다 | entry 항목

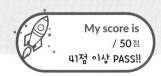
01 Which sentence is <u>incorrect</u>? 3점

① He is having shrimp chips.

② The new phone will be belonging to me.

③ Was he writing his autobiography?

④ Has he finished cleaning the room?

⑤ Mom had been scolding me when Dad came home.

02 Which is correct for the blank? 3점

> When the man heard the story, he remembered something his mother _____ to him before.

① had said
② saying
③ didn't say
④ has said
⑤ say

03 Which are the suitable words for the blanks? 3점

> Leo _____ never played chess before he met his aunt. He _____ his aunt that he had wanted to learn to play it for a long time.

① had – tells
② had – told
③ has – has told
④ had – had told
⑤ has – had told

04 Which sentences are <u>incorrect</u>? 4점

> ⓐ Have you ever been to New York?
> ⓑ We haven't known each other before he joined the club.
> ⓒ I have been studied since this morning.
> ⓓ I have been volunteering at a local hospital for a year.

① ⓐ, ⓑ, ⓓ
② ⓑ, ⓒ
③ ⓒ
④ ⓒ, ⓓ
⑤ ⓓ

05 Which translation is correct? 4점

> 그는 병원에 가기 전에 사흘 동안 아팠다.

① He is sick for three days before he went to the hospital.

② He was sick for three days before he had been to the hospital.

③ He has sick for three days before he went to the hospital.

④ He has been sick for three days before he went to the hospital.

⑤ He had been sick for three days before he went to the hospital.

06 Who finds the error and corrects it properly? 4점

> ⓐ I found out that she had been crying.
> ⓑ We have checked the door before we went out.

① 철수: ⓐ found → had found

② 미나: ⓐ had been → has been

③ 동해: ⓑ have checked → have been checking

④ 호박: ⓑ have checked → had checked

⑤ 승리: ⓑ went → had gone

VOCA shrimp 새우 | autobiography 자서전 | scold 나무라다 | each other 서로 | join 가입하다 | club 클럽, 모임, 동아리 | volunteer 자원봉사하다 | local 지역의

54

07 Which correction is right? 4점

> I have been preparing for the Hidden Singer contest for six months before I applied for it.

① have been preparing → had been preparing
② have been preparing → have prepared
③ applied → has applied
④ applied → had applied
⑤ for six months → since six months

08 Which CANNOT make a grammatically correct sentence? 4점

① have / you / doing / ? / been / What
② have / Recently, / . / tired / I / feeling / really
③ called / office, / left / her / He / already / . / but / she'd
④ Philadelphia / . / visited / have / We / several / times
⑤ police / thief / . / the / When / arrived, / had / away / run / the

09 Among the underlined, how many are grammatically incorrect? 4점

> I think ⓐ that the server ⓑ has forgotten us. We ⓒ had been waiting here ⓓ for 20 minutes, but nobody ⓔ have taken our order yet.

① one   ② two
③ three   ④ four
⑤ none

Challenge! 주관식 서술형

10 Fill in the blanks by using the given verb. 5점

> Last night, I started to do my homework at 8. I finished it at 9. Dad came home at 9:30. By the time he came home, I ＿＿＿＿＿＿＿＿ ＿＿＿＿＿＿＿＿ my homework. (finish)

11 Rewrite the sentence correctly. 6점

> She had failed the test because she never studied.

→ ＿＿＿＿＿＿＿＿＿＿＿＿＿＿＿＿＿
＿＿＿＿＿＿＿＿＿＿＿＿＿＿＿＿＿

12 Read the paragraph and fill in the blanks by putting the given words in the proper tenses. 6점

> The concert was planned to begin at 3 p.m., but some fans began to show up as early as 6 a.m. By 1 p.m., nearly two thousand fans had gathered and waited in line under the hot summer sun. By the time the concert began, many of the fans ＿＿＿＿＿＿＿＿ ＿＿＿＿＿＿＿ ＿＿＿＿＿＿＿ for about seven or eight hours. (wait, be)

VOCA apply for ~에 신청[지원]하다 | server 서빙하는 사람 | nearly 거의 | gather 모이다 | wait in line 줄을 서서 기다리다

CHAPTER 04
Review Test

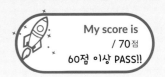

U07_1+3+GP
01 다음 중 어법상 어색한 문장은? 2점

① He passed the test that he had failed before.

② Chris has been here since three hours.

③ I told him that the sun rises in the east.

④ Some ancient people didn't know the Earth is round.

⑤ When it snows a little, it melts quickly.

U07_1
02 Which words are suitable for the blanks? 2점

A: You _____ very tired.
B: I know. I _____ for the exam until late last night.
A: Next time, study for it in advance.
B: I think I _____.

① look – studied – will

② look – study – will

③ looked – study – will

④ looked – studied – did

⑤ look – studied – do

U07_2+GP
03 Whose explanation is correct? (2 answers) 2점

함정

ⓐ When have you gotten married?
ⓑ I will be happy when school will be over.

① 용호: ⓐ 마지막에 before를 넣어야 한다.

② 현철: ⓐ when은 완료 시제에 쓸 수 없다.

③ 미현: ⓑ will을 would로 바꾸어야 한다.

④ 호열: ⓑ will be happy를 is happy로 고쳐야 한다.

⑤ 상호: ⓑ will be over를 is over로 고쳐야 한다.

U07_GP
04 밑줄 친 부분 중 어법상 어색한 것은? 2점

A: ① How long ② have you ③ stayed there?
B: I ④ have arrived here one month ago, and I ⑤ will stay here for another week.

U07_3
05 두 문장을 한 문장으로 연결할 때 빈칸에 알맞은 것은? 2점

He started to wait for her two hours ago. He is still waiting for her.
→ He _____ for her for two hours.

① is waiting

② was waiting

③ have waiting

④ has been waiting

⑤ have been waiting

[06~07] 빈칸에 들어갈 알맞은 말을 고르시오. 각 2점

U08_1
06

Ms. Shin didn't want to go to the theater with us because she _____ the movie.

① has already seen

② have already seen

③ had already seen

④ has yet seen

⑤ had yet seen

U08_1
07

Mina and Mike didn't know where to go because _____.

① they have lost their cell phones

② they had losed their cell phones

③ they have losed their cell phones

④ they had lost their cell phones

⑤ they has lost their cell phones

U08_1

08 ★ 고난도 Who groups the sentences that have the same usage of the past perfect tense(과거완료 시제)? 4점

ⓐ It had snowed for two days when I arrived in Syracuse.

ⓑ Had you ever seen a koala before you went to Australia?

ⓒ My husband had already bought the house when we met.

ⓓ Mom bought me new glasses because I had broken the old ones.

ⓔ Have you called your brother yet?

ⓕ How many times have you been to the amusement park?

---

① 소현: ⓐ, ⓔ　　② 찬호: ⓑ, ⓓ

③ 미소: ⓒ, ⓓ　　④ 노라: ⓒ, ⓔ

⑤ 소라: ⓓ, ⓔ

U08_GP

09 다음 중 어법상 <u>어색한</u> 문장을 찾아 바르게 고치시오. 4점

ⓐ I am understanding the fact very well.

ⓑ They were having pork cutlets for dinner.

(　　) _____ → _____

U07_2+GP

10 괄호 안의 단어를 빈칸에 알맞은 형태로 쓰시오. 각 3점

(1) When I _____ a chance, I will visit Iceland. (get)

(2) He is leaving for his hometown soon. I'm not sure when he _____ there. (get)

U08_3

11 ★ 고난도 Translate the sentence by using the given words according to the condition. 7점

해가 질 즈음에 우리는 그 유적지에 도착했을 것이다.

the historic site, arrive at, by the time, the sun, set

· Condition 1　주절을 먼저 쓸 것

· Condition 2　주절에 미래완료 시제를 쓸 것

→ _____

_____

U08_1

12 👁 한눈에 쏙 그림을 보고 조건에 맞게 문장을 영작하시오. 5점

그는 그가 자른 나무로 그의 집을 지었다.

· 조건 1　어휘 – build, with the wood, cut down

· 조건 2　11단어로 쓸 것

→ _____

_____

U08_2

13 Fill in the blanks in the dialog by using the given verb. 4점

A: Hello. What are you reading?

B: I'm reading a book about riddles.

I _____ _____

_____ it for half an hour. (read)

14

U07_GP

14 Rewrite the sentence correctly. 4점

> Have you ever gone to London before?

→ _____

_____

U08_1

15 주어진 단어를 빈칸에 알맞은 형태로 써서 문장을 완성하시오. 4점

> At 27, he became a teacher at the school where he _____ _____ a student. (be)

U08_2

16 그림에 나타난 상황을 한 문장으로 표현할 때 빈칸에 알맞은 말을 쓰시오. 6점

한눈에 쏙

| He started to play the game at 7 o'clock. | He was still playing the game when his mother came home at 9 o'clock. |

→ He _____ _____

_____ the game for two hours when his mother _____ home.

[17~18] 다음 글을 읽고 물음에 답하시오.

I type my password on my computer every day. I keep ⓐchecking my instant messages again and again. One day, I realized that the password I used ⓑto become a part of me because I ⓒhave been using it repeatedly. My password was "struckhimout11," and even though I did not always think about striking someone out intentionally, I considered ⓓthat baseball was my favorite activity. It was what made me ⓔto feel alive, and it was what I enjoyed the most. Later on, I changed my password to a goal _____(A)_____. It became a thing that reminded me of my dream every day.

*strike ~ out: (야구) 삼진을 잡다

U06_2+U08_1+2+U20_3+U02_1C

17 Among the underlined, how many are grammatically correct? 4점
★
고난도

① 1개 ② 2개

③ 3개 ④ 4개

⑤ 5개

U08_2

18 조건에 맞게 윗글의 빈칸 (A)에 들어갈 말을 쓰시오. 8점
★
고난도

·어휘	pursuing, that, been, I
·조건 1	한 단어를 추가할 것
·조건 2	주어진 단어는 변형하지 말 것

(A) _____

CHAPTER 05
조동사

UNIT

09 조동사(1)

개념이해책
52쪽 함께 보기

■ 아래 표의 빈칸에 알맞은 내용을 써 넣으세요. >>> 정답 12쪽

CONCEPT 1 can, may, will, must, should

조동사	의미	긍정	부정
can	능력, 가능	~할 수 있다 = 1)_____	cannot[can't]: ~할 수 없다 = be not able to
	2)_____	~해도 된다 3)_____	~하면 안 된다 = 4)_____
may	약한 추측	~일지도 모른다	may not: ~이 아닐지도 모른다
	허락	~해도 된다 5)_____	~하면 안 된다 6)_____
will	미래	~할 것이다 = 7)_____	will not[won't]: ~하지 않을 것이다 = 8)_____
must	의무/불필요	~해야 한다 = 9)_____	① don't/doesn't have to: ~할 필요 없다 = 10)_____ [need not] ② must not[mustn't]: ~해서는 안 된다
	강한 추측(확신)	~임에 틀림없다	cannot[can't]: 11)_____
should	도덕적 의무, 충고, 조언	~해야 한다 = 12)_____	should not[shouldn't]: ~해서는 안 된다 = 13)_____

CONCEPT 2 can, may가 사용된 중요 표현

- cannot help+-ing: 14)_____
- cannot ~ too...: 16)_____
- may[might] as well+동사원형: 18)_____
- may[might] well+동사원형: 15)_____
- cannot... without+-ing: 17)_____
- may[might] as well A as B: 19)_____

CONCEPT 3 that절에서 should의 생략

- 20) s_____(제안), 21) i_____(주장), demand(요구), order(명령), advise(충고)
- 이성적 판단: It is important, necessary, essential, natural, strange, a pity

 Level 1 Test

>>> 정답 12쪽

A 두 문장의 뜻이 같도록 빈칸에 알맞은 말을 쓰시오.

1 You don't need to write another essay.

→ You _____ _____ _____ write another essay.

2 You must eat here.

→ You _____ _____ eat here.

3 You shouldn't play the piano at night.

→ You _____ _____ _____ play the piano at night.

B 괄호 안의 단어를 이용하여 문장을 완성하시오.

1 나는 웃지 않을 수 없었다. (can, help)

→ I _____ _____ _____.

2 그녀가 그렇게 말하는 것은 당연하다. (may)

→ She _____ _____ say that.

3 그가 승자일 리 없다. (can)

→ He _____ _____ the winner.

VOCA essay 글, 에세이 | winner 승자, 우승자

60

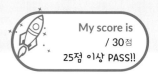

01 밑줄 친 부분의 쓰임이 [보기]와 같은 것은? 2점

> 보기   It <u>can't</u> be true.

① I <u>can't</u> believe it.
② You <u>can't</u> sit here.
③ Kate <u>can't</u> be satisfied now.
④ We <u>can't</u> reduce the budget.
⑤ I <u>can't</u> see well in the dark.

02 우리말과 같은 뜻이 되도록 할 때 빈칸에 알맞은 것은? 2점

> 당신은 그것에 대해 책임질 필요가 없습니다.
> = You _____ take charge of it.

① must not
② don't have to
③ may not
④ can't
⑤ have not to

03 다음 문장에서 어법상 어색한 부분을 바르게 고친 학생을 <u>모두</u> 고르시오. 2점

> I couldn't help follow my parent's decision.

① 동희: help → helping
② 기리: help → but
③ 철이: follow → to follow
④ 수희: follow → following
⑤ 리라: help → help but

04 어법상 <u>어색한</u> 문장으로 짝지어진 것은? 2점

> ⓐ Male drivers ought not to park here.
> ⓑ We have to stand the situation back then.
> ⓒ Kids should not eat too many marshmallows.
> ⓓ He need not wake up early.
> ⓔ She must afraid and scared now.

① ⓐ, ⓑ
② ⓐ, ⓒ
③ ⓑ, ⓔ
④ ⓒ, ⓓ
⑤ ⓓ, ⓔ

05 다음 문장과 반대되는 의미의 문장을 쓰시오. 4점

서술형

> He must be a fraud.

→ _____

06 조건에 맞게 우리말을 영작하시오. 4점

서술형

> 나는 대중 앞에서 연설하지 않겠다.
>
> · 조건 1   어휘 – make a speech, in public
> · 조건 2   7단어로 쓸 것

→ _____

07 다음 문장에서 어법상 어색한 부분을 고쳐 문장을 다시 쓰시오. (답 2개) 각 4점

서술형

> He was so angry that he couldn't help shout.

(1) _____

(2) _____

08 그림을 보고 조건에 맞게 우리말을 영작하시오. 6점

서술형

> 그녀가 달리고 난 다음에 목이 마른 것은 당연했다.
>
> · 조건 1   어휘 – natural, thirsty, after running
> · 조건 2   조동사를 쓰지 말 것
> · 조건 3   과거 시제로 쓸 것
> · 조건 4   9단어로 쓸 것

→ _____

VOCA   satisfied 만족한 | reduce 줄이다 | budget 예산 | take charge of ~을 책임지다 | male 남성의 | marshmallow 마시멜로 | scared 겁먹은 | fraud 사기꾼, 사기 | in public 대중 앞에서 | shout 소리지르다

 # Level 3 Test

>>> 정답 12쪽

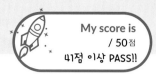
01 Which underlined "may" has a **different** meaning? 2점

① The rumor <u>may</u> be false.

② It <u>may</u> be windy tomorrow.

③ You <u>may</u> use my recipe.

④ Fumes <u>may</u> cause global warming.

⑤ She <u>may</u> not be rich.

02 Which words are proper for the blanks? 2점

- _____ you lend me some money?
- We _____ make good progress at that time.

① Could – can't
② Could – couldn't
③ May – couldn't
④ May – could
⑤ Can – can

03 Which is NOT suitable for the blank? 3점

A: May I pay with a check?
B: _____.

① Of course
② Yes, you may
③ No, you may not
④ No, you won't
⑤ I'm sorry, but you can't

04 Which sentences are **incorrect**? 4점

ⓐ Yuna must be very proud of herself.
ⓑ Should we participate in the debate?
ⓒ He has to reply to the invitation last week.
ⓓ Kids ought to not run in restaurants.
ⓔ He don't have to do ironing.

① ⓐ, ⓒ
② ⓒ, ⓓ
③ ⓒ, ⓓ, ⓔ
④ ⓑ, ⓓ
⑤ ⓐ, ⓒ, ⓓ, ⓔ

05 Which is best for the blank? 3점

You _____ make hasty decisions. Take your time and deal with the problems one by one.

① must not
② will
③ can
④ ought to
⑤ will not

06 Which one has the same meaning as the given sentence? 2점

You need not change the schedule.

① You may not change the schedule.
② You cannot change the schedule.
③ You don't have to change the schedule.
④ You will not change the schedule.
⑤ You ought not to change the schedule.

VOCA rumor 소문 | recipe 조리법 | fume 매연 | global warming 지구 온난화 | make progress 진전을 이루다 | check 수표 | participate in ~에 참가하다 | debate 토론, 논쟁 | reply 응답하다 | invitation 초대 | do ironing 다림질하다 | hasty 성급한 | take one's time 서두르지 않다 | deal with ~을 다루다

07 How many sentences are incorrect? 4점

> ⓐ I suggested he seeks medical attention.
> ⓑ Her teacher insisted that she is given a private lesson.
> ⓒ He asked his score is kept secret.
> ⓓ You may well refuse his offer.
> ⓔ They cannot meet without arguing.

① one　　　　② two
③ three　　　④ four
⑤ five

08 Which correction is right? 3점

> It was natural that he believes her story.

① was → were
② natural that → natural
③ believes → believed
④ believes → believe
⑤ believes → believing

09 How many words are NOT necessary when translating the given sentences? 3점

> 넌 농담하고 있음에 틀림없어. 그것은 사실일 리가 없어.
> → You _____ be kidding. That _____ be true.
>
> ⓐ will　　ⓑ can　　ⓒ may
> ⓓ must　　ⓔ can't

① one　　　　② two
③ three　　　④ four
⑤ five

Challenge! 주관식 서술형

10 Write the common word for the blanks. 4점

> • Eugene won first prize. He _____ be proud of himself.
> • You _____ not miss the class.

→ _____

11 Rewrite the sentence correctly. 6점

> He insisted that I accepted his proposal, but I declined.

→ _____

_____

12 Rearrange the given words to translate the sentence. 6점

> 나는 TV 보느니 자는 게 낫겠다.
> I, well, as, may, sleep, as, watch TV

→ _____

_____

13 Translate the sentence according to the conditions. 8점

> 부모가 자녀를 사랑하는 것은 당연하다.
>
> • Condition 1　어휘 – parents, their children
> • Condition 2　m으로 시작하는 5글자의 조동사를 포함시킬 것
> • Condition 3　6단어로 쓸 것

→ _____

VOCA　suggest 제안하다 | seek 찾다, 구하다 | medical attention 의학 치료 | private 개인의 | proposal 제안 | decline 거절하다

10 조동사(2)

■ 아래 표의 빈칸에 알맞은 내용을 써 넣으세요. ›› 정답 13쪽

개념이해책
55쪽 함께 보기

CONCEPT 1 would like to, had better, used to

조동사	긍정	부정
would like to	1)_____ (= want to)	would not[wouldn't] like to: 2)_____
had better	3)_____ (충고, 제안)	had better not: 4)_____
would rather	5)_____ (선택) would rather A than B (= prefer A to B): B 하느니 차라리 A 하는 게 낫다	would rather not: 6)_____
used to	① 과거의 습관: 7)_____ ② 과거의 상태: 8)_____	didn't use to 또는 used not to: 9)_____
would	과거의 습관: 10)_____	

CONCEPT 2 조동사 + have + p.p.

종류	의미	부정
11)_____ have+p.p.	~했어야 했다(후회·유감)	12)_____ have+p.p.
13)_____ have+p.p.	~했을지도 모른다(약한 추측)	14)_____ have+p.p.
15)_____ have+p.p.	~했음에 틀림없다(강한 추측)	16)_____ have+p.p.

Level 1 Test

›› 정답 13쪽

A 우리말과 뜻이 같도록 괄호 안의 단어들을 배열하시오.

1 너는 낮잠을 자는 게 낫겠다.

→ You _____ a nap.
(better, had, take)

2 내 조카는 뽀로로 인형을 안고 자곤 했다.

→ My niece _____ holding her Pororo toy. (sleep, to, used)

3 나는 그녀를 믿고 싶다.

→ I _____ her.
(would, to, trust, like)

B [보기]에서 알맞은 조동사를 이용해서 문장을 완성하시오.

보기 should   might   must   cannot

1 너는 그의 충고를 들었어야만 했다.

→ You _____ to his advice.

2 그들은 그때 긴장했음에 틀림없다.

→ They _____ nervous then.

3 그녀가 그날 도서관에 있었을 리 없다.

→ She _____ at the library that day.

4 그는 아팠을지도 모른다.

→ He _____ sick.

VOCA   take a nap 낮잠 자다 | niece 여자 조카 | trust 믿다 | advice 충고 | nervous 긴장한, 초조한

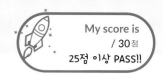
01 빈칸에 들어갈 말로 알맞은 것을 고르시오. 2점

> I _____ like to learn how to fly a drone.

① want   ② had
③ used   ④ would
⑤ ought

02 빈칸에 들어갈 말이 순서대로 짝지어진 것은? 3점

> A: I want to be stylish.
> B: You _____ change your hair color. You _____ look chic with a new hairstyle.

① had better – will
② can – have to
③ will – used to
④ may – would like to
⑤ would rather – ought to

03 다음 문장과 같은 의미의 문장은? 2점

> It is possible that she ordered a cheese pizza.

① She may order a cheese pizza.
② She might order a cheese pizza.
③ She must have ordered a cheese pizza.
④ It may have ordered a cheese pizza.
⑤ She might have ordered a cheese pizza.

04 다음 중 어법상 올바른 문장을 <u>모두</u> 고르면? 4점

> ⓐ You ought to not talk loudly on the subway.
> ⓑ I would rather stay indoors than go out in this cold weather.
> ⓒ You had better not come now.
> ⓓ He must have practice a lot.

① ⓐ, ⓑ, ⓒ   ② ⓑ, ⓒ
③ ⓒ   ④ ⓐ, ⓒ
⑤ ⓑ, ⓓ

05 다음 글에서 어법상 <u>어색한</u> 부분을 찾아 바르게 고치시오. 4점
서술형

> My brother loves assembling Lego blocks. He started doing that when he was 5 years old. Now he is 16 years old. He is used to assemble Lego blocks.

_____ → _____

06 다음 문장을 부정문으로 바꾸시오. 5점
서술형

> I would like to see you become a musician.

→ _____

07 다음 문장과 같은 의미의 문장을 조건에 맞게 쓰시오. 5점
서술형

> It is certain that she was innocent.
>
> ·조건 1   조동사를 쓸 것
> ·조건 2   5단어로 쓸 것

→ _____

08 다음 상황을 하나의 문장으로 표현하려 한다. 빈칸에 들어갈 알맞은 말을 써서 문장을 완성하시오. 5점
서술형

| I was in shape when I worked out every day. | I am not in shape anymore because I don't work out. |

→ I _____ when I worked out every day.

VOCA drone 드론 | stylish 유행을 따르는, 멋진 | chic 멋진, 세련된 | order 주문하다 | indoors 실내에서 | practice 연습하다 | assemble 조립하다 | musician 음악가 | certain 확실한 | innocent 무죄의 | be in shape 몸매를 유지하다

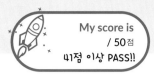

01 Which is the common word for the blanks?
2점

> • I'm sorry that I left early. I _____ to take care of my baby sister.
> • You _____ better tell me your plan.

① have
② could
③ had
④ used
⑤ would

02 Which underlined phrase has a similar meaning to the underlined phrase in the given sentence? 2점

> He <u>used to</u> work fourteen hours a day.

① He <u>had to</u> get ten stitches in his head.
② You <u>had better</u> call your dad right now.
③ I <u>would like to</u> avoid this situation.
④ She <u>would</u> go out with Oliver during high school.
⑤ We <u>ought to</u> respect our elders.

03 Choose the best expression for the blank in the dialog. 2점

> A: Jiho didn't pass the audition for the musical.
> B: Oh, that's too bad. He _____ more.

① should have practiced
② may have practiced
③ must have practiced
④ cannot have practiced
⑤ would have practiced

04 Among ①~⑤, which is incorrect? 2점

> This book is so boring. I ① would rather ② go ③ to sleep ④ than ⑤ to read this book.

05 Which correction is right? 2점

> She draws cartoons every day, so she is used to draw cartoons.

① is used to → used
② used to → used
③ is used to draw → used to drawing
④ draw → drawing
⑤ is used to draw → used drawing

06 Which has the same meaning as the given sentence? 2점

> I regret I didn't pay attention to what he said.

① I should have paid attention to what he said.
② I could have paid attention to what he said.
③ I must have paid attention to what he said.
④ I might have paid attention to what he said.
⑤ I cannot have paid attention to what he said.

07 Which is proper for the blank? 2점

> Ethan _____ about the party. He said he would come, but he didn't.

① must have forget
② must have forgotten
③ should have forgotten
④ cannot have forgotten
⑤ can have forgotten

VOCA make a reservation 예약하다 | in advance 미리 | stitch 바늘땀 | audition 오디션 | regret 후회하다 | pay attention to ~에 주의를 기울이다

08 Which sentences are <u>incorrect</u>? 4점

> ⓐ She will must clean her room.
> ⓑ He must have be sleepy then.
> ⓒ You can have ridden an elephant.
> ⓓ They should not cross the road.

① ⓐ, ⓑ 　　　　② ⓐ, ⓑ, ⓒ
③ ⓐ, ⓑ, ⓓ 　　④ ⓑ, ⓒ
⑤ ⓒ, ⓓ

09 Which set is necessary when translating the given sentence? 4점

> 어제 너에게 소리 지르지 말았어야 했어. 미안해.

① ought to / sorry
② must have / excuse
③ don't have to / yell
④ used not to / shout
⑤ shouldn't / apologize

Challenge! 주관식 서술형

10 Fill in the blank with <u>2 words</u> by using a modal verb(조동사). 4점

> A: My plane was delayed, so I had to wait in the airport for 6 hours.
> B: You _____ been very happy with the airline.

[11~12] Fill in the blanks to make the two sentences have the same meaning. 각 5점

11
> I want to attempt to do new things.

→ I _____ _____

_____ attempt to do new things.

12
> They must have been attacked by their enemy.

→ It _____ _____ that they

_____ _____ by their

enemy.

13 Rewrite the sentence correctly. 6점

> Nuclear energy is used to producing electricity.

→ _____

_____

14 Complete the girl's line according to the picture. 8점

> Girl: Be careful!
> Boy: Oops!
> Girl: 더 조심했어야지.

→ You _____.

VOCA　ride (-rode-ridden) (말을) 타다 ǀ apologize 사과하다 ǀ delay 지연시키다 ǀ attempt 시도하다 ǀ attack 공격하다 ǀ enemy 적 ǀ nuclear 원자력의 ǀ produce 생산하다 ǀ electricity 전기

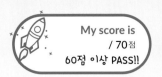

U09_1+GP

01 Which sentence has the same meaning as the one in the box? (2 answers) 2점

> Can I borrow the phone charger from you?

① Can you borrow the phone charger from me?

② May I lend the phone charger to you?

③ Will you lend the phone charger to me?

④ Are you able to borrow the phone charger from me?

⑤ Would you lend the phone charger to me?

U09_1

02 빈칸에 들어갈 말로 알맞은 것은? 2점

> You _____ save what you have written.
> The computer saves documents automatically.

① cannot

② don't have to

③ have to

④ won't

⑤ shouldn't

U10_1

03 다음 두 문장 중에서 어법상 어색한 부분을 찾아 바르게 고친 학생은? 2점

> ⓐ You'd better not to interrupt him.
> ⓑ You ought not to behave like that.

① 재석: ⓐ to interrupt → interrupt

② 동건: ⓐ to interrupt → interrupting

③ 유진: ⓑ ought not to → ought to not

④ 소라: ⓑ to behave → behaving

⑤ 미향: ⓑ not to → not

U09_2

04 주어진 문장과 같은 의미의 문장을 고르시오. 2점

> It is natural that you feel sad.

① You may feel sad.

② You must feel sad.

③ You may well feel sad.

④ You may as well feel sad.

⑤ You might as well feel sad.

U09_1

05 Which sentence has a <u>different</u> meaning than the others? 2점

① Don't ignore other people's feelings.

② You should not ignore other people's feelings.

③ You must not ignore other people's feelings.

④ You ought not to ignore other people's feelings.

⑤ You will not ignore other people's feelings.

U10_2

06 우리말을 영작할 때 빈칸에 알맞은 말을 고르시오. 2점

> 그녀가 그런 일을 했을 리가 없다.
> = She _____ such a thing.

① shouldn't have done

② cannot have done

③ may not have done

④ might have done

⑤ must not have done

U10_2

07 Which can be used when translating the following sentence? (Find ALL.) 2점

> 그는 그의 실수를 인정했을지도 모른다.

① might   ② admit

③ have   ④ must

⑤ should

U10_1+2

08 다음 문장들에서 어법상 어색한 부분이 바르게 수정된 것을 모두 고르시오. 3점

> ⓐ You will must prepare for the interview.
> ⓑ You had better not drink cold water.
> ⓒ I should have go there.

① ⓐ prepare → have prepared

② ⓐ will must → must

③ ⓑ had better not → had not better

④ ⓑ drink → to drink

⑤ ⓒ go → gone

U09_1

09 Write the common word for the blanks. 3점

> • He didn't eat all day. He _____ be hungry.
> • You _____ not jump on your bed.

→ _____

U09_1

10 다음 문장에서 어법상 어색한 부분을 바르게 고치시오. 4점

> You ought to not use your smartphone in class.

_____ → _____

U10_1

11 Rewrite the sentence correctly. 4점

> I would like donate all my money to charity.

→ _____
_____

U09_2

12 우리말을 영작할 때 빈칸에 알맞은 말을 쓰시오. 4점

> 점심 식사 후에는 수업 시간에 졸지 않을 수 없어요.

→ We _____ _____ dozing off

in class after lunch.

U10_1

13 ★ 고난도 조건에 맞게 주어진 문장을 영작하시오. 7점

> 모퉁이에 문방구가 없었는데.
>
> • 조건 1   어휘 – there, to, a stationery store, on the corner
> • 조건 2   11단어로 쓸 것

→ _____
_____

14 U10_1

★ 고난도

Translate the sentence according to the conditions. 7점

> 나는 시험에서 부정행위를 하는 것보다는 낙제하는 것이 낫겠다.
>
> · Condition 1 어휘 – fail, cheat, on the test, than
> · Condition 2 조동사 would를 쓸 것
> · Condition 3 9단어로 쓸 것

→ _____

_____

15 U09_3A+U10_2

✔ 함정

Find the sentence that has an error and correct it. 4점

> ⓐ She insisted that the prisoner is released from jail.
> ⓑ She must have had a good time in Hawaii last summer. She wants to go there again.

(   ) _____ → _____

16 U09_3B

★ 고난도

그림을 보고 조건에 맞게 영작하시오. 8점

> 그가 매 식사 전에 물을 마시는 것은 중요하다.
>
> · 조건 1 어휘 – important, before every meal
> · 조건 2 It ~ that 구문으로 쓸 것
> · 조건 3 현재 시제로 쓸 것
> · 조건 4 11단어로 쓸 것

→ _____

_____

[17~18] Read the following and answer each question.

Generally, sound ⓐreaches to the ear through the air. However, air is not the only medium ⓑwhat sound travels through. A loud noise will surprise fish and make ⓒthem dart away. From this, we can draw the conclusion that (A)소리가 물을 통해서 그것들에게 도달했음에 틀림없다. An American Indian puts his ear to the ground ⓓto listen to distant footsteps because such sounds are comparatively clear when traveling through the ground. A tapping at one end of a long wooden table can surely be heard at the other end if you press your ear against the table. We see therefore that sound ⓔcan reach the ear by solids, liquids, or gases.

*dart away: 재빠르게 도망치다

17 U01_2+U13_1+U03_1C+U09_1

★ 고난도

Which of the following correction is correct? (Up to 3 answers) 4점

① ⓐ reaches to → reaches
② ⓑ what → that
③ ⓒ them → themselves
④ ⓓ to listen → to be listened
⑤ ⓔ can → may

18 U10_2

Translate the underlined sentence (A) according to the conditions. 8점

> · Words must, through
> · Condition 1 동사는 지문의 동사를 활용할 것
> · Condition 2 the를 두 번 쓸 것
> · Condition 3 주어진 어휘를 포함하여 9단어로 완성할 것

(A) _____

CHAPTER 06
수동태

UNIT 11 조동사, 진행형, 완료형의 수동태

개념이해책
62쪽 함께 보기

■ 아래 표의 빈칸에 알맞은 내용을 써 넣으세요. ››› 정답 14쪽

CONCEPT 1 수동태의 의미와 기본 형태

기본형	1)_____ + 2)_____ + by + 행위자
전환법	주어 + 동사 + 목적어 → 주어 + 3)_____ + 4)_____ + by + 목적격
의미	주어가 ~이/-히/-지/-되다

CONCEPT 2 조동사의 수동태

조동사(can, may, must, will, shall, could, might, would, should) + 5)_____ + 6)_____

CONCEPT 3 진행형과 완료형의 수동태

진행형의 수동태		완료형의 수동태	
기본형	be 7)_____ + p.p.	기본형	have 10)_____ + p.p.
현재 진행 수동태	8)_____ being + p.p.	현재완료 수동태	11)_____ been + p.p.
과거 진행 수동태	9)_____ being + p.p.	과거완료 수동태	12)_____ been + p.p.

Level 1 Test

››› 정답 14쪽

A 주어진 단어를 빈칸에 알맞은 형태로 쓰시오.

1 The team _____ by 1 point in the last game. (beat)

2 This game _____ every four years. (hold)

3 A scary mask _____ by Mrs. Kim at a Halloween party last week. (wear)

4 In the past, the bell _____ at noon each day. (ring)

5 Somebody _____ a big stone at your car just now. (throw)

6 A model ship _____ together by my son now. (put)

B 주어진 문장의 태를 바꿀 때 빈칸에 알맞은 말을 쓰시오.

1 My father will sell my bike next week.

→ My bike _____ _____

_____ _____ _____

_____ next week.

2 Football isn't being played this year.

→ They _____ _____

_____ this year.

3 Ray has carried many boxes.

→ _____ _____ _____

_____ _____ by Ray.

4 Two people were moving the furniture.

→ _____ _____ _____

_____ by two people.

VOCA beat 이기다 | in the past 과거에 | ring 울리다 | model ship 모형 선박 | put together 조립하다

72

>>> 정답 14쪽

01 두 문장의 의미가 같도록 할 때 빈칸에 들어갈 수 <u>없는</u> 것은? (답 2개) 2점

> This fan fiction was written by my brother.
> → My brother _____ .

① by
② was
③ wrote
④ this
⑤ fan fiction

02 다음 문장을 수동태로 바꾸어 쓸 때, 빈칸에 알맞은 것을 고르시오. 2점

> They have not cleaned the lobby yet.
> → The lobby _____ yet.

① isn't cleaned
② wasn't cleaned
③ isn't had cleaned
④ has not been cleaned
⑤ has not being cleaned

03 다음 문장을 수동태로 전환할 때 앞에서 <u>7번째</u> 올 단어로 알맞은 것은? 2점

> She is taking a picture of him.

① being
② by
③ of
④ her
⑤ taken

04 다음 중 어법상 <u>어색한</u> 것은? 2점

① His homework was not done by him.
② A poem is being written by my daughter.
③ Your wisdom tooth must be pulled out.
④ We are constantly being bothered by the seagulls.
⑤ The door had completely destroyed when I got there.

05 다음 백과사전 항목의 제목을 조건에 맞게 완성하시오. 4점

서술형

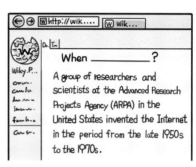

> When _____ ?
> A group of researchers and scientists at the Advanced Research Projects Agency (ARPA) in the United States invented the Internet in the period from the late 1950s to the 1970s.

> · 조건 1   수동태 의문문으로 쓸 것
> · 조건 2   빈칸에 4단어로 쓸 것
> · 조건 3   위에 나온 단어를 활용하여 쓸 것

→ When _____ ?

06 다음 문장을 수동태로 전환하시오. 5점

서술형

> Your kid is watering the flowers.

→ _____

07 주어진 단어 중 <u>필요한</u> 것만 골라 바르게 배열하여 우리말을 영작하시오. 7점

서술형

> 확인 문자가 고객님께 발송될 것입니다.
> going, a confirmation message, you, be, will, to, sent

→ _____

_____

08 다음 중 능동태 문장을 찾아 수동태로 전환하시오. 6점

서술형

> ⓐ He has composed a lot of musicals.
> ⓑ Has your dog ever been trained?

(   ) → _____

_____

VOCA fan fiction 팬픽 | wisdom tooth 사랑니 | pull out 뽑다 | constantly 꾸준히 | bother 괴롭히다 | seagull 갈매기 | completely 완전히 | destroy 파괴하다 | invent 발명하다 | researcher 연구원 | advanced 발달된 | research 연구 | agency 기관 | confirmation 확인

Level 3 Test

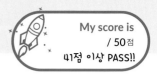

01 Which word is suitable for the blank? 2점

> 너희 어머니께 이 문제에 대해서 말씀 드려야 할까?
> = Should your mother _____ about this problem?

① tell
② be telling
③ be told
④ is told
⑤ have told

02 Which sentence is a grammatically correct answer for the given question? 2점

> Q. What is Stella doing?

① A glass of orange juice is drinking by Stella.
② A loaf of bread is eaten by Stella.
③ The baby is being carried by Stella.
④ A box of candy is being opening by Stella.
⑤ A spoonful of sugar being added by Stella.

03 Which correction is right? 2점

> ⓐ The exercise must be finished in time.
> ⓑ Is French spoken on this island?
> ⓒ When did the party held?

① ⓐ be finished → finish
② ⓑ Is → Does
③ ⓑ spoken → speaking
④ ⓒ did → was
⑤ ⓒ held → hold

04 Which TWO words are NOT necessary when changing the sentence into the passive voice? 2점

> A young Asian boy was playing the harp.

① was
② doing
③ played
④ being
⑤ been

05 Which word appears 7th when translating the sentence by using the given words? 2점

> 그 경주는 비 때문에 취소될 예정입니다.
> the race, be going to, cancel

① going
② to
③ be
④ canceled
⑤ because

06 Who understands the sentence correctly? 3점

> A new hotel has been built in the city.

① 가연: 주어가 동작을 하는 능동태 현재완료 문장이야.
② 동균: 현재완료는 맞는데 built를 building으로 써야 해.
③ 도연: 주어가 동작을 받으므로 has built로 써야 해.
④ 혜영: 위 문장은 어법상 오류가 없는 문장이야.
⑤ 수정: 능동태는 The city has built a new hotel.이야.

07 Which correctly changes the sentence into the active voice? 2점

> Your phone will be delivered by Monday.

① Monday will deliver your phone.
② Someone will deliver your phone by Monday.
③ It will deliver your phone by Monday.
④ Monday will deliver by your phone.
⑤ Your phone will deliver by Monday.

VOCA spoonful 한 스푼 | add 첨가하다 | exercise 연습, 운동 | in time 제시간에 | cancel 취소하다 | deliver 배달하다

08 Which sentences are <u>incorrect</u>? 3점

> ⓐ The salary is paid every month.
> ⓑ My bicycle was stolen last night.
> ⓒ The work has to finished in time.
> ⓓ Flowers are being grown in her garden.
> ⓔ The idea has suggested by Mr. Kim.

① ⓐ, ⓓ   ② ⓒ, ⓓ

③ ⓐ, ⓒ, ⓓ   ④ ⓑ, ⓒ, ⓔ

⑤ ⓒ, ⓔ

09 Which CANNOT make a grammatically correct sentence? 4점

① carpets / since / out / have / been / . / The / sold / this morning

② been / opened / hasn't / . / yet / present / The

③ prepared / Is / ? / by / chef / being / the / dinner

④ 16th / century / was / built / The / castle / . / in / the

⑤ His / exhibited / at / painting / the / . / gallery / being

Challenge! 주관식 서술형

10 Look at the picture and complete the sentence according to the conditions. 4점

> · Condition 1   현재완료로 쓸 것
> · Condition 2   어휘 – give

→ The house _____ _____

_____ a fresh coat of paint.

11 Rearrange the given words to make a complete sentence according to the conditions. 5점

> win, their, the championship, by, team, has
> · Condition 1   Change the form of the word if necessary.
> · Condition 2   Add 1 word.

→ _____

12 Change the sentence into the active voice. 5점

> The pony's tail was being combed by the vet.

→ _____

13 Fill in the blanks according to the directions to translate the sentence. 각 4점

> 그 마을 사람들은 그녀를 좋아하지 않는다.

(1) She _____ the villagers.

     (*passive voice*)

(2) _____

     (*active voice*)

14 Translate the sentence according to the conditions. 6점

> 당신은 스토킹을 당하고 있습니까?
> · Condition 1   being을 반드시 사용할 것
> · Condition 2   어휘 – stalk
> · Condition 3   4단어로 완전한 문장을 쓸 것

→ _____

VOCA   salary 월급 | pay 지불하다 | suggest 제안하다 | fresh 신선한 | coat 칠 | pony 조랑말 | comb 빗질하다 | vet (= veterinarian) 수의사 | villager 마을 사람 | stalk 스토킹하다

UNIT 12 여러 가지 수동태

개념이해책
65쪽 함께 보기

■ 아래 표의 빈칸에 알맞은 내용을 써 넣으세요. >>> 정답 15쪽

CONCEPT 1 5형식 문장의 수동태

목적격 보어	주요 5형식 동사	수동태 전환법
1)_____	make, keep, find, call, name, consider, leave, elect	주어＋동사＋목적어＋2)_____ → 주어＋be＋p.p.＋3)_____ (by＋목적격)
4)_____	tell, ask, expect, allow, advise, cause	주어＋동사＋목적어＋5)_____ → 주어＋be＋p.p.＋6)_____ (by＋목적격)
7)_____	사역동사: make, have, let	주어＋사역동사＋목적어＋8)_____ → 주어＋be＋p.p.＋9)_____ (by＋목적격)
10)_____	지각동사: see, watch, hear, listen to, feel	주어＋지각동사＋목적어＋11)_____ → 주어＋be＋p.p.＋12)_____ (by＋목적격)

CONCEPT 2 동사구의 수동태

주어＋동사구＋목적어 → 주어＋be＋p.p.＋13)_____ (by＋목적격)

CONCEPT 3 that절이 목적어인 경우

자주 쓰이는 동사	목적어
say, think, believe, consider, suppose	주어＋동사＋that S＋V → That S＋V be＋p.p. (by＋목적격) → It is＋p.p. (by＋목적격)＋that S＋V → 주어＋be＋p.p. (by＋목적격)＋14)_____

Level 1 Test

>>> 정답 15쪽

A 주어진 문장의 태를 바꿀 때 빈칸에 알맞은 말을 쓰시오.

1 The jury found the boy innocent.

→ The boy _____ _____ _____ by the jury.

2 He told me to leave him alone.

→ I _____ _____ by him _____ _____ him alone.

3 They say she is the bravest girl in history.

→ She _____ _____ _____ _____ the bravest girl in history.

B 밑줄 친 표현이 어법상 어색하면 바르게 고치시오.

1 She was laughed at by her friends.

→ _____

2 He was woken up me early this morning.

→ _____

3 The package can be picked up at the convenience store.

→ _____

4 It believes that spring water heals ADHD.

→ _____

VOCA jury 배심원단 | innocent 무죄의 | brave 용감한 | laugh at ～을 비웃다 | package 소포, 택배 | convenience store 편의점 | spring water 샘물 | heal 치유하다 | ADHD 주의력 결핍 및 과잉 행동 장애(attention deficit hyperactivity disorder)

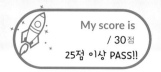
01 다음 문장을 수동태로 바르게 바꾼 것은? 2점

> Lou painted the walls all black.

① All black was painted the walls by Lou.
② The walls painted all black by Lou.
③ The walls was painted all black by Lou.
④ All was painted black the walls by Lou.
⑤ The walls were painted all black by Lou.

02 다음 문장을 수동태로 바꿀 때 5번째 올 단어는? 2점

> The kid saw the monster come back to him.

① monster ② come
③ the ④ to
⑤ seen

03 문장을 전환한 ⓐ~ⓓ에 대해 바르게 이해한 학생은? 3점

> They said that the story was ridiculous.
>
> ⓐ That the story was ridiculous were said by them.
> ⓑ It was said by them that the story was ridiculous.
> ⓒ It said that the story was ridiculous.
> ⓓ The story was said to be ridiculous.

① 담서: 주어진 문장에서 that절은 보여.
② 소영: ⓐ에서 were를 to be로 바꿔야 해.
③ 소원: ⓑ의 by them은 생략하면 안 돼.
④ 치현: ⓒ의 said를 is said로 바꿔야 해.
⑤ 원주: ⓓ는 문법적으로 이상이 없는 문장이야.

04 다음 대화의 빈칸에 알맞은 것은? 2점

> A: Do you take care of your pets?
> B: No. They are taken care _____ my mom.

① by ② of
③ for ④ of by
⑤ by of

05 다음은 어떤 문장을 혜림이가 수동태로 전환한 것이다. 잘못된 부분을 찾아 문장을 어법에 맞게 다시 쓰시오. 4점 *서술형*

> We call him J for short.
> → J is called him for short.

→ _____

06 주어진 표현을 이용해서 그림을 묘사하는 문장을 완성하시오. (현재 진행형으로 쓸 것) 5점 *서술형*

→ The girl _____

the boy. (make fun of)

07 조건에 맞게 우리말을 영작하시오. 8점 *서술형*

> 그 지역에서 땅이 흔들리는 것이 느껴졌다.
>
> · 조건 1 어휘 – the ground, feel, shake, the area
> · 조건 2 be + p.p. 구문을 이용할 것
> · 조건 3 필요 시 어휘를 변형할 것
> · 조건 4 주어진 어휘를 포함하여 8단어로 쓸 것

→ _____

_____

08 다음 세 문장의 빈칸에 공통으로 들어갈 말은? 4점 *서술형*

> ⓐ The sky is filled _____ clouds.
> ⓑ Is he satisfied _____ my work?
> ⓒ The street was crowded _____ taxis.

→ _____

VOCA monster 괴물 | ridiculous 우스꽝스러운 | take care of ~을 돌보다 | for short 줄여서 | shake 흔들리다 | satisfied 만족한 | crowded 붐비는

Level 3 Test

»» 정답 16쪽

01 Which translation is correct? 2점

> 부엌은 청결하게 유지되어야 한다.

① The kitchen is kept clean.
② The kitchen was kept clean.
③ The kitchen must keep clean.
④ The kitchen must kept clean.
⑤ The kitchen must be kept clean.

02 Which words are necessary when changing the sentence into the passive voice? 2점

> My mom made me wear this stupid hat.
>
> ⓐ was   ⓑ to   ⓒ by
> ⓓ wear   ⓔ me   ⓕ making

① ⓐ, ⓒ, ⓔ   ② ⓐ, ⓑ, ⓒ, ⓓ
③ ⓑ, ⓒ, ⓓ, ⓔ   ④ ⓒ, ⓔ, ⓕ
⑤ ⓔ, ⓕ

03 Which sentence correctly changes the given sentence into the passive voice? 2점

> They believe that the chief has magical powers.

① The chief is believed have magical powers.
② The chief is believed to have magical powers.
③ It believes that the chief has magical powers.
④ It is believed to have magical powers.
⑤ The chief is believed that he has magical powers.

04 Which word appears 5th when rearranging the given words to make a complete sentence? 2점

> questions, was, to, answer, he, expected, the

① expected   ② the
③ questions   ④ answer
⑤ to

05 Which word for each blank is correct? 2점

> ⓐ A new dress was made _____ Lynn.
> ⓑ My uncle's house is made _____ wood.

① of – of   ② of – from
③ for – from   ④ for – of
⑤ from – of

06 Which sentence is grammatically incorrect? (Find ALL). 3점

① Your dog was almost run over by the bus.
② The machine was turned off the manager.
③ We were looked down on by some people.
④ Honey has been made use of for more than 3,000 years.
⑤ My sister's 12th birthday party has canceled.

07 Which word for each blank is correct? 3점

> ⓐ The truck was covered _____ dust.
> ⓑ At first, nobody was surprised _____ the news.
> ⓒ The restaurant is known _____ its fantastic service.

① by – at – to   ② with – by – for
③ by – with – to   ④ with – to – for
⑤ with – for – to

VOCA stupid 꼴불견인 | chief 추장 | magical 마법의 | expect 기대하다 | dust 먼지 | fantastic 훌륭한

08 Which sentences are grammatically correct?
3점

> ⓐ Eric was asked keep me safe.
> ⓑ Your test result will send to you by Anna.
> ⓒ As usual, the rumor was found to be false.
> ⓓ The students were told to stay away from the windows.

① ⓐ, ⓑ 　　　　② ⓐ, ⓓ

③ ⓑ, ⓒ 　　　　④ ⓑ, ⓓ

⑤ ⓒ, ⓓ

09 Which CANNOT make a grammatically correct sentence? 4점

① has / been / She / spy / a / . / called

② Arizona / up / was / . / He / brought / in

③ quiet / Everybody / was / to / be / . / told

④ My / orange / trees / . / planted / have / daughters

⑤ made / rain / . / happily / by / are / Some / people

Challenge! 주관식 서술형

10 Rearrange the given words to make a complete sentence according to the conditions. 6점

> planning, a comeback, says, the, to, singer, is
>
> ·Condition 1　Change the form of the word if necessary.
> ·Condition 2　Add 1 word.

→ _____

11 Change the sentence into the passive voice. Use the verb "ask." 5점

> The captain had me sing over and over.

→ _____

　_____

12 This is a dialog between Gyujin and Gyumin about the passive voice. Find TWO errors in the dialog and correct them. 각 4점

> 규진: She made me happy.를 수동태로 어떻게 바꿔?
> 규민: ⓐ 능동태의 목적어가 me니까 ⓑ 주어는 I이고 ⓒ 동사는 am made, ⓓ 보어는 happy를 쓰면 돼.
> 규진: 그럼 happy를 주어로 해서 바꿔도 돼?
> 규민: 노노노. 그건 ⓔ 목적어가 아니라 목적격 보어니까 전환할 때 ⓕ 능동태의 주어로 쓸 수 없어.

(　　) _____ → _____

(　　) _____ → _____

13 Fill in the blanks to change the sentence into the active voice. 4점

> Lucy is said to run the biggest restaurant in town.

→ They _____ _____ Lucy

　_____ the biggest restaurant in

　town.

14 Find the sentence that has an error and correct it. 4점

> ⓐ The scholar has been looked up to many people.
> ⓑ The new employee was laughed at because he made a mistake.

(　　) _____ → _____

VOCA　as usual 평소대로 | over and over 계속해서 | scholar 학자 | employee 직원

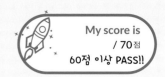

U11_1+2+3

01 다음 중 수동태 전환이 올바르지 <u>않은</u> 것은? 2점

① She wrote this report.
→ This report was written by her.
② Jiyun will invite him to the party.
→ He will be invited to the party by Jiyun.
③ You two ought to share everything.
→ Everything is ought to shared by you two.
④ Somebody is using the computer.
→ The computer is being used by somebody.
⑤ You can see the Milky Way from here.
→ The Milky Way can be seen from here.

U11_4

02 Which is suitable for the blank? 2점

> The room looks very neat. It _____.

① cleaned
② has been cleaned
③ being cleaned
④ is cleaned
⑤ be cleaned

U11_2+4+U12_2

03 다음 빈칸 중 어느 것에도 들어갈 수 <u>없는</u> 것은? 2점

> ⓐ Nari _____ been looked up to _____ her coworkers.
> ⓑ The issue _____ be dealt _____ immediately.

① has ② with
③ of ④ will
⑤ by

U12_1+GP

04 다음을 수동태로 전환할 때 앞에서 <u>5번째</u> 올 단어는? 2점

> My grandfather named our dog Izzy.

① my ② by
③ program ④ this
⑤ Izzy

U11_1+GP+U12_1

05 Which is correct for the blank when changing the sentence into the passive voice? 2점

> What do you call this in English?
> → What _____ in English?

① does this call
② is this called
③ are you called this
④ is this calling
⑤ are you this called

U11_3+4+U12_1

06 우리말을 영어로 <u>잘못</u> 옮긴 학생은? (정답 최대 3개) 3점

① 모두가 일어서도록 만들어졌다.
→ 지현: Everybody was made stand up.
② 저는 야채를 더 먹으라는 권고를 받았어요.
→ 창록: I was advised to eat more vegetables.
③ 다락방에서 누군가가 우는 소리가 들렸다.
→ 준섭: Somebody was heard crying in the attic.
④ 배들은 남자들에 의해 청소되고 있었다.
→ 희수: The boats were being cleaning by the men.
⑤ 그녀는 2008년부터 브루스와 결혼한 상태이다.
→ 상원: She has been married to Bruce since 2008.

07 밑줄 친 부분 중 어법상 올바르지 않은 것은? 2점

U11_1+2+3+4

① We <u>were made to feel</u> responsible.

② The story <u>is based on</u> an Apache folk tale.

③ Bottles of French wine <u>can be found</u> for under $20 near here.

④ The brilliant idea <u>has reused</u> without change.

⑤ My car <u>was being driven</u> by my mother.

U12_1+3+GP

08 ★ 고난도 How many sentences are grammatically <u>incorrect</u>? 4점

ⓐ Why has she been called Shao-Mimi?
ⓑ Tim was made sad by everything today.
ⓒ Workers were seen make wooden boxes.
ⓓ He was told to do the dishes by his mom.
ⓔ It is estimating that there are more than 80,000 chicken restaurants in Korea.

① 1개   ② 2개
③ 3개   ④ 4개
⑤ 5개

U12_1+GP

09 주어진 단어들을 바르게 배열하여 문장을 만드시오. 4점

mayor, was, Seoul, elected, residents, of, by, he, its

→ _____

_____

U11_3

10 Find the sentence that has an error and correct it. 4점

ⓐ Your voice is being recording at the moment.
ⓑ Children won't be negatively affected by this game.

(   ) _____ → _____

U12_1+GP

11 두 사람의 대화를 보고 여자가 입은 티셔츠의 문구를 완성하시오. 4점

M: Excuse me, miss. Do you have the time?

W: Sorry. My mom won't let me date anybody. It's written on my T-shirt.

M: Oh, I think you're mistaken. I just want to know what time it is now.

W: Oh, my god. I'm so embarrassed.

→ I'm _____ _____

_____ _____ anybody.

U11_GP

12 주어진 단어들을 바르게 배열하여 올바른 문장을 만드시오. 4점

not, by, to, the, is, be, going, house, him, sold

→ _____

U12_2+GP

13 다음 문장에서 어법상 <u>어색한</u> 것을 찾아 바르게 고치시오. 4점

Mowgli brought up by wolves and educated by the bear Baloo.

_____ → _____

14 Translate the sentence according to the conditions. 5점

그녀의 드레스들은 가장 값비싼 천으로 만들어졌다.

- Condition 1　어휘 – her dresses, make, the most expensive cloth
- Condition 2　주어를 her dresses로 할 것
- Condition 3　전치사의 쓰임에 유의할 것
- Condition 4　과거 시제로 쓸 것
- Condition 5　주어진 어휘를 포함하여 9단어로 완성할 것

➡ _____

_____

15 다음 문장을 전환할 때 빈칸에 알맞은 말을 쓰시오. 각 4점

People say that this image of Buddha is over 700 years old.

(1) It _____

_____ .

(2) This image of Buddha _____

_____ .

16 다음은 사역동사의 수동태에 관한 인터넷 강의 장면이다. 주어진 문장을 수동태로 전환하시오. 6점

➡ Min _____

_____ .

[17~18] 다음 글을 읽고 물음에 답하시오.

Before you choose a souvenir to take home, think over (A)그것이 어떻게 만들어졌고 어디서 왔는지(and / it / it / how / where / made / came / from).  If animal bone or skin ⓐused to make it, just leave it on the shelf. ⓑPick your souvenirs directly from nature is not a good idea. Wildflowers are ⓒvery more beautiful in the wild than on your desk. Instead, pick something ⓓthat does not have negative effects on the place you visit. Paintings or crafts ⓔproduced by local people are good examples.

17 윗글의 밑줄 친 (A)와 같은 뜻이 되도록 괄호 안에 제시된 단어들을 배열하시오. (단, 1단어를 추가할 것) 8점
★고난도

(A) _____

_____

18 윗글의 밑줄 친 ⓐ~ⓔ 중 어법상 옳은 것은? (정답 2개) 4점
★고난도

① ⓐ　　　　　　② ⓑ

③ ⓒ　　　　　　④ ⓓ

⑤ ⓔ

CHAPTER 07
관계사

13 관계대명사의 역할과 용법

■ 아래 표의 빈칸에 알맞은 내용을 써 넣으세요. >>> 정답 17쪽

개념이해책
72쪽 함께 보기

CONCEPT 1 관계대명사의 종류

선행사	주격 (+동사)	목적격 (+주어+동사)	소유격
사람	1)_____	2)_____ (생략 가능)	3)_____
사물, 동물	4)_____	5)_____ (생략 가능)	whose (= of which)
사람, 사물, 동물	6)_____	7)_____ (생략 가능)	

CONCEPT 2 관계대명사의 용법

제한적 용법	• 관계대명사절이 선행사를 8)_____에서 수식
계속적 용법	• 관계대명사절이 선행사를 보충 설명 • 앞에 9)_____가 있음 • '10)_____+대명사'로 바꾸어 쓸 수 있음

CONCEPT 3 관계대명사 that

that을 쓸 수 없는 경우	that을 주로 쓰는 경우
• 11)_____격이 없다 • 12)_____ 용법에는 쓰이지 않는다. • 13)_____와 나란히 함께 쓰일 수 없다.	• 선행사에 형용사의 14)_____, 서수, the very, the only, the same 등이 있을 때 • 선행사에 all, every, any, no, -thing 등이 있는 경우

CONCEPT 4 관계대명사 what

what = the 15)_____(s) 16)_____ [17)_____]: ~하는 것

Level 1 Test

>>> 정답 17쪽

A 빈칸에 알맞은 관계사를 넣으시오. (답이 둘 이상인 경우도 있음)

1 Tony argued with the boy _____ you like.

2 Do you like the song _____ they are playing on the radio?

3 This is the girl about _____ I told you before.

4 Miso showed me _____ she had in her closet.

B 빈칸에 알맞은 관계사를 넣으시오. (that 또는 what)

1 Show me _____ you brought from India.

2 He will eat the *kimbap* _____ you brought.

3 Tell me everything _____ you know about the project.

4 Can you tell me _____ you know about the rumor?

VOCA argue 논쟁하다, 말다툼하다 | closet 벽장 | rumor 헛소문

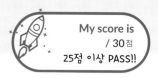

01 두 문장을 하나로 올바르게 만든 것을 <u>모두</u> 고르시오. 2점

> Mr. Choi is a teacher. I am fond of him.

① Mr. Choi is a teacher of I am fond.
② Mr. Choi is a teacher that I am fond of.
③ Mr. Choi is a teacher whom I am fond of.
④ Mr. Choi is a teacher of that I am fond.
⑤ Mr. Choi is a teacher I am fond of.

02 다음 중 밑줄 친 단어가 관계대명사가 <u>아닌</u> 것을 <u>모두</u> 고르시오. 2점

① A woman <u>who</u> I know doesn't let her children watch TV.
② She told me <u>that</u> her brother lives in Seoul.
③ Do you know <u>who</u> made the mistake?
④ I will tell you <u>which</u> one I will choose.
⑤ This is the pen with <u>which</u> I take notes.

03 두 문장을 한 문장으로 만들 때 빈칸에 알맞은 말은? 3점

> Justin is a tour guide, and he speaks Chinese.
> → Justin, _____, is a tour guide.

① who speaks Chinese
② which he speaks Chinese
③ who he speaks Chinese
④ which speaks Chinese
⑤ and speaks Chinese

04 빈칸에 'that'이 들어갈 수 <u>없는</u> 것을 <u>모두</u> 고르시오. 3점

① The girl _____ backpack is filled with snacks is Patty.
② Math is a subject _____ I understand easily.
③ I believe _____ you will succeed.
④ She is the girl _____ he can't get along with.
⑤ Kate knows the man in _____ you're interested.

05 빈칸에 공통으로 들어갈 단어를 쓰시오. 4점

서술형

> • Jenny is the most attractive girl _____ I have ever seen.
> • Please tell him _____ I know everything.

→ _____

06 조건에 맞게 우리말을 영작하시오. 8점

서술형

> 쇼팽(Chopin)의 야상곡들은 내가 자주 듣는 클래식 음악이다.
>
> • 조건 1 어휘 – nocturnes, the classical music pieces, often, listen to
> • 조건 2 관계대명사를 사용할 것
> • 조건 3 listen과 to를 분리하지 말 것

→ _____

_____

07 그림을 보고 조건에 맞게 우리말을 영작하시오. 8점

서술형

> 나를 무섭게 만들었던 것은 그의 커다란 개였다.
>
> • 조건 1 어휘 – scare, huge
> • 조건 2 7단어로 쓸 것
> • 조건 3 관계사를 포함할 것
> • 조건 4 과거 시제로 쓸 것

→ _____

_____

VOCA be fond of ~을 좋아하다 | take notes 필기하다 | backpack 배낭 | get along with ~와 어울리다, 잘 지내다 | be interested in ~에 흥미가 있다 | attractive 매력적인 | nocturne 야상곡 | huge 커다란, 거대한

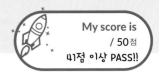
01 Which words are proper for the blanks? 2점

> • She lost the coupon _____ I had given to her.
> • You're the man _____ I have been looking for.

① that – which   ② which – whom

③ whose – who   ④ whom – which

⑤ whom – that

02 Which is the proper word for the blank? 2점

> I will buy _____ you want to have.

① which   ② that

③ what   ④ whom

⑤ who

03 Which sentence is grammatically incorrect? 2점

① She got angry with Henry, who had hidden her shoes.

② I know Mina, who used to live around here.

③ I went to the movies with Ted, who I like a lot.

④ He argued with his mom, who hardly ever happens.

⑤ I hate my brother, who often makes fun of me.

04 Which words are correct for the blanks? 2점

> • He asked me _____ I was the most afraid of.
> • I will try something new _____ can make my life better.

① what – what   ② what – that

③ that – what   ④ that – which

⑤ that – that

05 Which sentence is incorrect? (Find ALL.) 3점

① She couldn't remember the bank which she went last week.

② They are the people who provide services in our communities.

③ This is the same book that I have.

④ She's the girl who is my best friend.

⑤ This is a blouse which the sleeves are adjusted.

06 Which of the underlined words CANNOT be replaced by "that"? 2점

① I have a problem about which I need to talk with her.

② This is the sofa which I used to sleep on.

③ He is the man whom she respects the most.

④ I have a friend who wants to be a cellist.

⑤ David accepted the job which she offered.

07 Which sentence has the same usage of "that" as the given sentence? (Find ALL.) 2점

> The person that is responsible for a school is called a principal.

① It was yesterday that we met her.

② I think that we don't need side airbags.

③ He has a car that has three doors.

④ I want to drink something that calms me.

⑤ Summer is the season that comes after fall.

VOCA make fun of ~을 놀리다 | provide 제공하다 | community 지역사회, 공동체 | sleeve 소매 | adjust 조정하다 | cellist 첼리스트 | accept 받아들이다 | offer 제안하다 | be responsible for ~에 책임이 있다 | side airbags 측면 에어백 | calm 진정시키다

08 Which sentence needs a <u>different</u> word for the blank? 2점

① She will drive the very car _____ you bought.

② Is this _____ she needs for the party?

③ We need _____ you have in your office.

④ Thanks for _____ you have done for me.

⑤ I will tell you _____ you can do here.

09 Which CANNOT make a grammatically correct sentence? 4점

① that / you / . / understand / I / said / don't

② know / man / to / . / who / you / I / sitting / the / next / is

③ whose / the / Choose / you / like / . / character / name

④ went / father / . / to / goes / the / school / which / She / to / her

⑤ the / is / . / who / wrote / Mexican / song / musician / The

Challenge! 주관식 서술형

10 Rearrange the given words to make a complete sentence according to the conditions. 5점

cry, to, what, made, which, her, said, you

· Condition 1　Use only the necessary words.

· Condition 2　Write a sentence with 6 words.

→ _____

11 Rewrite the sentence correctly. 5점

The shoes which I lent to Judy is my sister's.

→ _____

_____

12 Rewrite the sentence by changing the underlined word into two words. 4점

She danced really well, <u>which</u> amused us.

→ She danced really well, _____

_____ amused us.

13 Write the proper words for the blanks. 각 4점

(1) She doesn't use anything _____ I have.

(2) This function is _____ I have been searching for.

14 Look at the picture and complete the translation according to the conditions. 7점

그가 부엌에서 만든 것은 운동화 밑창이었다.

· Condition 1　과거 시제로 쓸 것

· Condition 2　관계대명사를 쓸 것

· Condition 3　빈칸에 7단어로 쓸 것

→ _____

the soles of the sneakers.

VOCA amuse 즐겁게 하다 | function 기능 | sole 밑창

관계부사, 관계사의 생략

■ 아래 표의 빈칸에 알맞은 내용을 써 넣으세요. >>> 정답 18쪽

개념이해책
75쪽 함께 보기

① 관계부사: 전치사 + 관계대명사

용도	선행사	관계부사	예문
장소	the place	1)_____ (= in[on, at] which)	This is the place 1)_____ we met.
시간	the time	2)_____ (= in[on, at] which)	The time 2)_____ she leaves for America isn't exact.
이유	the reason	3)_____ (= for which)	Do you know the reason 3)_____ he regrets his actions so much?
방법	(the way)	4)_____	He showed me 4)_____ she danced.

② 관계사의 생략

관계 대명사	5)_____격 관계대명사	동사의 6)_____격	There is a meeting (which[that]) we should attend.
		전치사의 7)_____격	This is the coat of which I am fond. (생략 불가능) This is the coat (which[that]) I am fond of. (생략 가능)
	8)_____격 관계대명사 +9)_____동사		The official language (which is) spoken in India is English.
관계 부사	선행사		Tell me (the time) when the flight will depart.
	10)_____		Tell me the time (when) he will arrive.

Level 1 Test

>>> 정답 18쪽

A 빈칸에 알맞은 말을 [보기]에서 골라 쓰시오.

보기	which	what	who
	whom	whose	when
	where	why	how

1 She visited the palace _____ many tourists like to visit.

2 This is the reason _____ she got angry.

3 I don't remember the moment _____ she put my phone in the refrigerator.

4 Don't move! Stay _____ you are.

5 _____ parents treat siblings should be fair.

B 빈칸에 알맞은 말을 쓰시오.

1 She likes the way he dresses.

→ She likes _____ he dresses.

2 She often visits the broadcasting station at which he works.

(1) She often visits the broadcasting station _____ he works _____.

(2) She often visits the broadcasting station he works _____.

(3) She often visits the broadcasting station _____ he works.

(4) She often visits _____ he works.

VOCA palace 궁전 | tourist 관광객 | refrigerator 냉장고 | treat 대하다 | sibling 형제 자매 | fair 공평한 | broadcasting station 방송국

 Level **2** Test

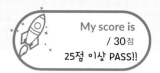

01 각 빈칸에 들어갈 말이 바르게 짝지어진 것은? 2점

> • Today is the day _____ we got married.
> • The library _____ he built is very modern.
> • The reason _____ she missed the bus was that she didn't know the schedule.

① when – why – where
② when – where – how
③ when – that – why
④ where – how – when
⑤ where – why – when

02 밑줄 친 부분 중 생략할 수 없는 것을 모두 고르면? 2점

① The man that gives me advice is my uncle.
② Donghae is the place which he misses.
③ The course in which I'm interested is full.
④ Can you like a girl who everybody hates?
⑤ The waiter who is serving dinner is kind.

03 다음 문장에 대한 설명으로 올바른 것은? 2점

> Which is the seat on he is going to sit?

① the seat과 on 사이에 관계사가 생략된 문장이다.
② 전치사 on은 문장 끝에만 쓸 수 있다.
③ on 다음에 관계대명사 that을 써야 한다.
④ on 대신에 관계부사 where를 써야 한다.
⑤ 주격 관계대명사와 be동사가 생략되어 있다.

04 다음 중 어법상 어색한 문장으로 짝지어진 것은? 3점

> ⓐ I won't forget the day when I lost the game on.
> ⓑ This is the way he solved the problem.
> ⓒ The city where she was born in is Paris.

① ⓐ, ⓑ   ② ⓐ, ⓒ
③ ⓒ   ④ ⓑ, ⓒ
⑤ ⓑ

05 다음 문장에서 생략된 단어를 모두 포함해서 문장을 다시 쓰시오. 5점
_{서술형}

> He found a bug crawling up his leg.

→ _____

_____

06 다음 중 어법상 어색한 문장을 모두 찾아 바르게 고쳐 쓰시오. 6점
_{서술형}

> ⓐ I will introduce the man what I share my office with.
> ⓑ We told him what he had to do.
> ⓒ This is the furniture of you should get rid.

→ _____

_____

07 다음 두 문장을 하나로 만드시오. (10단어로 쓸 것) 5점
_{서술형}

> Nobody knows the reason. She made such a decision for that reason.

→ _____

_____

08 조건에 맞게 다음 문장을 영작하시오 5점
_{서술형}

> 그녀는 그를 설득할 방법을 나에게 말해주었다. (그녀는 어떻게 자기가 그를 설득할 것인지 나에게 말해주었다.)

· 조건 1   어휘 – persuade
· 조건 2   빈칸에 5단어로 쓸 것
· 조건 3   관계부사를 쓸 것
· 조건 4   시제 일치에 유의할 것

→ She told me _____

_____

VOCA modern 현대적인 | bug 벌레 | crawl 기어오르다 | share 나누어 쓰다 | furniture 가구 | get rid of ~을 없애다 | decision 결정 | persuade 설득하다

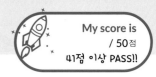
Level 3 Test

>>> 정답 18쪽

01 Which is the proper word for the blank? 3점

> My grandmother says she can't forget the day _____ the atom bomb was dropped.

① which ② when
③ where ④ how
⑤ why

02 Which of the underlined words CANNOT be omitted? 3점

① Harper drank the milk <u>which</u> I had put on the table.
② This is the man <u>whom</u> I told you about.
③ Tell me something about the house <u>that</u> you want to buy.
④ I'm sorry, but I'm not a person on <u>whom</u> you can depend.
⑤ She forgot to bring the ticket <u>which</u> I had given her.

03 Which of the underlined words is used <u>differently</u> than the others? 3점

① Do you remember the moment <u>when</u> we first met?
② I'm waiting for the day <u>when</u> you will be a monk.
③ She was playing <u>when</u> I was working hard.
④ I will tell you the date <u>when</u> I'm leaving.
⑤ Sunday is the day <u>when</u> I can get up late.

04 Which is the proper word to make the two sentences have the same meaning? 3점

> I went to the restaurant, and there I met my teacher.
> = I went to the restaurant, _____ I met my teacher.

① which ② when
③ where ④ how
⑤ why

05 Who corrects the error properly? 3점

> ⓐ The way she illustrates books is wonderful.
> ⓑ How he fixed the car was amazing.
> ⓒ I will tell you some places where you should visit.
> ⓓ What is the reason she got fired?

① 성희: ⓐ The way → How
② 승훈: ⓑ How → The way
③ 미나: ⓒ where → which
④ 광수: ⓓ the reason → why
⑤ 수희: ⓓ the reason → the reason why

06 Which underlined word or phrase CANNOT be omitted? 3점

① The box <u>which</u> she is holding contains clothes.
② Here are the books <u>that</u> you need to read.
③ The girl <u>that</u> often does the voluntary work is my daughter.
④ This is the tree <u>which was</u> planted long ago.
⑤ Monday is the day <u>when</u> we have 7 classes.

VOCA atom bomb 원자폭탄 | drop 투하하다 | depend on ~에 의존하다, 의지하다 | monk 스님 | illustrate 삽화를 그리다, 설명하다 | fix 고치다 | fire 해고하다 | contain 포함하다 | voluntary 자발적인

07 Which words are proper for the blanks? 3점

- I remember the day _____ he called me.
- We will visit the farm _____ his father lives.

① why – where
② which – when
③ when – how
④ how – that
⑤ when – where

08 Which correction is right? 3점

ⓐ I know how she invented the machine.
ⓑ Visit the museum which you can see many paintings.
ⓒ This is the city in which she grew up.

① ⓐ how → the way how
② ⓐ how → what
③ ⓑ which → that
④ ⓑ which → where
⑤ ⓒ in which → which

09 Which is grammatically wrong?
(Up to 3 answers) 3점

① This is the hotel where we stayed last year.
② November 27 is the day on when I was born.
③ I'll tell you the reason why you feel tired all the time.
④ Social media is the way how they express themselves.
⑤ Those pictures were taken in the park in which I used to play.

Challenge! 주관식 서술형

10 Write the proper words for each blank. 4점

The reason _____ she got confused was _____ your explanation was not sufficient.

11 Rewrite the sentence WITHOUT using the underlined word. 5점

This is the ice cream of which I am fond.

→ _____

_____

12 Rewrite the sentence by adding the omitted words. 6점

He has just gotten a package sent by his parents.

→ _____

_____

13 Translate the sentence according to the conditions. 8점

그가 기다리고 있는 승강장은 사람들로 붐빈다.

- 조건 1 어휘 – be waiting, be crowded with
- 조건 2 현재 시제로 쓸 것
- 조건 3 빈칸에 8단어로 쓸 것

→ The platform _____

_____.

VOCA   invent 발명하다 | machine 기계 | get confused 혼동하다 | explanation 설명 | sufficient 충분한 | platform 승강장 | be crowded with ~로 붐비다

복합관계사

■ 아래 표의 빈칸에 알맞은 내용을 써 넣으세요. >>> 정답 19쪽

개념이해책
78쪽 함께 보기

1 복합관계대명사: 관계대명사 + -ever

복합관계대명사	명사절	양보의 부사절
1)_____	~하는 사람은 누구든 (= 2)_____)	누가[누구를, 누구에게] ~할지라도 (= 3)_____)
4)_____	~하는 것은 어느 것이든 (= 5)_____)	어느 것이[것을] ~할지라도 (= 6)_____)
7)_____	~하는 것은 무엇이나 (= 8)_____)	무엇이[무엇을] ~할지라도 (= 9)_____)

2 복합관계부사: 관계부사 + -ever

복합관계부사	시간·장소의 부사절	양보의 부사절
10)_____	~할 때는 언제나 (= 11)_____)	언제 ~할지라도 (= 12)_____)
13)_____	~하는 곳은 어디든지 (= 14)_____)	어디에서 ~할지라도 (= 15)_____)
16)_____		아무리 ~할지라도 (= 17)_____)

Level 1 Test

>>> 정답 19쪽

A 두 문장의 뜻이 같도록 빈칸에 알맞은 말을 쓰시오.

1 The innocent girl would believe anything that they said.

→ The innocent girl would believe _____ they said.

2 Whoever supported the theory opposed the new policy.

→ _____ _____ supported the theory opposed the new policy.

3 No matter how humble it may be, there is no place like home.

→ _____ humble it may be, there is no place like home.

4 No matter when you come, I'll open this place.

→ _____ you come, I'll open this place.

B 빈칸에 알맞은 말을 [보기]에서 골라 쓰시오.

보기	whoever	whatever	whichever
	whenever	wherever	however

1 네가 원하는 것은 무엇이든지 요리해 줄게.

→ I will cook you _____ you want.

2 네가 아무리 열심히 노력해도 그것을 얻을 수 없다.

→ _____ hard you may try, you can't get it.

3 내가 그를 만날 때마다, 그는 나의 아빠를 생각나게 한다.

→ _____ I meet him, he reminds me of my father.

4 너는 네가 가고 싶은 곳 어디든지 갈 수 있다.

→ You can go _____ you want to go.

VOCA innocent 순수한 | support 지지하다 | theory 이론 | oppose 반대하다 | policy 정책 | humble 초라한 | remind A of B A에게 B를 생각나게 하다

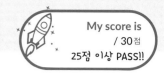
01 밑줄 친 부분의 쓰임이 올바르지 <u>않은</u> 것은? 2점

> A: Do you ① <u>think</u> I should ② <u>make</u> a study plan?
> B: ③<u>Yes</u>. Make a plan, and ④ <u>what</u> ⑤ <u>your plan is</u>, stick to it.

02 빈칸에 알맞은 것을 고르시오. 2점

> _____ she goes into town, she can't help buying clothes.

① Whenever　　　　② Wherever
③ Whichever　　　　④ Whatever
⑤ Whoever

03 다음 문장에 대한 설명으로 <u>잘못된</u> 것을 <u>모두</u> 고르시오. 3점

> Whoever wants to visit my house has to call me first.

① 미나: Whoever는 양보의 부사절을 이끈다.
② 민수: Whoever는 문장에서 주어 역할을 한다.
③ 희석: Whoever는 복합관계대명사이다.
④ 민서: Whoever는 Anyone who로 바꾸어 쓸 수 있다.
⑤ 철하: Whoever는 No matter who로 바꾸어 쓸 수 있다.

04 밑줄 친 부분을 같은 의미의 표현으로 바꾸어 쓴 것 중 <u>어색한</u> 것은? 3점

① You may choose <u>whichever</u> you like.
　→ anything that
② You may do <u>whatever</u> you want to do.
　→ anything that
③ <u>Whoever</u> comes first gets the best seat.
　→ No matter who
④ You can invite <u>anyone whom</u> you know.
　→ whomever
⑤ <u>Whenever</u> you come here, we will welcome you.
　→ No matter when

05 다음 대화가 자연스럽도록 괄호 안의 단어들을 배열하여 빈칸 (A)에 알맞은 말을 쓰시오. 5점 〔서술형〕

> A: Do you have any idea about how to help those people?
> B: No, I don't. ____(A)____, I'll agree to it.
> (is, your, no, matter, what, idea)

(A) _____

06 우리말과 같은 의미의 두 문장을 쓸 때 빈칸에 알맞은 말을 쓰시오. 각 3점 〔서술형〕

> 너는 아무리 경험이 많더라도 조심해야 해.

(1) _____ experienced you may be, you have to be careful.

(2) _____ _____
_____ experienced you may be, you have to be careful.

07 두 문장의 의미가 같도록 빈칸에 알맞은 말을 쓰시오. 4점 〔서술형〕

> No matter what his opinion is, I no longer care.

→ _____ his opinion is, I no longer care.

08 조건에 맞게 우리말을 영작하시오. 5점 〔서술형〕

> 네가 아는 사람 누구에게나 물어보아라.
>
> ·조건1　어휘 – ask
> ·조건2　4단어로 쓸 것

→ _____

VOCA　study plan 공부 계획 | stick to ~을 계속하다, 고수하다 | can't help+-ing ~하지 않을 수 없다 | welcome 환영하다 | experienced 경험 있는

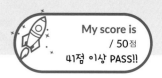
Level 3 Test

>>> 정답 19쪽

01 Which sentence is <u>unnatural</u>? 2점

① Whoever says that is a liar.

② You may do whatever you want to do.

③ Whichever movie is playing isn't important.

④ Whatever he lives, he won't be satisfied.

⑤ No matter how hard you try, you can't stop us now.

[02~03] Read the following paragraph and answer the questions.

A 7.2 earthquake on the Richter scale hit the town ___(A)___ I live. After the earthquake hit, I rushed to my son's kindergarten. When I got there, the building had been completely destroyed. It looked terrible, but I kept remembering the promise that I had made to my son: " ___(B)___ , I'll always be there for you." I knew the place ___(C)___ my son's classroom had been, and I went there.

02 Choose ALL of the proper words for blanks (A) and (C). 2점

① where   ② in which

③ what   ④ which in

⑤ on that

03 Which of the following are appropriate for blank (B)? 3점

ⓐ No matter what happens
ⓑ In any situation
ⓒ Whatever happens
ⓓ Whenever you are in need
ⓔ Even if you save me

① ⓐ, ⓑ, ⓒ   ② ⓐ, ⓑ, ⓒ, ⓓ

③ ⓐ, ⓒ   ④ ⓐ, ⓒ, ⓓ

⑤ ⓑ, ⓒ, ⓓ, ⓔ

04 Choose ALL of the correct translations. 2점

네가 원하는 것은 무엇이든지 가져도 좋다.

① You may keep whatever you want.

② You may keep no matter what you want.

③ You may keep anything that you want.

④ You may keep at anything you want.

⑤ You may keep no matter which you want.

05 Which of the following CANNOT be used when translating the sentence? 2점

그가 어디에 있을지라도 나는 그를 찾을 것이다.

① no matter where

② wherever

③ at any place where

④ find

⑤ will

06 Which of the following has the same meaning as the underlined part? 3점

How much time do you spend exercising each day? It may be just 15 minutes or as much as 2 hours. However, the amount of time is not important. <u>Whatever it is</u>, it is important to keep it every day.

① No matter what it is

② No matter what is it

③ No matter is it what

④ Any time it is

⑤ Any time is it

VOCA earthquake 지진 | Richter scale 리히터 척도 | kindergarten 유치원 | completely 완전히 | destroy 파괴하다 | situation 상황 | amount 양

94

07 How many sentences are <u>incorrect</u>? 4점

> ⓐ Whenever I feel depressed, I go shopping.
> ⓑ No matter whatever your dream is, it is precious.
> ⓒ You should not look down on people, no matter what their jobs are.
> ⓓ How hard I tried, I couldn't beat Sigyeong at tennis.

① none ② one
③ two ④ three
⑤ four

08 Which sentence is grammatically <u>wrong</u>?
(Up to 3 answers) 4점

① Put that thing away, what it is!
② Whenever I wash my car, it rains.
③ Whoever opened the door didn't close it.
④ Whatever you go, don't forget where you're from.
⑤ I hope she is happy wherever she decides to live.

Challenge! 주관식 서술형

09 Translate the sentence into English according to the conditions. 8점

> 장바구니에 네가 원하는 것은 무엇이든지 담아.
> · Words   put, your shopping cart
> · Condition 1   복합관계대명사를 이용할 것
> · Condition 2   8단어로 완성할 것

→ _____

10 Write one word for the blank to make the two sentences have the same meaning. 4점

> It doesn't matter what you do; I'm on your side.

→ _____ you do, I'm on your side.

11 Change the underlined word into THREE words to make the two sentences have the same meaning. 4점

> <u>However</u> skilled you are, you should not ignore the safety rules.

→ _____

12 Translate the sentence according to the conditions. 6점

> 너를 행복하게 하는 일은 무엇이든지 해라.
> · Condition 1   어휘 – make, happy
> · Condition 2   5단어로 쓸 것

→ _____

13 Read the following paragraph and write two expressions that can replace the underlined phrase (A) without changing the meaning.
각 3점

> Sometimes I get so tired that I want to quit my job as a reporter. (A) <u>Every time</u> I feel this way, I think about the dream I had when I was young. My dream was to be a great reporter and to win a Pulitzer Prize.

(1) _____

(2) _____

VOCA depressed 우울한 | precious 소중한 | look down on ~을 무시하다 | beat 이기다 | be on one's side ~의 편이다 | skilled 능숙한 | ignore 무시하다 | safety rule 안전 규칙 | Pulitzer Prize 퓰리처상(미국에서 매년 문학. 언론 분야 등에 수여하는 상)

CHAPTER 07
Review Test

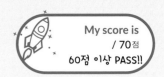

U13_1+3+U20_3

01 빈칸에 'that'이 쓰일 수 없는 것을 모두 고르시오. 2점

① This is a film _____ makes me laugh.
② He is the only person _____ ignores my opinions.
③ I believe _____ you will succeed in the future.
④ The girl _____ legs are very long is a model.
⑤ This is the café in _____ I often study.

U13_4

02 밑줄 친 What[what]의 쓰임이 나머지와 다른 것은? 2점

① This is what I lost at the subway station.
② What he told me about the camping trip excited me.
③ That's just what I was thinking.
④ What makes me happy is your smile.
⑤ I don't know what she will like.

U13_1

03 Who corrects the error properly? 2점

> Tell me all the things that you know them.

① 민수: know them → know
② 지형: them → it
③ 현주: that → what
④ 효정: all the things that → what
⑤ 유정: that → which

U14_2

04 밑줄 친 부분을 생략할 수 없는 것을 모두 고르시오. 2점

① The dentist whom you recommended to me is excellent.
② We need a person that will help us clean the house.
③ I don't know the reason why she likes me.
④ What is the language which is spoken in Hong Kong?
⑤ This is the company at which my father works.

U13_1

05 How many sentences are grammatically incorrect? 4점

> ⓐ This is the bus stop at which I meet my friend.
> ⓑ I like the boy whom is polite to the elderly.
> ⓒ The man who made these cakes are my father.
> ⓓ What she told me was amazing.
> ⓔ The girl who takes care of her sisters always look tired.

① one   ② two
③ three   ④ four
⑤ five

U14_2

06 우리말과 같은 뜻이 되도록 할 때 'living'이 들어갈 위치로 가장 알맞은 곳은? 2점

> In 1950, (①) Mother Teresa set up (②) the Missionaries of Charity (③) to help (④) those (⑤) on the streets.
>
> 1950년에 테레사 수녀는 거리에서 살아가는 사람들을 돕기 위해 자선 선교 단체를 세웠다.

07 U14_1

밑줄 친 말과 바꾸어 쓸 수 있는 것은? 2점

> This is the house in which my cousin lives.

① when ② where
③ what ④ how
⑤ why

08 U15_1

Choose ALL of the proper words for the blank. 3점

> 무슨 일이 일어나도 나는 울지 않겠다.
> = _____ may happen, I will not cry.

① No matter what
② Whomever
③ Whatever
④ No matter anything
⑤ Anything what

09 U13_4

빈칸에 알맞은 한 단어를 4글자로 쓰시오. 4점

> We must do _____ is right.

10 U13_2+GP

밑줄 친 부분이 가리키는 것을 정확히 쓰시오. 4점

> She sent some unique flowers, which I had never received before.

→ _____

11 U13_1

Combine the two sentences into one.
(2 answers) 각 4점

> They bought a couch. Its price was reasonable.

(1) _____
_____

(2) _____
_____

12 U14_1+GP

Translate the sentence according to the conditions. 6점

> 이것이 그가 그 음식점을 운영하는 방법이다.
> ·Condition 1 어휘 – run the restaurant
> ·Condition 2 관계부사를 사용할 것
> ·Condition 3 빈칸에 5단어로 쓸 것

→ This is _____.

13 U15_2

주어진 단어 중 필요한 것만 골라 빈칸에 6단어로 쓰시오.
4점

> good, matter, are, however, well, no, how, you

→ _____,
people will judge you according to their
moods and needs.

U14_1

14 각 빈칸에 알맞은 말을 쓰시오. 각 3점

(1) Our parents need to remember the days
_____ they were young.

(2) This is the park _____ I first met my
boyfriend.

U15_1

15 Rewrite the translation by correcting the
error. 4점

> 너는 이용할 수 있는 무엇이든 이용할 수 있다.
> = You can use whenever is available.

→ _____

U14_1

16 도표를 보고 빈칸에 들어갈 알맞은 말을 쓰시오. 4점

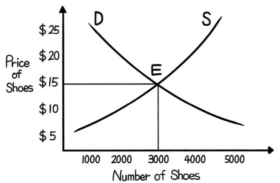

In the figure above, the equilibrium is point E,
_____ the supply curve (S) and the
demand curve (D) meet.

*equilibrium: 균형 상태

[17~18] Read the following and answer each
question.

No research has shown that ⓐthere is a clear relationship between laughter and pain reduction. However, many patients say that ⓑtheir pain has decreased after a good laugh. Some doctors argue that the decrease could be related to chemicals ⓒwhich is produced in the blood. Or the patients may ⓓexperience less pain because their muscles are more relaxed or simply because they have forgotten their pain at the moment. (A)그 이유가 무엇일지라도, there aren't many people ⓔwhom disagrees with the saying "A clown is like an aspirin."

U13_1

17 Among the underlined, which one has the
most errors? 4점

고난도

① ⓐ 　　　　② ⓑ

③ ⓒ 　　　　④ ⓓ

⑤ ⓔ

U15_1

18 Translate the underlined (A) into English.

(4 words) 5점

(A) _____

CHAPTER 08
비교 구문

UNIT 16 비교 변화, 원급 이용 비교 구문

개념이해책
86쪽 함께 보기

■ 아래 표의 빈칸에 알맞은 내용을 써 넣으세요. >>> 정답 20쪽

CONCEPT 1 원급, 비교급, 최상급

불규칙 변화	• good/well −1)＿＿＿＿＿ −2)＿＿＿＿＿ • many/much −5)＿＿＿＿＿ −6)＿＿＿＿＿ • late −9)＿＿＿＿＿ −10)＿＿＿＿＿ (시간) • far −13)＿＿＿＿＿ −14)＿＿＿＿＿ (거리)	• bad/ill −3)＿＿＿＿＿ −4)＿＿＿＿＿ • little −7)＿＿＿＿＿ −8)＿＿＿＿＿ • late −11)＿＿＿＿＿ −12)＿＿＿＿＿ (순서) • far −15)＿＿＿＿＿ −16)＿＿＿＿＿ (정도)
다른 형태 변화	than 대신 to를 쓰는 비교급	비교, 최상급 관용 표현
	• 17)＿＿＿＿＿ to: ~보다 직급[학년]이 높은 • 18)＿＿＿＿＿ to: ~보다 직급[학년]이 낮은 • 19)＿＿＿＿＿ to: ~보다 우수한[상급의] • 20)＿＿＿＿＿ to: ~보다 열등한[하급의] • 21)＿＿＿＿＿ A to B: B보다 A를 더 좋아하다	• would rather A than B: 22)＿＿＿＿＿ • rather than: 23)＿＿＿＿＿ • other than: 24)＿＿＿＿＿ • at 25)＿＿＿＿＿ : 최소한 ↔ at 26)＿＿＿＿＿ : 많아야 • at 27)＿＿＿＿＿ : 마침내

CONCEPT 2 원급을 이용한 구문

A ~ as+원급+as B	28)＿＿＿＿＿＿＿＿＿＿＿
A ~ not as[so]+원급+as B (= A ~ less+원급+than B = B ~ 비교급+than A)	29)＿＿＿＿＿＿＿＿＿＿＿
as+원급+as possible (= as+원급+as+주어+can[could])	30)＿＿＿＿＿＿＿＿＿＿＿
A ~ 배수사+as+원급+as B (= A ~배수사+비교급+than B)	31)＿＿＿＿＿＿＿＿＿＿＿

Level 1 Test

>>> 정답 21쪽

A 우리말에 맞도록 빈칸에 알맞은 말을 쓰시오.

1 그는 나이는 나보다 많지만 내 후배다.

→ He is older than me, but he is ＿＿＿＿＿

＿＿＿＿＿ me.

2 나는 빈둥거리는 것보다 차라리 일을 하는 것이 더 좋다.

→ I ＿＿＿＿＿ working ＿＿＿＿＿ being

lazy.

3 그녀는 과학에서 나보다 우수하다.

→ She is ＿＿＿＿＿ ＿＿＿＿＿ me in

science.

B 두 문장의 뜻이 같도록 빈칸을 완성하시오.

1 English is harder than math.

→ Math is ＿＿＿＿＿ hard than English.

→ Math ＿＿＿＿＿ ＿＿＿＿＿ as hard as

English.

2 I made my fiancée as happy as possible.

→ I made my fiancée ＿＿＿＿＿

＿＿＿＿＿ ＿＿＿＿＿

＿＿＿＿＿.

3 He is twice as tall as his son.

→ He is two times ＿＿＿＿＿ ＿＿＿＿＿

his son.

VOCA fiancée 약혼녀

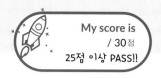
01 각 문장의 밑줄 친 단어를 올바르게 고친 것은? 2점

ⓐ Math is <u>easy</u> for me than science.
ⓑ Joy is <u>a kindest</u> of my friends.
ⓒ His house is <u>far</u> from school than my house.

① ⓐ more easy ⓑ kindest ⓒ farther
② ⓐ easier ⓑ the kindest ⓒ further
③ ⓐ easier ⓑ the kindest ⓒ farther
④ ⓐ easyer ⓑ the kindest ⓒ further
⑤ ⓐ easyer ⓑ kindest ⓒ farther

02 다음 문장을 바르게 설명한 학생을 <u>모두</u> 고르시오. 2점

My niece cried as loudly as possible.

① 슬기: loudly는 cried를 수식하고 있다.
② 지예: possible은 올바르게 쓰였다.
③ 선아: possible은 can으로 바꿀 수 있다.
④ 종호: possible은 she could로 바꿀 수 있다.
⑤ 재설: as loudly as는 more loudly로 바꾸어야 한다.

03 다음 중 어법상 <u>어색한</u> 문장을 <u>모두</u> 고르시오. 2점

① His computer is superior than mine.
② I prefer fried chicken to grilled chicken.
③ The tree is three times as tall as me.
④ He was more handsome than I had expected.
⑤ She is much slender than before.

04 다음 중 어법상 <u>어색한</u> 문장으로 묶인 것은? 3점

ⓐ Her hair is even longer than me.
ⓑ My dad came home earlier than my mom.
ⓒ It is not cheaper than your iPad.
ⓓ Mini looks less cuter than yesterday.
ⓔ I avoided him as much as possibly.

① ⓐ, ⓑ, ⓓ   ② ⓐ, ⓓ
③ ⓐ, ⓓ, ⓔ   ④ ⓑ, ⓓ
⑤ ⓒ, ⓓ, ⓔ

05 다음 문장에서 어법상 <u>어색한</u> 부분을 바르게 고치시오. 3점

서술형

He can play the instrument as good as a professional musician.

_____ → _____

06 다음 문장의 빈칸에 들어갈 알맞은 말을 조건에 맞게 쓰시오. 5점

서술형

Cats _____.

· 어휘   twice, sleep, people
· 조건 1   원급 표현을 추가할 것
· 조건 2   m으로 시작하는 한 단어를 추가할 것

→ _____

07 그림을 묘사하는 문장을 조건에 맞게 완성하시오. 5점

서술형

그녀는 가능한 한 오래 철봉에 매달려 있었다.

· 조건 1   어휘 – hang on to the iron bar
· 조건 2   과거 시제로 쓸 것
· 조건 3   빈칸에 11단어로 쓸 것

→ She _____
_____.

08 다음 문장들에서 어법상 <u>어색한</u> 부분을 고쳐 문장을 다시 쓰시오. 각 4점

서술형

ⓐ She is junior than me.
ⓑ I rather die than surrender.

ⓐ → _____
ⓑ → _____

VOCA niece 여자 조카 | expect 기대하다 | slender 날씬한 | instrument 악기 | professional 전문적인 | musician 음악가, 연주자 | hang (-hung- hung) 매달리다 | iron bar 철봉 | surrender 항복하다

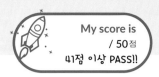

01 Which is NOT proper for any of the blanks?
2점

ⓐ The situation is _____ than I thought.
ⓑ This car is faster than any other _____.
ⓒ My bag is _____ as big as _____.

① still worse　　　② vehicle
③ five times　　　④ Jane
⑤ yours

02 Which sentences are incorrect? (Find ALL.) 3점

① She assisted me as much as she can.
② This building isn't as larger as that one.
③ She makes more worse noise than you.
④ Emma is inferior to David in math.
⑤ The yellow car is two times bigger than the black one.

03 Which words are proper for the blanks? 2점

• His English is superior _____ mine.
• Your coat is as light as _____.
• Dairy products are in the _____ aisle.

① to – me – latest
② to – mine – last
③ to – me – last
④ than – mine – latest
⑤ than – mine – latest

04 Which translation is correct? (2 answers) 2점

그 부부는 가능한 한 우아하게 춤을 추었다.

① The couple danced as graceful as possible.
② The couple danced as gracefully as possible.
③ The couple danced as gracefully as they can.
④ The couple danced as gracefully as they could.
⑤ The couple danced as gracefully as possibly.

05 Choose ALL of the incorrect sentences. 2점

baseball gloves $20　boxing gloves $30　ski gloves $15　golf gloves $10

① Golf gloves are the cheapest gloves.
② Baseball gloves are not as expensive as boxing gloves.
③ Ski gloves are not as expensive as golf gloves.
④ Boxing gloves are less expensive than baseball gloves.
⑤ Baseball gloves are more expensive than golf gloves.

06 Which is appropriate for the blank? 2점

He is younger than me, but he is _____ me in the company.

① senior to　　　② senior than
③ junior to　　　④ junior than
⑤ junior with

VOCA situation 상황 | assist 도와주다 | dairy product 유제품 | aisle 복도, 통로 | gracefully 우아하게

07 Which of the following is <u>incorrect</u>? 2점

① Most of his estate went to the eldest son.

② I prefer reading books than strolling.

③ Beer sells better in summer than in winter.

④ She is as devoted to her family as Victoria.

⑤ My daughter studies less than my son.

08 Which TWO of the following sentences have <u>different</u> meanings than the others? 3점

① I didn't answer the question as fast as you.

② You answered the question faster than I.

③ I answered the question faster than you.

④ I answered the question more slowly than you.

⑤ You didn't answer the question faster than me.

09 Which CANNOT make a grammatically correct sentence? 4점

① her neighbors / to / feels / She / . / superior

② your decision / soon / possible / as / as / . / Make

③ This sweater / thicker / that one / is / . / less / than

④ did / his brother / work / . / as / as / much / twice / He

⑤ kindness / Good looks / are / as / . / important / as / not

Challenge! 주관식 서술형

10 Complete the sentence to make the two sentences have the same meaning. 4점

> My composition looks worse than yours.

→ My composition looks _____

_____ yours.

11 This is Ari's translation. Find ALL of the errors and rewrite the whole sentence correctly. 6점

> 기술은 아이들을 과거보다 덜 창의적으로 만들었다.
> → Technology has made children less creatively as they were in the past.

→ _____

_____

12 Fill in the blanks according to the graph. 각 4점

Number of Movie Tickets Sold

(1) On Sunday, movie tickets sell _____

_____ _____

_____ on Wednesday. (배수사 사용)

(2) Movie tickets sell the _____ on Thursday. (최상급 사용)

13 Translate the sentence according to the conditions. 각 5점

> 그녀는 가능한 한 많이 웃으려고 노력했다.
>
> · Condition 1   어휘 – try to, laugh, much
> · Condition 1   같은 의미의 두 문장을 쓰되 (1)은 8단어로, (2)는 9단어로 쓸 것

(1) _____

(2) _____

VOCA   estate 재산 | stroll 산책하다 | devoted 헌신적인 | composition 작문 | creative 창의적인 | sell 팔리다, 팔다 | try to ~하려고 노력하다

17 비교급, 최상급 구문

■ 아래 표의 빈칸에 알맞은 내용을 써 넣으세요. >>> 정답 21쪽

개념이해책
89쪽 함께 보기

CONCEPT 1 비교급을 이용한 구문

A ~ 비교급+than B	1)
The+비교급 ~, the+비교급 …	2)
get/become/grow+비교급+and+비교급	3)
the+비교급+of the two	4)
(all) the+비교급+because (of)	5)

CONCEPT 2 최상급

one of the+최상급+복수 명사	6)	the+서수+최상급+단수 명사	7)

CONCEPT 3 최상급을 나타내는 표현

A ~ the+최상급+단수 명사	8)
A ~ 비교급+than any other+단수 명사	9)
A ~ 비교급+than all (of) the other+복수 명사	10)
No (other)+단수 명사 ~ 비교급+than A	11)
No (other)+단수 명사 ~ as[so]+원급+as A	12)
There is nothing+비교급+than A (= Nothing is+비교급+than A)	13)

Level 1 Test

>>> 정답 21쪽

A 두 문장의 뜻이 같도록 빈칸을 채우시오.

1 Fried chicken is the most delicious food.

→ Fried chicken is _____ _____ _____ any other food.

2 New York is the most populous city in the U.S.

→ _____ _____ city in the U.S. is as populous as New York.

3 Canada is one hundred times as large as Korea.

→ Canada is one hundred times _____ _____ Korea.

B 괄호 안의 단어를 이용하여 빈칸을 완성하시오.

1 네 이야기는 내가 들은 것 중 가장 재미있다. (funny)

→ Your story is _____ _____ that I have ever heard.

2 그는 나이를 먹을수록 더욱 까다로워진다. (particular)

→ The older he is, _____ _____ _____ he becomes.

3 건강보다 더 소중한 것은 없다. (there, precious)

→ _____ _____ _____ _____ _____ than health.

VOCA populous 인구가 많은 | particular 까다로운 | precious 소중한

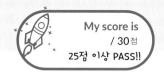
01 주어진 문장과 의미가 <u>다른</u> 것을 고르시오. 2점

> No gem is as transparent as the diamond.

① The diamond is the most transparent gem.

② The diamond is more transparent than any other gem.

③ No gem is more transparent than the diamond.

④ No gem is as transparent as the diamond.

⑤ The diamond is as transparent as all other gems.

02 밑줄 친 부분과 바꾸어 쓸 수 <u>없는</u> 말은? 2점

> His explanation made me <u>even</u> more confused.

① a lot   ② very

③ still   ④ much

⑤ far

03 다음 두 문장에서 어법상 <u>어색한</u> 부분을 바르게 고친 학생을 <u>모두</u> 고르시오. 2점

> ⓐ I like her so more because of her intelligence.
> ⓑ The recent economic crisis became much serious more.

① 윤중: ⓐ because of → because

② 미래: ⓑ much → very

③ 나현: ⓐ so → a lot

④ 의중: ⓑ serious more → more serious

⑤ 종규: ⓐ more → more than

04 다음 문장을 영작할 때 사용될 수 <u>없는</u> 단어는? 2점

> 네가 더 일찍 출발할수록 거기에 더 먼저 도착할 거야.

① the   ② start

③ earlier   ④ soon

⑤ arrive

05 두 문장이 같은 뜻이 되도록 빈칸에 알맞은 말을 쓰시오. 4점

> As the supply becomes less, the price goes up higher.

→ _____ _____ the supply becomes, _____ _____ the price goes up.

06 다음 중 어법상 <u>어색한</u> 부분을 바르게 고치시오. 4점

> ⓐ Audrey Hepburn was one of the most beautiful woman in the world.
> ⓑ The symptom will get worse and worse.

(   ) _____ → _____

[07~08] 주어진 문장과 같은 의미의 문장을 조건에 맞게 쓰시오. 각 7점

07

> There is nothing more important than family.

· 조건 1   문장을 부정어로 시작할 것

· 조건 2   둘 다 6단어로 쓰되, (1)에는 비교급을, (2)에는 원급을 사용할 것

(1) _____

_____

(2) _____

_____

08

> This painting is more abstract than that one.

· 조건 1   어휘 – of the two

· 조건 2   9단어로 쓸 것

→ _____

VOCA   gem 보석 | transparent 투명한 | explanation 설명 | confused 혼동된 | intelligence 지성 | recent 최근의 | economic 경제의 | crisis 위기 | serious 심각한 | supply 공급 | symptom 증상 | painting 그림 | abstract 추상적인

Level 3 Test

My score is
/ 50점
41점 이상 PASS!!

01 Choose the correct translation. (2 answers) 2점

실패를 많이 하면 할수록 너는 성공에 더 가까워진다.

① As you fail a lot, you get close to success.

② The more you fail, the closer you get to success.

③ You fail the more, you get to the closer success.

④ The more you fail, you get to success the closer.

⑤ As you fail more, you get closer to success.

02 Which is incorrect according to the chart? 2점

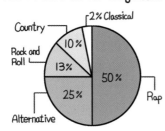

Music Preferences for Young Adults

① Young adults like classical music the least.

② No other music is liked as much as rap.

③ Young adults don't like rock and roll as much as alternative music.

④ No other music is more popular than classical music.

⑤ Young adults like rock and roll more than country music.

03 How many sentences are incorrect? 2점

ⓐ She is one of the most famous actress.

ⓑ He has become more and more arrogant.

ⓒ As cheaper the product became, the more customers wanted to buy it.

ⓓ I like him all the better because he is kind.

① zero   ② one

③ two   ④ three

⑤ four

04 The following graph shows the sales of mobile games by company A. According to the graph, which is NOT true? 2점

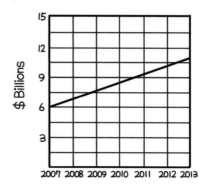

① In no other year did the company have lower sales than in 2007.

② Its sales were the highest in 2013.

③ In 2012, it had the second lowest sales.

④ Its sales are getting bigger and bigger.

⑤ In 2013, it had almost two times bigger sales than in 2007.

05 Which sentences are incorrect? 2점

ⓐ Male birds are colorfuler than female birds.

ⓑ Who is the taller of the two girls?

ⓒ You can jump highlier than him.

① ⓐ, ⓑ   ② ⓐ, ⓒ

③ ⓑ   ④ ⓑ, ⓒ

⑤ ⓐ, ⓑ, ⓒ

06 Which is the correct translation of the underlined Korean sentence? 2점

A: I have two English dictionaries. Which one should I use?

B: 이 사전이 둘 중에서 더 좋아.

① This dictionary is better of two.

② This dictionary is better of the two.

③ This dictionary is the better of the two.

④ This dictionary is the best of the two.

⑤ This dictionary is as good as the other.

VOCA success 성공 | preference 선호 | young adult 청소년, 젊은이 | arrogant 거만한 | sales 판매량 | male 수컷의 | colorful 색이 다채로운 | female 암컷의 | dictionary 사전

07 Which CANNOT make a grammatically correct sentence? 4점

① freedom / precious / more / than / Nothing / . / is

② and / more / . / more / expensive / getting / are / Things

③ important / in / One / life / of / thing / the / most / . / hope / is

④ know, / to / you / the / less / more / The / say / need / . / you

⑤ more / than / . / other / any / country / Saudi Arabia / oil / produces

08 Who analyzes the sentence correctly?
(Up to 3 answers) 4점

> ⓐ Nothing is more precious than you.
> ⓑ The more people have, the more they want.

① 희주: ⓐ Nothing is as precious as you.로 바꿔 쓸 수 있어.

② 수영: ⓐ 너(you)보다 소중한 것은 많다는 뜻이야.

③ 진환: ⓐ 비교급을 이용해서 최상급을 표현하고 있어.

④ 은옥: ⓑ 사람들은 더 가지면 가질수록 더 원한다는 뜻이야.

⑤ 소을: ⓑ As people have much, they want much.와 같은 뜻이야.

Challenge! 주관식 서술형

09 Rearrange the given words according to the conditions. 6점

> South Korea, city, second, the, is, in, larger, Busan
>
> · Condition 1　Change the form of one word among the given words.
> · Condition 2　Start the sentence with a name of a city.

→ _____

10 Complete the sentence according to the graph. 6점

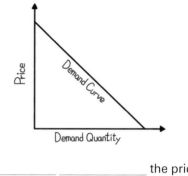

→ _____ _____ the price

gets, _____ _____ the

demand gets. (high, low)

[11~12] Answer the questions according to the graph.

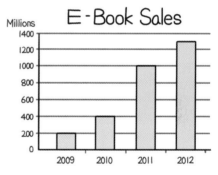

11 Fill in the blanks by using the given word. 6점

→ _____

_____ e-books were sold in 2011

than in 2009. (times)

12 Complete the sentence summarizing the graph by using the given words. 6점

→ E-book sales are _____

_____ _____

_____ . (grow, big)

VOCA　demand 수요 | curve 곡선 | price 가격

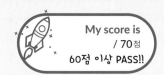

[01~02] 두 문장이 같은 뜻이 되도록 빈칸에 알맞은 것을 고르시오. 각 2점

01 U16_2

I am not as lucky as Billy.
= Billy is _____ I am.

① luckier than
② not luckier than
③ not as lucky as
④ more lucky than
⑤ not more lucky than

02 U16_1

I like football more than baseball.
= I prefer football _____ baseball.

① by   ② than
③ to   ④ with
⑤ for

03 U17_1 다음 글의 밑줄 친 부분과 같은 의미의 문장은? 2점

The lower prices are, the more people will buy. The higher prices are, the less they will buy.

① As prices are lower, people will buy more.
② As prices are low, people will not buy much.
③ As prices are higher, people will buy more.
④ As people will buy more, the prices are lower.
⑤ As people will buy more, the prices are higher.

04 U17_GP Which correction is right? 2점

함정

ⓐ Peter is the kindest in all the boy in my class.
ⓑ There is no one junior to me at my company, so I have to do the most trivial tasks.

① ⓐ in all the boy → in the boy
② ⓐ in all the boy → of all the boys
③ ⓑ to me → than me
④ ⓑ the most trivial → the more trivial
⑤ 어법상 어색한 부분이 없다.

05 U17_GP 다음 중 밑줄 친 'much' 대신 쓸 수 <u>없는</u> 것은? 2점

The accident could have been <u>much</u> worse. Fortunately, no one was hurt.

① even   ② still
③ far   ④ a lot
⑤ great

06 U17_3 Which has a <u>different</u> meaning than the given sentence? 2점

I like running the most.

① There is nothing I like more than running.
② Nothing is more enjoyable than running to me.
③ I like running more than any other thing.
④ I like running as much as other things.
⑤ I like nothing as much as running.

07 다음 중 어법상 어색한 문장을 모두 고르시오. 2점

U16_1+2+U17_3

① Iron is more useful than any other metals.
② Mary reads books as many as Jane.
③ I'll finish writing the essay as soon as possible.
④ Her job is more difficult than yours.
⑤ GN-z11 is the farthest galaxy from the Earth.

08 How many sentences are grammatically incorrect? 3점

U16_1+2

ⓐ She is shouting as loudly as she can.
ⓑ He didn't run as fast as he can.
ⓒ The weather got more and more cold.
ⓓ My score is more worse than yours.
ⓔ They have more money than she is.

① one ② two
③ three ④ four
⑤ five

09 Rewrite the sentence by correcting the error.

U16_2

(2 answers) 각 3점

I sat down as low as can to hide.

(1) _____

_____

(2) _____

_____

10 괄호 안의 단어를 이용해 우리말과 같은 뜻이 되도록 빈칸에 알맞은 표현을 쓰시오. 4점

U16_2

그가 거기에 도착했을 때, 그는 그 건물이 팬케이크처럼 납작해진 것을 발견하였다.

→ When he got there, he found the building had

become _____ _____

_____ a pancake. (flat)

11 우리말과 일치하도록 주어진 단어를 사용하여 문장을 완성하시오. 4점

U17_1

환경 파괴가 점점 더 심각해지고 있다.
become, serious

→ The destruction of the environment is _____

_____ .

12 Complete the translation by using the given words. 4점

U17_1

흰색 모니터가 둘 중에서 더 넓다.
wide, of the two

→ The white monitor _____

_____ .

13 Read the following dialog and rewrite the underlined sentence according to the conditions. 7점

U16_2

A: Which is more important to you, books or food?
B: Books are more important to me than food.

· Condition 1   Compare books and food.
· Condition 2   Use the word "as."
· Condition 3   Write a negative sentence.
· Condition 4   Write 7 words in the blank.

→ _____ to

me.

U17_1

14 우리말과 같은 뜻이 되도록 빈칸에 내용과 어법상 알맞은 말을 써 넣어 문장을 완성하시오. 4점

> 더 열심히 연습할수록 더 좋은 결과를 얻을 것이다.

→ _____ _____ you practice,

_____ _____ results you

will get.

[15~16] Look at the following graph and answer the questions.

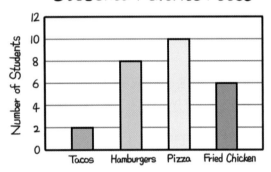

Students' Favorite Foods

U17_3+GP

15 According to the above graph, complete the sentence like the example. 6점

> 보기 Pizza is the most popular food.
> → Pizza is more popular than any other food.
>
> Tacos are the least popular food.

→ Tacos are _____

_____.

U16_2+U17_1

16 Compare hamburgers and fried chicken. 각 4점

(1) Fried chicken is _____

_____ _____ hamburgers.

(2) Hamburgers are _____

_____ _____ fried chicken.

[17~18] Read the following and answer each question.

When Clara was a little girl, her teacher, David Mills, used @to encourage his pupils to drink a lot of milk. Somehow, he believed  ⓑwhat milk enhanced one's intelligence. For him, (A)지능보다 더 가치 있는 것은 없었다. From time to time, Clara would ask him, "Mr. Mills, what is intelligence?" Each time, he would answer in a different way: "Intelligence is your baby sister's first words," "Intelligence is one of the greatest ©thing in life," or, "Intelligence is the question ⓓwhich you asked in ethics class this morning." The teacher's responses would drive her crazy, but now, twenty years later, she think it's fun ⓔto consider why Mr. Mills said those things.

U20_3+U17_2

17 Among the underlined, how many are grammatically **wrong**? 4점

고난도

① 1개   ② 2개

③ 3개   ④ 4개

⑤ 5개

U17_3

18 Rearrange the given words to translate the underlined (A) 6점

> than, was, valuable, nothing, more, there, intelligence

(A) _____

CHAPTER 09
분사

■ 아래 표의 빈칸에 알맞은 내용을 써 넣으세요. ››› 정답 23쪽

개념이해책
96쪽 함께 보기

CONCEPT ❶ 현재분사와 과거분사

	형태	의미	역할
현재분사	동사원형+1)_____	• 능동: ~하는, ~하게 하는 • 진행: ~하고 있는	• 2)_____ 역할: 명사 수식, 보어 • 3)_____ 형에 쓰임
과거분사	• 규칙: 동사원형+4)_____ • 불규칙: 동사의 과거분사형	• 수동: ~되어진/지는, • 완료: ~되어 있는	• 5)_____ 역할: 명사 수식, 보어 • 6)_____ 형, 7)_____ 태에 쓰임

CONCEPT ❷ 감정을 나타내는 분사

boring	8)_____	pleasing	20)_____
bored	9)_____	pleased	21)_____
exciting	10)_____	annoying	22)_____
excited	11)_____	annoyed	23)_____
surprising	12)_____	interesting	24)_____
surprised	13)_____	interested	25)_____
shocking	14)_____	amazing	26)_____
shocked	15)_____	amazed	27)_____
disappointing	16)_____	moving	28)_____
disappointed	17)_____	moved	29)_____
satisfying	18)_____	frightening	30)_____
satisfied	19)_____	frightened	31)_____

CONCEPT ❸ 현재분사와 동명사

현재분사	형용사적 성질: 32)_____ 수식, 33)_____ 역할, 34)_____ 형
동명사	명사적 성질: 주어, 35)_____, 보어 역할

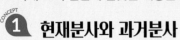

Level 1 Test

››› 정답 23쪽

A [ ] 안에서 알맞은 것을 고르시오.

1 Reading [boring / bored] books makes me sleepy.

2 The man found [hiding / hidden] treasure.

3 I got a letter [writing / written] in Latin.

4 There was a cat [crying / cried] in a box.

5 The tomato festival in Spain is very [interesting / interested].

VOCA treasure 보물 | Latin 라틴어 | festival 축제 | novel 소설 | Dickens 디킨스(19세기 영국 소설가)

B 어법상 어색한 부분을 찾아 바르게 고치시오.

1 In my town, there is a library build in 1900.

_____ → _____

2 The boy chased the run dog.

_____ → _____

3 The man spoken to her is my grandfather.

_____ → _____

4 I like the novels writing by Dickens.

_____ → _____

 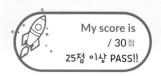

>>> 정답 23쪽

01 빈칸에 알맞은 것은? 2점

I have to sweep the _____ leaves.

① fall
② fallen
③ to fall
④ be falling
⑤ be fallen

02 밑줄 친 단어의 쓰임이 주어진 문장과 같은 것은? 2점

The girl dancing on the stage is my sister.

① I remember sending you a message.
② Drinking a lot of water is good for your health.
③ The girls chatting in the classroom are twins.
④ I like listening to music when I'm alone.
⑤ My hobby is riding my bike in the mountains.

03 다음을 영작할 때 사용될 수 없는 것은? 2점

나는 줄 서 있는 그 남자를 알고 있다.

① I
② the man
③ in line
④ know
⑤ stood

04 다음 중 어법상 어색한 문장을 고른 것은? 3점

ⓐ I'm going to take the train left at ten.
ⓑ I heard a phone ringing inside the wall.
ⓒ David fixed the broken computer.
ⓓ The movie was disappointed.

① ⓐ, ⓒ
② ⓐ, ⓓ
③ ⓒ, ⓓ
④ ⓐ, ⓑ, ⓒ
⑤ ⓑ, ⓒ, ⓓ

05 밑줄 친 부분을 바르게 고쳐 문장을 다시 쓰시오. 5점

[서술형]

Look at the kites fly in the sky.

→ _____

06 그림을 묘사하는 문장을 조건에 맞게 영어로 쓰시오. 6점

[서술형]

- 조건 1   과거 시제로 쓸 것
- 조건 2   어휘 – she, the, child, give, candy, cry, piece
- 조건 3   필요하면 어형을 변화할 것
- 조건 4   10단어로 쓸 것

→ _____
_____

07 다음 문장에서 어법상 어색한 부분을 바르게 고치시오. 4점

[서술형]

She was surprising by the thank-you cards from her children.

_____ → _____

08 괄호 안의 단어를 빈칸에 알맞은 형태로 써서 문장을 완성하시오. 각 3점

[서술형]

(1) The classical music concert was long and _____. (tire)

(2) I was _____ of sitting down at the classical music concert. (tire)

VOCA sweep 쓸다 | stage 무대 | chat 이야기하다, 수다 떨다 | stand in line 줄을 서다 | kite 연 | thank-you card 감사 카드 | classical 클래식의, 클래식 음악의

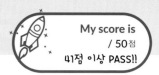
[01~02] Choose the suitable word or phrase for the blank. 각 2점

01

I have a good neighbor _____ Dorothy.

① naming
② named
③ be naming
④ have named
⑤ be named

02

A _____ stone gathers no moss.

① roll
② rolled
③ rolling
④ be rolling
⑤ be rolled

03 Which is suitable for each blank? 2점

- A _____ man will clutch at a straw.
- Don't cry over _____ milk.

① drown – spill
② drown – spilling
③ drowning – spilling
④ drowned – spilled
⑤ drowning – spilled

04 Which underlined word is grammatically incorrect? (2 answers) 2점

① Their stage costumes were underlined{embarrassing}.
② We were underlined{surprised} by his refusal.
③ I was underlined{satisfying} with his explanation.
④ She felt underlined{bored} because she had to stay home alone.
⑤ The instructions were very underlined{confused}.

05 Who corrects the error properly? 2점

Some books writing in English are selling well in Vietnam nowadays.

① 유미: Some books → Any books
② 민수: in English → English
③ 윤후: well → good
④ 진희: writing → written
⑤ 준성: are selling → is selling

06 Which underlined word is used underlined{differently} than the others? 2점

① underlined{Getting} up early in the morning is difficult.
② They were underlined{dancing} together at the party.
③ I always enjoy underlined{trying} new things.
④ Do you mind underlined{opening} the window?
⑤ His favorite activity is underlined{gardening} in the morning.

07 Which sentences are underlined{incorrect}? 4점

ⓐ The man working in the garden is my father.
ⓑ You are more beautiful than these blossoming flowers.
ⓒ The drunk man tried to hit me with a bending pipe.
ⓓ The book publishing last month was sold out.

① ⓐ, ⓑ
② ⓑ, ⓒ
③ ⓒ, ⓓ
④ ⓐ, ⓑ, ⓒ
⑤ ⓑ, ⓒ, ⓓ

VOCA neighbor 이웃 | gather 모으다 | moss 이끼 | drown 익사하다 | clutch at ~을 붙잡다 | straw 지푸라기 | spill 쏟다 | stage costume 무대 의상 | refusal 거절 | explanation 설명 | instruction 지시 | nowadays 요즘 | blossom (꽃이) 피다 | publish 출판하다

08 Which is NOT necessary when translating the sentence? 3점

> 잠자고 있는 사자를 깨우지 마라.

① don't　　　　② wake

③ a　　　　　　④ slept

⑤ lion

09 Which CANNOT make a grammatically correct sentence? 4점

① everybody / by / . / moved / speech / was / his

② on / a / I / . / sat / my / saw / bird / window

③ girl / dog / waved / me / at / the / . / her / walking

④ of / was / truck / the / . / speed / frightening / the

⑤ music / . / composed / she / Beethoven / likes / by

Challenge! 주관식 서술형

10 Translate the sentence into English according to the conditions. 8점

> 그의 팬들에 의해 둘러싸인 그 가수는 짜증 난 것처럼 보인다.
>
> ·Words　　　　surround, seem, annoy
> ·Condition 1　주어진 어휘를 모두 변형할 것
> ·Condition 2　총 8단어로 완성할 것

→ _____

11 Find the error and correct it. 4점

> The roof was damaging by the storm.

_____ → _____

12 Rearrange the words to translate the sentence. 5점

> 나는 짖고 있는 개가 무섭다.
>
> of　I'm　dogs　barking　afraid

→ _____

13 Complete the description of the picture by using the right form of the verb "bore." 5점

→ The lecture was so _____ that nobody paid attention. Some students fell asleep because they were _____.

14 Look at the picture and complete the sentence in the present tense by using the given word. 5점

→ People _____ _____ _____ the fireworks. (excite)

VOCA　damage 손상을 입히다 | storm 폭풍우 | be afraid of ~을 두려워하다 | lecture 강의 | pay attention 주의를 기울이다 | fall asleep 잠이 들다 | firework 불꽃(놀이)

■ 아래 표의 빈칸에 알맞은 내용을 써 넣으세요. ▶▶▶ 정답 24쪽

개념이해책
99쪽 함께 보기

CONCEPT 1 분사구문의 용법

1)_____	Arriving at the station, I called him to pick me up.
2)_____	Not knowing where I was, I asked a police officer.
3)_____	(Being) Left behind, you should let me know.
4)_____	Jane having a bad cold, her boss made her work harder.
5)_____	Listening to K-pop, Sakahi read a Korean novel.
6)_____	The bellman opened the door, delivering my luggage.

CONCEPT 2 독립분사구문과 비인칭 독립분사구문

종류	형태	의미
독립분사구문	7)_____ +분사 ~	분사구문의 주어 ≠ 8)_____의 주어
9)_____ 독립분사구문	(10)_____ 생략)+분사 ~	분사구문의 주어가 11)_____인 경우

CONCEPT 3 with + 목적어 + 분사

with+목적어+	현재분사	목적어와 12)_____ 관계	~이 …한 채로
	과거분사	목적어와 13)_____ 관계	~이 …된 채로

Level 1 Test

▶▶▶ 정답 24쪽

A 빈칸에 자연스럽게 이어질 말을 [보기]에서 고르시오.

> 보기
> ⓐ she took a 5-minute break
> ⓑ the dog started barking
> ⓒ with the lights turned on
> ⓓ Dad drove as fast as possible

1 Seeing his own reflection, _____.

2 Being tired from work, _____.

3 Having no time to lose, _____.

4 Eric went to bed _____.

B 밑줄 친 부분이 어색하면 바르게 고치시오.

1 Having not received an answer, I called him again.

→ _____

2 Being found someone's ID card, she brought it to the teachers' room.

→ _____

3 Jack is waiting for the passengers in his taxi with the engine run.

→ _____

VOCA take a break 잠깐 쉬다 | reflection (거울 등에 비친) 모습 | receive 받다 | ID card 신분증 | passenger 승객

01 다음 중 빈칸에 가장 적절한 것은? 2점

> _____ well, I didn't go on the blind date.

① Feeling not
② Not feeling
③ No feeling
④ Didn't feel
⑤ Haven't felt

02 밑줄 친 부분과 바꿔 쓸 수 있는 것은? 2점

> After he had bowed deeply to the queen, he put the marbles in front of her.

① Bowed deeply to the queen
② Bowing deeply to the queen
③ Having bowed deeply to the queen
④ Being bowed deeply to the queen
⑤ After bowed deeply to the queen

03 다음을 영작할 때 사용될 수 없는 것은? 2점

> 그의 제복으로 판단해 보면, 그는 경찰관임에 틀림없다.

① uniform
② being
③ must
④ if
⑤ judging

04 다음 중 문장 전환이 옳은 것으로 짝지어진 것은? 3점

> ⓐ As she woke up late, she had to hurry.
>   → Waking up late, she had to hurry.
> ⓑ Singing softly, she walked her dog.
>   → She walked her dog as she sang softly.
> ⓒ As I didn't know what to do, I stood still.
>   → Knowing not what to do, I stood still.
> ⓓ As he had lost his wallet, he asked for help.
>   → Having losing his wallet, he asked for help.

① ⓐ, ⓑ
② ⓑ, ⓒ
③ ⓒ, ⓓ
④ ⓐ, ⓑ, ⓓ
⑤ ⓑ, ⓒ, ⓓ

05 밑줄 친 부분을 분사구문으로 고쳐 쓰시오. 4점 〔서술형〕

> My brother broke his leg while he was playing soccer.

→ My brother broke his leg, _____

_____.

06 밑줄 친 부분과 같은 뜻이 되도록 빈칸에 알맞은 말을 쓰시오. 6점 〔서술형〕

> The last subway having already left, I had to take a taxi.

→ _____

_____, I had to take a taxi.

07 그림을 보고 괄호 안의 단어를 활용하여 빈칸에 알맞은 말을 4단어로 쓰시오. 5점 〔서술형〕

→ The employee was talking on the phone

_____. (leg, cross)

08 주어진 단어들 중 필요한 것만 골라 빈칸에 알맞게 배열하시오. 6점 〔서술형〕

> with, having, results, in, being, the, satisfied, satisfying

→ _____,

she kept smiling.

VOCA   blind date 소개팅 | bow 절하다 | deeply 깊이 | marble 구슬 | uniform 제복 | judge 판단하다 | still 가만히 | employee 직원 | result 결과

Level 3 Test

>>> 정답 24쪽

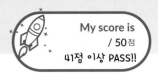

My score is
/ 50점
41점 이상 PASS!!

---

01 Which is suitable for the blank? (2 answers) 2점

> Entering the attic, _____.

① she turned on the light
② there was a book covered with dust
③ I saw my father's childhood album
④ a black cat was sleeping under the lamp
⑤ an unfinished letter was on the floor

---

02 Which is correct for the blank? 2점

> _____ sunny, we went for a ride.

① It was   ② It being
③ It   ④ Being
⑤ Was

---

03 Which CANNOT fit in any of the blanks? 3점

> ⓐ _____ the guitar, the singer sang happily.
> ⓑ _____ hungry, Rick didn't have lunch.
> ⓒ _____ fast, the girl bumped into a tree.
> ⓓ _____ your mind, everything will look different.
> ⓔ _____ my bike, I saw him in front of the house.

① Not feeling   ② Changing
③ Playing   ④ Rode
⑤ Running

---

04 Which underlined part is incorrect? (2 answers) 2점

① <u>Generally speaking</u>, women live longer than men.
② <u>Frankly speaking</u>, she doesn't really like you.
③ <u>Strictly speak</u>, this car is better than that.
④ <u>Judging from its cover</u>, this book must be very old.
⑤ <u>Rough speaking</u>, the stadium can hold about 100,000 people.

---

05 Which correction is right? 2점

> Having sick in bed for almost two weeks, Mrs. Kimberly looked so weak.

① Having → Being
② sick → been sick
③ for → since
④ almost → most
⑤ looked → looked like

---

06 Who changes the underlined part correctly? 3점

① <u>Not having received my salary</u>, I asked her again.
  → 미나: Though I hadn't received my salary
② <u>Hiking in the woods</u>, we ran into a bear.
  → 웅기: While we were hiking in the woods
③ <u>Living near the building</u>, she has never been there.
  → 은수: As she lives near the building
④ <u>Not having enough money</u>, Sally can't buy it.
  → 동규: As she has not enough money
⑤ <u>Unable to do it alone</u>, I asked him for help.
  → 은정: Because I unable to do it alone

VOCA attic 다락방 | dust 먼지 | unfinished 끝나지 않은 | go for a ride 드라이브를 하다 | bump into ~에 부딪치다 | stadium 경기장 | hold 수용하다 | salary 급여 | run into ~와 마주치다

07 How many sentences are <u>incorrect</u>? 4점

> ⓐ Driving in Manhattan, I saw many skyscrapers.
> ⓑ Praising by her teacher, she felt great.
> ⓒ Having not time, I couldn't do it.
> ⓓ Written in Japanese, I had Rie translate the note for me.
> ⓔ Having seen him before, I recognized him.

① one ② two
③ three ④ four
⑤ five

08 Which CANNOT make a grammatically correct sentence? 4점

① wrong / frankly / speaking, / you / . / are
② stayed / home / at / sick, / . / she / being
③ eyes / . / kept / her / talking / blinking / she / with
④ skipped / . / not / lunch / he / having / money, / any
⑤ alone, / baby / cry / began / the / to / . / leaving

Challenge! 주관식 서술형

09 Translate the sentence according to the conditions. 8점

> 엄격히 말해서 너의 답은 옳지 않아.
>
> · Condition 1 접속사를 사용하지 말 것
> · Condition 2 분사를 사용할 것
> · Condition 3 7단어로 완성할 것

→ _____

10 Find the sentence that has an error and correct it. 5점

> ⓐ Taken the wrong bus, I found myself in Sinsa-dong in Eungpyeong-gu, not in Gangnam-gu.
> ⓑ Having bought a new car, my uncle decided to give his old one to my sister.

(   ) _____ → _____

11 Complete the sentence according to the conditions. 8점

> · Condition 1 '그녀를 전에 만난 적이 없었으므로'라는 표현을 쓸 것
> · Condition 2 5단어로 쓸 것

→ _____,

he didn't know how to spot her in the crowd.

12 Look at the picture and complete the sentence by using a participle(분사). 7점

→ My bike _____ yesterday, I have to walk to school today. (steal)

VOCA skyscraper 초고층 건물 | translate 번역하다 | recognize 알아보다 | spot 발견하다, 찾다

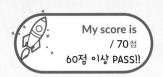

U18_1

01 빈칸에 알맞은 것은? 2점

> Don't touch the _____ window.

① break ② broke
③ be breaking ④ be broken
⑤ broken

U18_1+GP

02 Which sentence is grammatically <u>incorrect</u>?

2점

① Some people invited to the party didn't come.
② I was deeply moved by his speech.
③ Can you see the boiling water?
④ There are many swans swum in the lake.
⑤ My dog found my lost shoe.

U18_3

03 다음 중 밑줄 친 부분의 쓰임이 나머지와 <u>다른</u> 하나는? 2점

① She is <u>cooking</u> garlic pizza.
② How about <u>going</u> to a new restaurant?
③ Look at the <u>sleeping</u> babies.
④ Do you know the boy <u>dancing</u> in the hall?
⑤ The game is very <u>interesting</u>.

U18_1+GP

04 Which is NOT necessary when translating the sentence? 2점

> 그녀는 인도네시아에서 만든 청바지를 입고 있다.

① wearing ② blue jeans
③ making ④ in
⑤ Indonesia

[05~06] 각 빈칸에 적절한 말이 순서대로 짝지어진 것을 고르시오. 각 2점

U18_2+GP

05

> Yesterday, Jiseong asked a foreign teacher what he disliked about Korea. It was an _____ question. The teacher was _____.

① embarrassing – embarrassed
② embarrassed – embarrassing
③ embarrassing – embarrassing
④ embarrassed – embarrassed
⑤ embarrass – to embarrass

U19_1+2

06

> • _____ what to say, I kept silent.
> • _____ in Mexico, he can speak Spanish.

① Not known – Living
② Not knowing – Living
③ Known Not – Lived
④ Knowing not – Lived
⑤ Not to know – To live

U19_1+4

07 빈칸에 들어갈 표현을 바르게 쓰지 <u>못한</u> 학생은? 2점

> The child looked at the candy _____.

① 유재영: with his mouth watering
② 이상엽: and wanted to have a bite
③ 유진선: while eating a hamburger
④ 이승은: thought it'd be delicious
⑤ 이은영: without saying a word

08 Which word for the blank is <u>different</u> than the others? 2점

U19_1+2+3

① He _____ honest, everybody likes him.

② _____ old, my cat can't jump high.

③ It _____ sunny, they went out in the park.

④ Not _____ what to do, he asked for my advice.

⑤ The book _____ easy, my little brother can read it.

09 어법상 어색한 것을 찾아 바르게 고친 것은? (답 2개) 4점

U19_1+2+U02_1C

★ 고난도

> The consultant said too many things. Having confused, I asked her explaining everything to me again.

① many → much

② Having → Being

③ confused → confusing

④ asked → ask

⑤ explaining → to explain

10 Which of the following is proper for the blank? 2점

U19_2+GP

함정

> _____ to bed late last night, I wanted to sleep in this morning.

① Going

② Not going

③ Being gone

④ Having gone

⑤ Not having gone

11 우리말에 맞게 단어 조각을 배열하시오. 4점

U18_1+GP

> 그는 대기 중이던 버스에 올라탔다.
>
> | got on | he | bus | waiting | the |

→ _____

12 Look at the picture and fill in the blanks to translate the sentence. 5점

U18_1+GP

★ 고난도

> 부상당한 사람들이 병원으로 이송되었다.

→ The _____ people _____

_____ to the hospital. (wound, carry)

13 Rewrite the sentence by correcting the underlined word properly. 4점

U18_2+GP

> I was <u>amazing</u> by his success.

→ _____

14 다음 문장을 조건에 맞게 영작하시오. 5점

U18_1+GP

함정

> 한국에서 만든 애니메이션 영화는 매우 재미있다.
>
> ・조건 1   과거분사를 두 번 쓸 것
> ・조건 2   어휘 – animated movies, very, interesting
> ・조건 3   8단어로 완성할 것

→ _____

15 괄호 안의 단어들을 바르게 배열하여 문장을 완성하시오.
4점

> Jamila was surfing the Internet _____.
> (her, her, on, lap, sitting, dog, with).

→ Jamila was surfing the Internet _____

_____ .

16 주어진 단어를 활용하여 각 빈칸에 알맞은 말을 쓰시오.
각 2점

> (A) _____ the window, she found the
> driveway (B) _____ with lots of
> (C) _____ trees. (open, cover, fall)

17 다음 두 문장 중 어법상 어색한 것을 찾아 고치시오. 4점

> ⓐ Living near the sea, my father is a good
> swimmer.
> ⓑ Being our dinner over, we went out for a
> walk.

( ) _____ → _____

18 다음은 독립분사구문에 관한 혜련이의 노트 필기이다. 필기에서 잘못된 것을 2개 찾아 고치시오. 각 3점

독립분사구문
1. 분사형의 주어와 주절의 주어가 같은 경우.
2. 이하 전환법은 일반 분사구문과 동일
(예문) As the bench was painted just now, we should not sit on it.
→ The bench being painted just now, we should not sit on it.

_____ → _____

_____ → _____

[19~20] 다음 글을 읽고 물음에 답하시오.

True success consists of many little successes along the way. ⓐDuring adolescence, experiencing success helps you gain confidence and ⓑgrow as an individual. (A)As you experience success in achieving your goals, you will start to feel ⓒhappy about yourself. You will feel like setting new goals and trying new things. However, there may be times when you do not reach your goals. ⓓFailing to achieve a goal, try to find out what went wrong. ⓔKnowing why you failed and what you learned from the failure will help you improve your chances for success the next time.

19 윗글의 밑줄 친 부분을 바르게 설명한 학생은? 4점

① 주희: ⓐ는 '~ 동안'의 의미로 while로 바꿔 쓸 수 있다.

② 정아: ⓑ는 helps와 병렬구조이므로 grows로 고쳐야 한다.

③ 수미: ⓒ는 '행복하게'로 해석하므로 happily로 고쳐야 한다.

④ 세빈: ⓓ는 If you fail로 바꿔 쓸 수 있다.

⑤ 혜련: ⓔ는 why 이하를 이끄는 현재분사로 쓰였다.

20 윗글의 밑줄 친 (A)와 같은 뜻이 되도록 주어진 철자로 시작하여 쓰시오. 6점

(A) E_____

_____

CHAPTER 10
접속사

UNIT 20 등위 접속사, 상관 접속사, 종속 접속사

개념이해책
106쪽 함께 보기

■ 아래 표의 빈칸에 알맞은 내용을 써 넣으세요. ▶▶▶ 정답 26쪽

CONCEPT 1 등위 접속사

A 1)_____ B	A 그리고 B	My joints were stiff 1)_____ sore.
A 2)_____ B	A 그러나 B	Many are invited, 2)_____ few are chosen.
A 3)_____ B	A 또는 B	Would it be better to buy 3)_____ to rent a house?

CONCEPT 2 상관 접속사

4)_____	A와 B 둘 다	5)_____	A와 B 둘 중 하나
6)_____	A가 아니라 B	7)_____	A도 B도 아닌
8)_____ A 9)_____ B = B 10)_____ A	A뿐만 아니라 B도		

CONCEPT 3 명사절을 이끄는 종속 접속사

| 11)_____ : ~라는 것, ~라고 | 11)_____ he is alive is certain. (주절)
I think (11)_____) he is a great hero. (목적절)
His strength is 11)_____ he is honest. (보어절) |
| 12)_____
(목적절일 때는 13)_____ 도 가능):
~인지 (아닌지) | 12)_____ the vaccine is safe (or not) is important. (주절)
I don't know 12)_____ [13)_____] it is true (or not). (목적절)
The problem is 12)_____ he will come (or not). (보어절) |

Level 1 Test

▶▶▶ 정답 26쪽

A [ ]에서 알맞은 것을 고르시오.

1 Did you know that comets are made of ice [and / but] dust?

2 Jenny can drive a car, but John [doesn't / can't].

3 Be careful, [and / or] you will slip on the ice.

4 I went to the museum to see an exhibition, [but / and] it was closed.

5 Does he like either drinking tea or [eating fruit / to eat fruit]?

6 I don't know [that / if] Jasmine will come to my birthday party or not.

B 어법상 어색한 부분을 찾아 바르게 고치시오.

1 You must tell either your parents nor your teacher about it.

_____ → _____

2 May I ask that you are against the decision?

_____ → _____

3 Hyori told me if she met her teacher by chance in the airport.

_____ → _____

4 Not only they but also she are from Canada.

_____ → _____

VOCA comet 혜성 | dust 먼지 | slip 미끄러지다 | museum 박물관 | exhibition 전시 | closed 닫힌 | against ~에 반대하여 | decision 결정 | by chance 우연히

01 밑줄 친 부분이 어법상 어색한 것은? 2점

① Either you or he <u>has</u> to adjust to the different lifestyle.

② Both Kant and Mill <u>measure</u> morality in different ways.

③ Neither she nor I <u>am</u> going to the movies.

④ Not only his sisters but also he <u>play</u> the piano.

⑤ You as well as he <u>were</u> great.

02 밑줄 친 부분을 바르게 고친 학생은? 2점

> I think <u>if</u> you have made the right decision.

① 영재: when ② 진하: whether

③ 주현: because ④ 수현: so

⑤ 지수: that

03 다음 중 어법상 어색한 문장으로 묶인 것은? 3점

> ⓐ Both of my daughters live in Paris now.
> ⓑ Mary is not happy all the time.
> ⓒ My dad neither smoke nor drink.
> ⓓ Not all of them is impolite.
> ⓔ I didn't spend all the money.

① ⓐ, ⓑ ② ⓑ, ⓒ

③ ⓓ ④ ⓒ, ⓓ

⑤ ⓒ, ⓓ, ⓔ

04 다음 두 문장의 뜻이 일치하도록 할 때 빈칸에 가장 적절한 표현은? 2점

> He has been to not only Switzerland but also the Czech Republic.
> = He has been to the Czech Republic _____ Switzerland.

① as well as ② as good as

③ as many as ④ as much as

⑤ as long as

05 우리말과 같은 의미가 되도록 빈칸을 채우시오. 4점

 서술형

> 엄마 자신뿐 아니라 다른 식구들도 엄마의 퇴직을 기다리고 있다.

→ _____ _____ Mom herself

_____ _____ the other

family members _____ looking

forward to her retirement.

06 괄호 안의 말을 배열하여 우리말을 영작하시오. 5점

 서술형

> 그 계획은 장점도 있고 단점도 있다.
> both, merits, demerits, the plan, and, has

→ _____

07 다음 두 문장에서 어법상 어색한 부분 2곳을 찾아 바르게 고치시오. 각 3점

 서술형

> ⓐ I haven't decided that he is innocent or guilty yet. (그에게 죄가 있는지 없는지 나는 아직 단정하지 않았다.)
> ⓑ People in the past used to believe that the Earth was not round or flat. (옛날 사람들은 지구가 둥글지 않고 평평하다고 믿곤 했다.)

( ) _____ → _____

( ) _____ → _____

08 조건에 맞게 우리말을 영작하시오. 6점

 서술형

> 마음이 따뜻한 사람이 모든 사람에게 사랑받아야 하는 것은 당연하다.
>
> ·어휘 natural, should, a, warmhearted, everyone
> ·조건 가주어를 사용할 것

→ _____

VOCA adjust 적응하다 | lifestyle 생활방식 | measure 측정하다, 파악하다 | morality 도덕성 | Switzerland 스위스 | the Czech Republic 체코 공화국 | retirement 은퇴, 퇴직 | merit 장점 | demerit 단점 | innocent 무죄의 | guilty 유죄의 | flat 평평한 | warmhearted 마음이 따뜻한

 **Level 3 Test**

>>> 정답 26쪽

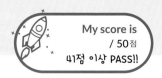

My score is
/ 50점
41점 이상 PASS!!

01 Which sentences are <u>incorrect</u>? 3점

> ⓐ Neither I nor Mia am tired.
> ⓑ He lived in both Canada and America.
> ⓒ My wife as well as I cherish every moment of our married life.
> ⓓ You can either eat here or take the food out.

① ⓐ, ⓑ   ② ⓐ, ⓒ
③ ⓑ, ⓒ   ④ ⓑ, ⓓ
⑤ ⓒ, ⓓ

02 Which word is NOT appropriate for any of the blanks? (2 answers) 3점

> ⓐ The old lady never smiles _____ laughs.
> ⓑ Smile, _____ the world will smile with you.
> ⓒ I had a bad cold, _____ I still went to school.
> ⓓ You can eat your cake with either a spoon _____ a fork.
> ⓔ He wanted to go to the beach, _____ she refused.

① or   ② if
③ and   ④ but
⑤ that

03 Which of the underlined words has a <u>different</u> usage than the others? 2점

① The police think <u>that</u> he is the main suspect.
② Martin Luther is the man <u>that</u> sparked the Protestant Reformation.
③ I hope <u>that</u> he doesn't fail his driving test.
④ It is true <u>that</u> the pen is mightier than the sword.
⑤ You will find <u>that</u> there's no place like home.

04 Whose analysis of the translation is <u>incorrect</u>? (2 answers) 3점

> 너 나한테 관심 있는지 없는지 말해봐.
> Tell me _____ you're interested in me.

① 금홍: 명사절을 이끄는 접속사가 필요해.
② 계금: 아무것도 안 써도 돼.
③ 미치: if가 명사절을 이끄는 접속사니까 if를 쓰면 돼.
④ 신이: whether or not을 써도 돼.
⑤ 학비: 신이야, 넌 틀렸어. if or not을 써야 돼.

05 Which word for the blank is <u>different</u> than the others? 3점

① Both Lily and Skylar _____ from Iceland.
② I as well as you _____ responsible for this.
③ Not the chairs but the sofas _____ on sale.
④ Not only Brooks but also you _____ a very special person.
⑤ Neither the driver nor the passengers _____ in danger.

06 Choose TWO sentences which have the same usage of "That[that]." 2점

① <u>That</u> is a genuine antique vase.
② Don't you think <u>that</u> this dress is too delicate to be washed by machine?
③ I know some boys <u>that</u> are soccer players.
④ She said <u>that</u> movie looked very fun.
⑤ I'm sure <u>that</u> she's coming to the party tonight.

07 How many pairs are proper for the blank? 2점

She can speak _____ Japanese _____ Spanish.	
either – or	neither – or
both – and	neither – nor
either – and	not only – but also

① 0개   ② 1개
③ 2개   ④ 3개
⑤ 4개

VOCA   cherish 소중히 여기다 | refuse 거절하다 | main suspect 유력 용의자 | spark 촉발시키다, 유발하다 | Protestant Reformation 종교 개혁 | mighty 강력한 | sword 검, 칼 | responsible 책임 있는 | passenger 승객 | genuine 진짜의 | antique 골동품 | delicate 연약한

08 How many sentences are <u>incorrect</u>? 3점

> ⓐ Both you and he have responsibility for it.
> ⓑ I think either he or you are hiding something.
> ⓒ Not only you but also I are exhausted.
> ⓓ Neither Marie nor her sisters is tall.

① zero ② one
③ two ④ three
⑤ four

09 Find the one who marks the sentence <u>incorrectly</u>. 4점

① 지영: Kate as well as Daniela are a chef. (✕)
② 정아: She is not only tall but also cute. (○)
③ 진희: Fortunately, neither she nor I was hurt. (○)
④ 봉서: Both she and I are members of the club. (○)
⑤ 영주: Either you or your friend Lindsay were doing the job. (○)

Challenge! 주관식 서술형

10 Translate the sentence into English according to the conditions. 6점

> 우리가 아이슬란드(Iceland)로 갈지 말지는 비용에 달려 있다.
>
> · Words   depend on, the cost
> · Condition 1   필요 시 어형 변화할 것
> · Condition 2   세 번째 단어는 부정어로 쓸 것
> · Condition 3   주어진 단어를 포함하여 12단어로 쓸 것

→ _____

_____

11 Fill in the blank with the proper conjunction (접속사). 4점

> I think _____ people need religion because it gives them hope.

12 Fill in the blanks to make the two sentences have the same meaning. 4점

> His idea is not only creative but also effective.

→ His idea is effective _____

_____ _____ creative.

13 Translate the sentence by choosing the <u>necessary</u> words and rearranging them. 5점

> Bill도 Sue도 그 수학 문제를 풀지 못했다.
> Bill, neither, able, either, nor, or, Sue, to, is, was, solve, not

→ _____

_____ the math problem.

14 Look at the picture and translate the sentence by using the given words. 6점

> 기사는 공주가 용을 무찌를지 궁금해한다.
> wonder, if, defeat the dragon

→ _____

VOCA   responsibility 책임 | exhausted 기진맥진한 | religion 종교 | creative 창의적인 | effective 효과적인 | wonder 궁금해하다 | defeat 패배시키다, 물리치다

UNIT 21 종속 접속사

■ 아래 표의 빈칸에 알맞은 내용을 써 넣으세요. >>> 정답 27쪽

개념이해책
109쪽 함께 보기

① 부사절을 이끄는 종속 접속사

시간	1)_____(~할 때), 2)_____(~하는 동안에), 3)_____(~하면서, ~할 때), 4)_____(~한 이래로), 5)_____(~한 후에), 6)_____(~하기 전에), 7)_____(~할 때까지), 8)_____(~하자마자)
이유	9) b_____, 10) s_____, 11) a_____(~하기 때문에)
조건	12)_____(~한다면), 13)_____(~하지 않는다면)
양보	14) t_____, 15) a_____, 16) e_____(비록 ~일지라도), 17)_____(~한다고 해도)
목적 (~이 …하도록)	18)_____+주어+can/may/will+동사원형 = in order that+주어+can/may/will+동사원형 = (in order) to+동사원형 = so as to
결과 (너무 ~해서 …하다)	19)_____+형용사/부사+20)_____+주어+동사 = 21)_____(a/an)+명사+22)_____+주어+동사

② 여러 가지 의미로 쓰이는 접속사

since	① ~한 이래로 ② 23)_____	as	① ~하면서, ~할 때 ② ~함에 따라 ③ ~하는 대로 ④ 25)_____	if	① 26)_____절(~인지) ② 27)_____절(~라면)
while	① ~하는 동안 ② 24)_____			when	① 28)_____절(언제) ② 29)_____절(~할 때)

Level 1 Test

>>> 정답 27쪽

A [ ]에서 알맞은 것을 고르시오.

1 She has to wait [since / until] her mother comes.

2 [Since / While] the traffic sign is written in French, I can't read it.

3 The performance was canceled [because / because of] the weather.

4 Let me know when Julie [attend / will attend] the conference.

5 You will regret it someday if you [waste / will waste] your time.

6 When I go to London, I [will visit / visit] Tower Bridge.

B 밑줄 친 부분의 의미에 유의하여 문장을 우리말로 해석하시오.

1 He helped me so that I could solve the riddle.

→ _____

2 We got up so late that we missed the flight.

→ _____

3 I want to know when Minsu will arrive here.

→ _____

4 Don't take your car when you go downtown.

→ _____

VOCA traffic sign 교통 표지판 | performance 공연 | conference 회의, 학회 | regret 후회하다 | Tower Bridge 타워 브리지(런던에 있는 개폐식 다리) | riddle 수수께끼 | flight 항공편, 비행기 | downtown 시내에, 시내로

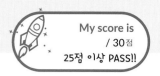
01 밑줄 친 'As[as]'의 의미가 다음 문장과 같은 것은? 2점

> "Thank you," he replied <u>as</u> he blew out one of the two candles on the table.

① Cook <u>as</u> the book says.
② She closed her eyes <u>as</u> she listened to music.
③ I like him just <u>as</u> a friend.
④ <u>As</u> she is kind, I like her.
⑤ <u>As</u> I told you, she won't be here today.

02 빈칸에 들어갈 말을 바르게 설명한 학생은? 2점

> _____ I was exhausted, I couldn't sleep.

① 진유: 조건의 If가 들어가야 함
② 영준: 양보의 Although가 들어가야 함
③ 윤성: '~한 이래로'의 Since가 들어가야 함
④ 규리: 이유의 Because가 들어가야 함
⑤ 장현: 시간 접속사 As soon as가 들어가야 함

03 빈칸에 가장 알맞은 것은? 2점

> I can't lend you any money _____ I don't have any.

① despite   ② although
③ unless   ④ in spite of
⑤ since

04 밑줄 친 'While[while]'의 의미가 같은 것은? 2점

> ⓐ Mom came in <u>while</u> the baby was sleeping.
> ⓑ <u>While</u> I was speaking, he said nothing.
> ⓒ <u>While</u> I don't agree with you, I understand what you mean.
> ⓓ After a <u>while</u>, she went out without saying a word.
> ⓔ He thought about her for a <u>while</u>.

① ⓐ, ⓑ   ② ⓑ, ⓒ
③ ⓑ, ⓒ, ⓓ   ④ ⓒ, ⓓ
⑤ ⓒ, ⓔ

05 다음 중 어법상 어색한 것을 찾아 바르게 고치시오. 4점
서술형

> ⓐ If she will pass the test, I will buy her a car.
> ⓑ Let me know if she will change her mind.

( ) _____ → _____

06 두 문장의 뜻이 같도록 빈칸에 알맞은 말을 쓰시오. 4점
서술형

> I will end this Zoom meeting if you don't have any more questions.

→ I will end this Zoom meeting _____ you have any more questions.

07 괄호 안의 접속사를 이용하여 문장을 다시 쓰시오. 6점
서술형

> The man apologized to his wife, but she didn't forgive him. (although)

→ _____ ,

_____ .

08 그림을 보고 조건에 맞게 우리말을 영작하시오. 8점
서술형

> 그 기계는 너무 복잡해서 내가 고칠 수 없었다.
> ・조건 1 과거 시제로 쓸 것
> ・조건 2 어휘 – so, complicated, repair, machine
> ・조건 3 10단어로 쓸 것

→ _____

VOCA reply 대답하다 | blow out 불어서 끄다 | exhausted 기진맥진한 | lend 빌려주다 | despite ~에도 불구하고 | apologize 사과하다 | complicated 복잡한 | repair 수리하다

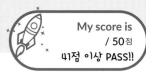

My score is
／ 50점
41점 이상 PASS!!

01 Which is the common word for the blanks? 2점

> • _____ it rained, we had to stay home.
> • Your body weakens _____ you get older.

① As[as]   ② Since[since]
③ While[while]   ④ That[that]
⑤ If[if]

02 Which of the underlined "As[as]" has a <u>different</u> meaning than the others? 2점

① <u>As</u> I was getting ready for work, I heard a strange noise.
② <u>As</u> I don't like the actor, I won't see the movie.
③ I talked with Sarah <u>as</u> we walked to school.
④ <u>As</u> I entered the room, he was sleeping.
⑤ Tommy spoke to me <u>as</u> he was watching TV.

03 Which is NOT grammatically correct? 2점

> ① It ② has been ③ years ④ as they last ⑤ made contact.

04 Which sentences are <u>unnatural</u>? 2점

> ⓐ Though she had enough money, she didn't buy the coat.
> ⓑ Although it is expensive, it doesn't look good.
> ⓒ I didn't help him though he asked me to.
> ⓓ They enjoyed their day at the zoo despite the weather was bad.
> ⓔ Even though she is selfish, she has a lot of friends.

① ⓐ ⓒ ⓓ   ② ⓑ, ⓓ
③ ⓓ   ④ ⓔ
⑤ ⓓ, ⓔ

05 Which translation is correct? 2점

> 결과를 입수하는 대로 알려드리겠습니다.

① As soon as I will get the results, I let you know.
② As soon as I will get the results, I'll let you know.
③ As soon as I get the results, I'll let you know.
④ I'll let you know as soon as I'll get the results.
⑤ I let you know as soon as I have gotten the results.

06 Choose the common word for the blanks. 2점

> • My brother and I went out _____ as to buy groceries.
> • I held her hand _____ that she could keep her balance.

① so   ② if
③ when   ④ though
⑤ as

07 Choose ALL of the sentences that have the same meaning as the given sentence. 2점

> The chocolate is so sweet that I can't eat it.

① As the chocolate is so sweet, I can eat it.
② If the chocolate is so sweet, I can't eat it.
③ Though the chocolate is so sweet, I can't eat it.
④ The chocolate is very sweet, so I can't eat it.
⑤ The chocolate is too sweet for me to eat it.

VOCA weaken 약해지다 ┃ make contact 연락하다 ┃ selfish 이기적인 ┃ result 결과 ┃ grocery 식료품 ┃ keep one's balance 균형을 잡다

08 Which is the common word for the blanks? 2점

> • _____ he was late, he didn't hurry.
> • _____ he studied hard, he failed the test.
> • _____ it was very cold, he wasn't wearing a coat.

① Though ② As
③ Since ④ When
⑤ Whether

Challenge! 주관식 서술형

09 Find ALL of the errors in the following sentences and correct them. 6점

> ⓐ Hold the door in order to I can pass.
> ⓑ I stopped talking and looked at her so that I can concentrate on her.

→ _____

_____

10 Rearrange the given words according to the conditions. 6점

> 우리는 Jenny가 올 때까지 기다려야 하지 않나요?
> here, we, shouldn't, will, come, until, Jenny, wait
>
> · Condition 1 Delete any unnecessary word(s).
> · Condition 2 Change the form of the word if necessary.

→ _____

11 Combine the two sentences into one by using the given word. 6점

> Would you cut this sandwich in half for me? I'd like as to share it with my friend. (so, can)

→ _____

_____

12 Translate the sentence into English according to the conditions. 8점

> Daphne는 수줍음을 타지만, Roxy는 활동적이다.
>
> · Words   shy, energetic
> · Condition 1 등위 접속사를 사용하지 말 것
> · Condition 2 문장의 첫 단어는 아래 영영풀이를 참조할 것
>   w_____ : compared with the fact that
> · Condition 3 모두 7단어로 쓸 것

→ _____

13 Look at the picture and complete the dialog according to the conditions. 각 4점

> Boy: I love you. I want to marry you. Please say yes.
> Woman: Oh, that's so sweet. But you are _____.
>
> · Condition 1 같은 의미의 두 가지 표현을 쓸 것
> · Condition 2 (1)에는 too를, (2)에는 so를 쓸 것
> · Condition 3 어휘 – young, marry, me

(1) _____

(2) _____

VOCA concentrate 집중하다 | energetic 활동적인 | compared with ~에 비해서

CHAPTER 10
Review Test

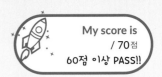

U20_2+GP

01 ★ 고난도 Which sentences are <u>incorrect</u>? 3점

> ⓐ Both John and Jenny is on my side.
> ⓑ Either he or his parents knows the fact.
> ⓒ Not only I but also he likes to play computer games.
> ⓓ She is not my niece but my sister.
> ⓔ Neither she nor you are going to give up.

① ⓐ, ⓑ   ② ⓐ, ⓒ, ⓓ
③ ⓓ   ④ ⓔ
⑤ ⓓ, ⓔ

U20_2+3

02 Choose the proper word from each bracket.

2점

> • I wonder [if / that] you can help me.
> • I like [either / neither] carrots nor spinach.
> • Twenty passengers were [either / neither] killed or injured.

① if – either – neither
② if – neither – either
③ if – neither – neither
④ that – neither – either
⑤ that – either – neither

U21_1+GP

03 빈칸에 알맞은 접속사를 <u>모두</u> 고르시오. 2점

> _____ he is a busy man, he always has time to write a reply to any letter he receives.

① Even though   ② Despite
③ In spite of   ④ Although
⑤ Though

U21_1

04 다음 빈칸 중 어느 것에도 어울리지 <u>않는</u> 것을 고르시오.

2점

> • I went to see Antonio _____ I was in Cancun.
> • We have to wait here _____ the rain stops.

① while   ② when
③ unless   ④ until
⑤ but

U21_2

05 밑줄 친 'While[while]'의 의미가 주어진 문장과 <u>다른</u> 것은? 2점

> At home, Steve does his homework <u>while</u> listening to music.

① Strike <u>while</u> the iron is hot.
② <u>While</u> I'm playing the piano, you can sing along.
③ <u>While</u> I'm away, watch my backpack.
④ Leo reads a newspaper <u>while</u> he eats breakfast.
⑤ She likes playing computer games <u>while</u> her brother doesn't.

U21_GP

06 Which best fits in the blank? 2점

> _____ the fact that she is honest, no one trusts her. That's pretty sad.

① Despite   ② Although
③ Unless   ④ Until
⑤ Since

07 다음 대화의 각 빈칸에 알맞은 말이 순서대로 짝지어진 것은? 2점

U21_1

> A: How about going shopping now?
> B: Now? Sorry, but I'm _____ busy today that I _____ you.

① so – join　　　② too – can join

③ so – can't join　　④ too – to join

⑤ so – can join

U20_2+GP

08 Rearrange the given words to make a complete sentence. 4점

> not only, are, she, but also, you, attractive

→ _____

_____

U20_GP+U21_GP

09 괄호 안에 주어진 동사를 빈칸에 알맞게 고쳐 쓰시오.
각 3점

(1) I'll wait until he _____ the work. (finish)

(2) Neither Susan nor I _____ able to attend the meeting because we have an appointment. (be)

U21_2

10 Write the common word for the blanks. 3점

> • _____ I like fishing, I try to go fishing as often as possible.
> • _____ he was sleepy, he went to bed.
> • _____ I was walking on the street, I saw my homeroom teacher.

→ _____

U21_GP

11 Find ALL of the errors in the following sentences and correct them. 5점

> ⓐ Tomorrow, he has to get up before the sun will rise.
> ⓑ If she will come, I will give a gift to her.

→ _____

_____

U20_3

12 빈칸에 들어갈 말을 쓰시오. 각 4점

(1) I'll ask Minsu _____ he likes me or not.

(2) My idea is _____ we eat out this evening.

13 다음 두 문장을 'that'을 이용하여 한 문장으로 쓰시오. 4점

> Bob was so kind to me. It was hard to say goodbye.

→ _____

_____

14 괄호 안의 단어를 사용해서 다음 문장을 같은 의미의 문장으로 바꿀 때 빈칸에 알맞은 말을 쓰시오. 4점

> Change your attitude in order to survive to the next round. (so, may)

→ Change your attitude _____

_____ to the next round.

15 다음의 주어진 접속사와 표현을 이용하여 [보기]와 같이 어법과 조건에 맞는 문장을 3개 만드시오. 각4점

although	since	as	because

go to school

get good grades on her tests

study very hard

be late for school

take a taxi

be very sick

보기 As she was very sick, she couldn't go to school.

· 조건 1 주어는 she로 할 것
· 조건 2 필요한 경우 단어를 추가할 것
· 조건 3 [보기]에 사용된 접속사는 사용하지 말 것

(1) _____

_____

(2) _____

_____

(3) _____

_____

[16~17] Read the following and answer each question.

> People say ___(A)___ yes is not always the right answer. This also applies to friendship. If you always say yes, your friendship can be put in danger ___(B)___ you have to sacrifice your personal life. Some of your time may be spent doing things for your friends. Don't be afraid to say no to your friends ___(C)___ you need to. It's better to say no and be uncomfortable for a while. Explain ___(D)___ you can't do it this time rather than to say yes and regret it later. ___(E)___ they are your true friends, you'll be understood. In the end, (가)아니라고 말하는 것은 너뿐만 아니라 너의 친구들을 위해서도 더 좋을 것이다.

16 Which word for each blank is <u>wrong</u>? 4점

① (A) – that   ② (B) – because

③ (C) – when   ④ (D) – why

⑤ (E) – Unless

17 Rearrange the given words to translate the underlined (가) according to the conditions. 5점

> for, only, better, be, saying, friends, no, not, will, your, also, you, for

· Condition 1   Do NOT change the given words.
· Condition 2   Add one word.

(가) _____

_____

CHAPTER 11
가정법

22 가정법 과거, 가정법 과거완료

■ 아래 표의 빈칸에 알맞은 내용을 써 넣으세요. ⟩⟩⟩ 정답 28쪽

개념이해책
116쪽 함께 보기

CONCEPT 1 가정법 과거와 가정법 과거완료

	가정법 과거	가정법 과거완료
형태	If+주어+동사의 1)_____형 ~, 주어+조동사의 2)_____형+3)_____ ….	If+주어+4)_____+5)_____~, 주어+조동사의 6)_____형+7)_____+8)_____ ….
의미	9)_____	10)_____
문장 전환	가정법 과거 → 직설법 11)_____(긍정 ↔ 부정)	가정법 과거완료 → 직설법 12)_____(긍정 ↔ 부정)

CONCEPT 2 대용 표현

가정법 과거	if it 13)_____ not for = 14)_____ it not for = 15)_____ for = 16)_____
가정법 과거완료	if it 17)_____ not 18)_____ for = 19)_____ it not been for = 20)_____ for = 21)_____

Level 1 Test

⟩⟩⟩ 정답 28쪽

A 주어진 단어를 이용하여 빈칸에 알맞은 형태로 쓰시오.

1 I _____ _____ fishing if it weren't so hot. (will, go)

2 If the TV program _____ not showing now, I would go with you. (be)

3 Without Wi-Fi, I _____ _____ _____ my ticket then. (can, not, book)

B 두 문장의 의미가 통하도록 빈칸을 채우시오.

1 If I knew him well, I would be friends with him on Instagram.

→ As I _____ _____ him well, _____ _____ friends with him on Instagram.

2 As he is lazy, he can't get a job.

→ If he _____ lazy, he _____ _____ a job.

3 We didn't have a good time as it rained.

→ We _____ _____ _____ a good time if it _____ _____.

C 우리말과 같은 뜻이 되도록 빈칸에 알맞은 말을 쓰시오.

1 우리 아빠가 영어 선생님이라면 난 영어를 잘할 텐데.

→ If my dad _____ an English teacher, I _____ _____ good at English.

2 어제 날씨가 화창했다면, 우린 교외로 나갔을 텐데.

→ If it _____ _____ sunny yesterday, we _____ _____ _____ to the countryside.

3 너의 부모님이 일찍 집에 오지 않으셨다면, 파티는 더 재미있었을 거야.

→ The party _____ _____ _____ more fun if your parents _____ _____ home early.

4 여러분의 지지가 없었다면, 저는 선거에서 승리하지 못했을 것입니다.

→ _____ _____ your support, I couldn't have won the election.

VOCA go fishing 낚시를 하러 가다 | show 방송되다 | Wi-Fi 무선 인터넷 | countryside 교외, 시골 | support 지지 | election 선거

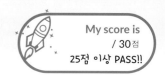

🏃 Level 2 Test

01 빈칸에 가장 적절한 것은? 2점

I want to learn how to fix a bike. If my bike broke down now, _____.

① I would fix it
② I would know what to do
③ I will not know what to do
④ I would not know what to do
⑤ I would know everything about bikes

02 빈칸에 들어갈 말이 바르게 짝지어진 것은? 2점

If I _____ doing my homework, I _____ soccer with you yesterday.

① finish – can play
② finished – could play
③ finished – could have played
④ had finished – could play
⑤ had finished – could have played

03 다음 문장을 잘못 이해하고 있는 학생은? 2점

If you had asked me, I would have helped you.

① 경민: if절에 had asked를 쓴 것은 의미상 적절해.
② 다은: would have+p.p.도 있으니까 경민이가 맞아.
③ 동수: If절은 As you asked me로 바꿀 수 있어.
④ 태욱: 문장 끝에 과거 부사를 추가할 수 있어.
⑤ 나라: 결국에는 '너'를 도와주지 못했다는 뜻이야.

04 다음 중 어법상 어색한 것은? 2점

① I will buy you those shoes if you like them.
② She wouldn't buy this car if she were you.
③ If I had two houses, I would let you use one.
④ What would you do if you knew his username?
⑤ If I am the president of Korea, I would paint the Blue House green.

05 조건에 맞도록 우리말을 영작하시오. 7점

🖋서술형

네가 나라면 뭘 하겠니?

· 조건 1 가정법을 이용할 것
· 조건 2 What으로 시작할 것
· 조건 3 8단어로 쓸 것

→ _____

06 우리말과 일치하도록 빈칸에 알맞은 단어를 쓰시오. 5점

🖋서술형

Ellen이 미술 학교에 갔다면 화가가 되었을 텐데.

→ If Ellen _____ _____ to an

art school, she _____

_____ _____ a painter.

07 두 문장의 의미가 같도록 빈칸에 알맞은 말을 쓰시오. 5점

🖋서술형

If I were thin, I would try on these jeans.

→ As I _____ _____ thin, I

_____ _____

_____ these jeans.

08 그림을 보고 빈칸에 알맞은 말을 4단어로 쓰시오. 5점

🖋서술형

→ If I _____, I could

have understood him.

VOCA fix 고치다 | username 사용자명 | Blue House 청와대 | art school 미술 학교 | try on ~을 입어보다 | thoughtful 사려 깊은

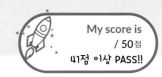
01 Which has the same meaning as the given sentence? (2 answers) 2점

> If I didn't like online games, my dream wouldn't be to run an Internet café.

① As I like online games, my dream is to run an Internet café.

② As I don't like online games, my dream isn't to run an Internet café.

③ I like online games, so my dream is to run an Internet café.

④ As I liked online games, my dream was to run an Internet café.

⑤ I liked online games, so my dream was to run an Internet café.

02 Which word appears 5th in the blank when rearranging the given words? 2점

> If _____.
> (it, could, water, nothing, were, for, not, live)

① were ② for

③ not ④ water

⑤ nothing

03 Who understands the sentence correctly? 2점

> If Ella hadn't eaten too much crab, she would have enjoyed the lobster.

① 재경: Ella는 실제로 게를 먹었어.

② 대만: Ella는 실제로 게를 먹지 않았어.

③ 승린: Ella는 게도 먹고 바닷가재도 맛있게 먹었다는 얘기야.

④ 성광: Ella는 원래 바닷가재를 즐겨 먹지 않는다는 말이야.

⑤ 상우: 바닷가재는 먹었지만 게는 맛있게 먹지 못했다는 말이야.

04 Which is correct for the blank? (2 answers) 2점

> But for your advice, I would drop out of school.
> = _____, I would drop out of school.

① Had it not been for your advice

② Were it not for your advice

③ If you hadn't advised me

④ If there isn't your advice

⑤ If it were not for your advice

05 Which translation is correct? 2점

> 사투리가 아니었다면 네 목소리를 못 알아들었을 거야.

① If it were not for your accent, I wouldn't have recognized your voice.

② If it had not been for your accent, I didn't recognize your voice.

③ Had it not been for your accent, I wouldn't have recognized your voice.

④ Had it not been for your accent, I wouldn't recognize your voice.

⑤ But for your accent, I hadn't recognized your voice.

06 Who corrects the error properly? 2점

> ⓐ If you have a good breakfast, you will have a lot of energy all day.
> ⓑ Were it not for the rope, the tiger would have eaten the siblings alive.

① 태석: ⓐ have → had

② 유민: ⓐ will have → would have had

③ 성일: ⓑ Were it not for → Had it not been for

④ 현준: ⓑ would have eaten → had eaten

⑤ 다율: ⓑ Were it → If it were

VOCA run 운영하다 | Internet café 피시방, 인터넷 카페 | crab 게 | lobster 바닷가재 | drop out of school 학교를 중퇴하다 | accent 사투리, 억양 | recognize 알아보다 | sibling 형제자매

138

07 Which underlined part is incorrect? 2점

> I had ① no navigation system in my car, ② so I ③ got lost. If I ④ had had one, I ⑤ would not get lost that rainy night.

08 Which CANNOT make a grammatically correct sentence? 4점

① were / worry / you / I / I / . / wouldn't / if
② air, / could / live / nothing / . / Without
③ a / bring / Would / it / ? / if / okay / be / I / friend
④ everything / But / him, / would / for / lose / . / we
⑤ clothes / the / have / money / more / would / buy / he / if / . / didn't / He

Challenge! 주관식 서술형

09 Rearrange the given words to translate the Korean sentence. 6점

> 우리가 시간이 더 있었더라면, 우리는 Central Park에 갔었을 거야.
> Central Park, had, to, we, gone, we, would, time, have, if, had, more

→ _____
_____

10 Translate the sentence according to the conditions. 8점

> 천국이 없다면 지옥도 없을까?
>
> · Condition 1   어휘 – Heaven, Hell
> · Condition 2   If로 시작하고, 문장에 would를 포함할 것
> · Condition 3   If절과 주절에 각각 there와 no를 사용할 것

→ _____,
_____ as well?

11 Find TWO errors and correct them. 각 4점

> My boyfriend and I went on a trip to Chuncheon. Before the trip, I told him I would reserve our seats, but it just slipped my mind. We had to stand on the train all the way. If I reserved our seats, we would have a comfortable journey.

_____ → _____

_____ → _____

12 Fill in the blanks to make the two sentences have the same meaning. 각 5점

> You don't listen carefully; perhaps that's why you ___(A)___ .
> = ___(B)___ , you wouldn't make the same mistake again and again.

(A) _____

(B) _____

VOCA navigation system 내비게이션 | as well ~도 또한 | reserve 예약하다 | slip one's mind 잊어버리다 | journey 여행 | perhaps 아마도

23 I wish 가정법, as if 가정법

개념이해책
119쪽 함께 보기

■ 아래 표의 빈칸에 알맞은 내용을 써 넣으세요. >>> 정답 29쪽

① I wish 가정법

	I wish 가정법 과거	I wish 가정법 과거완료
형태	I wish (that)+주어+동사의 1)_____형	I wish (that)+주어+2)_____+3)_____
의미	4)_____ → 5)_____의 실현 불가능한 소망·사실에 대한 유감 표현	6)_____ → 이루지 못한 7)_____의 일에 대한 유감을 표현
문장 전환	I wish 가정법 과거 → I am sorry 직설법 8)_____(긍정 ↔ 부정)	I wish 가정법 과거완료 → I am sorry 직설법 9)_____(긍정 ↔ 부정)

② as if 가정법

	as if 가정법 과거	as if 가정법 과거완료
형태	as if[though]+주어+동사의 10)_____형	as if[though]+주어+11)_____+12)_____
의미	13)_____ → 14)_____ 사실과 반대인 상황을 가정	15)_____ → 16)_____ 사실과 반대인 상황을 가정
문장 전환	as if[though] 가정법 과거 → In fact, 직설법 17)_____(긍정 ↔ 부정)	as if[though] 가정법 과거완료 → In fact, 직설법 18)_____(긍정 ↔ 부정)

Level 1 Test

>>> 정답 29쪽

A 괄호 안의 단어를 빈칸에 알맞은 형태로 쓰시오.

1 I wish I _____ _____ here. I miss my old town. (not, move)

2 He was talking as if he _____ _____ to Cuba before. (be)

3 She dances as if she _____ a professional dancer, but she's not. (be)

B 밑줄 친 부분이 어색하면 바르게 고치시오.

1 I wish I didn't buy the dress back then.

→ _____

2 She talks as though she read all the books in her father's room when she was 9 years old.

→ _____

C [보기]의 단어를 빈칸에 알맞은 형태로 쓰시오.

보기	can	talk	witness
	live	be	understand

1 때로는 네가 나의 감정을 이해할 수 있었으면 좋겠어.

→ Sometimes I wish you _____ _____ my feelings.

2 대기 오염이 꽉 찬 도시에 살지 않으면 좋을 텐데.

→ I wish I _____ _____ in a city full of air pollution.

3 그녀는 나와 함께 있을 때 아기인 것처럼 행동해.

→ When she _____ with me, she acts as if she _____ a baby.

4 그 남자는 그 교통 사고를 목격했던 것처럼 말했다.

→ The man _____ as if he _____ _____ the car accident.

VOCA move 이사하다 | professional 전문적인, 프로의 | feeling 감정 | air pollution 대기 오염 | witness 목격하다

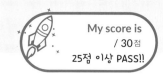

Level 2 Test

01 다음 문장을 바르게 이해한 학생은? 2점

> I wish my brother were here with me.

① 경현: 과거 사실에 대한 유감을 표현하는 문장이야.
② 동준: 나에게 남동생이 하나 있었으면 좋겠다는 뜻이야.
③ 미서: 동생이 지금 나랑 같이 없어서 유감이란 뜻이야.
④ 유민: 여기서 were를 is not으로 바꿔도 돼.
⑤ 서연: I'm sorry my brother is here with me.로 바꿔 쓸 수 있어.

02 다음 문장과 같은 뜻을 가진 것은? 2점

> I'm sorry I didn't buy the wristwatch phone.

① I wish I bought the wristwatch phone.
② I wish I didn't buy the wristwatch phone.
③ I wish I had bought the wristwatch phone.
④ I wished I bought the wristwatch phone.
⑤ I wished I hadn't bought the wristwatch phone.

03 어법상 어색한 부분을 바르게 고친 것은? 2점

> Kevin isn't rich, but he spends a lot of money as though he is rich.

① isn't → wasn't
② spends → spending
③ a lot of → many
④ though → if
⑤ is → were

04 빈칸에 알맞은 답을 쓴 학생은? 2점

> You looked as if you had been extremely busy yesterday.
> = In fact, you _____ extremely busy.

① 강희: are   ② 동윤: aren't
③ 상우: were   ④ 태연: weren't
⑤ 찬민: had been

05 두 문장의 의미가 같도록 빈칸을 채우시오. 5점

> I wish I had completed the course last year.

→ I am sorry _____
 _____ last year.

06 괄호 안의 단어를 이용해서 대화의 밑줄 친 우리말에 해당하는 표현을 7단어로 영작하시오. 6점
서술형

> M: Kate, why do you want to break up with me? We've been good so far.
> W: Jack, listen. 난 네가 나에게 좀 더 신경을 써줬으면 좋겠어. That's all. (wish, care more about)

→ _____

07 다음 중 어법상 어색한 것을 찾아 바르게 고치시오. 4점

> ⓐ He talked to me as if he met me before.
> ⓑ You talk as if you knew about it.

(____) _____ → _____

08 조건에 맞도록 우리말을 영작하시오. 7점
서술형

> 그녀는 마치 성공한 여성 사업가인 것처럼 행동해.
>
> ・조건 1 as if 구문을 사용할 것
> ・조건 2 진행형을 사용하지 말 것
> ・조건 3 어휘 – behave, successful, businesswoman

→ _____

VOCA wristwatch 손목시계 | extremely 엄청나게 | complete 완료하다 | course 강좌 | break up with ~와 헤어지다 | care about ~에 대해 신경을 쓰다 | behave 행동하다 | successful 성공한 | businesswoman 여성 사업가

Level 3 Test

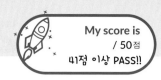

My score is
/ 50점
41점 이상 PASS!!

01 Which changes the sentence <u>incorrectly</u>? 2점

① I am shorter than my friends.
  → I wish I were not shorter than my friends.
② I can't find a part-time job.
  → I wish I could find a part-time job.
③ I don't have enough money to buy a laptop.
  → I wish I had enough money to buy a laptop.
④ I ate too much last night.
  → I wish I didn't eat too much last night.
⑤ I didn't learn to swim as a child.
  → I wish I had learned to swim as a child.

02 Which word appears <u>6th</u> when translating the sentence by using the given words? 2점

> 그때 Sue가 내 편이었으면 좋을 텐데.
> that, on one's side, back then

① Sue   ② had
③ were   ④ been
⑤ on

03 Which sentences are <u>incorrect</u>? 2점

> ⓐ I wish that I am good with numbers.
> ⓑ Don't look at me as if I were a stranger.
> ⓒ Without the fridge, all the fruit would have gone bad.
> ⓓ Olga kept on working as though nothing has happened.

① ⓐ, ⓑ   ② ⓑ, ⓒ
③ ⓐ, ⓓ   ④ ⓑ, ⓒ, ⓓ
⑤ ⓐ, ⓒ, ⓓ

04 Which correction is right? 2점

> I wish that I had some medicine for you yesterday morning.

① wish → sorry   ② that → if
③ that → as if   ④ had → had had
⑤ had → have had

05 Which is correct for the blank? 2점

> Sunny didn't see the movie, but she described it _____.

① as she saw it
② as she had seen it
③ as though she saw it
④ as if she had not seen it
⑤ as though she had seen it

06 Which CANNOT be used when translating the sentence? 2점

> 내 강아지가 그때 말을 할 줄 알았더라면 좋을 텐데.

① wish   ② that
③ were   ④ had
⑤ able

[07~08] Choose the sentence that has the same meaning as the given one. 각 2점

07
> She talked to me as if she had known everything.

① In fact, she knows everything.
② In fact, she had known everything.
③ In fact, she doesn't know everything.
④ In fact, she didn't know everything.
⑤ In fact, she hadn't known everything.

VOCA part-time 시간제의 | laptop 노트북 컴퓨터 | on someone's side ~의 편에 | stranger 낯선 사람 | fridge (= refrigerator) 냉장고 | go bad 상하다 | medicine 약 | describe 묘사하다

08

> Dave seems to be talking to somebody, but there's nobody around.

① Dave is talking as if there were nobody around.
② Dave is talking as though there had been somebody around.
③ Dave is talking as if there had been nobody around.
④ Dave is talking as though there weren't somebody around.
⑤ Dave is talking as though there were somebody around.

09 Which CANNOT make a grammatically correct sentence? 4점

① that / wish / not / . / done / I / I / had
② I / happier / I / . / wish / were
③ had / . / it / happened / never / I / wish
④ the / pass / exams / that / wish / you / . / I
⑤ could / . / I / you / speak / Spanish / wish / that

Challenge! 주관식 서술형

10 Choose the right one for each blank. 각 2점

> **Wishes about the past: wish (that)+past perfect**
> We use "(A)[hope / wish]" with the past perfect tense to talk about regrets from the (B)[present / past]. These are things that (C)[had / have] already happened but that we wish (D)[had / have] happened in a different way.
>
> *past perfect: 과거완료

(A) _____ (B) _____

(C) _____ (D) _____

11 Find TWO errors and correct them. 각 3점

> I wish I were able to go to the party with you the other day, but I can't.

_____ → _____

_____ → _____

12 Look at the picture and complete the sentence. 5점

> It would have been so much fun if you had seen the fireworks with me.

→ I wish you _____ with me last night.

13 Fill in the blanks to translate the sentence according to the conditions. 7점

> 입장 바꿔 생각해봐. (네가 내 자리에 있는 것처럼 생각해봐.)
> ----
> · Condition 1   as though 구문을 사용할 것
> · Condition 2   어휘 – place
> · Condition 3   8단어로 쓸 것

→ _____

14 Find the error and correct it. 4점

> ⓐ My father always talks as if he were a good student when he was young.
> ⓑ The little girl said hi to me as though I were one of her friends.

(   ) _____ → _____

VOCA   firework 불꽃놀이 | in one's place ~의 자리[입장]에 있는

Review Test

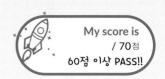

U22_2A+2B

01 Which is the right correction? 2점

> 그녀의 도움이 없었다면 내가 무엇을 했을지 모르겠다.
> = I don't know what I would have done if it were not for her help.

① don't → didn't

② what → which

③ have done → had done

④ would → would be

⑤ were not → had not been

U22_2A

02 빈칸에 알맞은 것은? 2점

> She wouldn't have been tired if she _____ to bed earlier the night before.

① goes

② went

③ has gone

④ had gone

⑤ would have gone

U22_1+2

03 다음 중 어법상 어색한 것끼리 짝지어진 것은? 4점

★
고난도

> ⓐ If I were hungry, I would have eaten more.
> ⓑ If the movie hadn't been boring, I wouldn't have fallen asleep.
> ⓒ If you hadn't loved her, I would marry her then.
> ⓓ What would you do if you were in my shoes?
> ⓔ If she were here now, would you say the same thing to her?
> ⓕ But for your kindness at that time, I would be lost there.

① ⓐ, ⓑ, ⓒ

② ⓐ, ⓒ, ⓕ

③ ⓒ, ⓓ, ⓔ

④ ⓒ, ⓓ, ⓕ

⑤ ⓓ, ⓔ, ⓕ

U23_1B

04 빈칸에 들어갈 말로 알맞은 것은? 2점

> The gala show was fantastic. I wish you _____ to see it.

① came

② will come

③ had come

④ have come

⑤ would come

U22_1+2

05 Which words are proper for the blanks? 2점

한눈에
쏙

> • If I _____ you, I would accept the offer.
> • If Beth had called me, I _____ it upstairs.

① was – would hear

② had been – would hear

③ were – would hear

④ were – would have heard

⑤ had been – would have heard

U23_1

06 다음 중 필요한 단어만 골라 문장을 완성한 것은? 2점

> I, more, I, had, wish, have, friends, am

① I wish more friends I had.

② I wish I had more friends.

③ I had I wish more friends.

④ I have more friends I wish.

⑤ I wish I have more friends.

U22_1+2

07 Which sentence is incorrect? (2 answers) 2점

함정

① If I had been you, I would have punished him.

② She could take more pictures if she bought a bigger memory card.

③ I could have helped you if I had known.

④ Were it not for water, the flower would have died.

⑤ Would you have dinner with him if he had asked you out?

08 다음을 영작할 때 <u>7번째</u> 올 단어로 적절할 것은? 2점

U23_2A

> 그는 나를 마치 아이처럼 다룬다.

① as ② were

③ a ④ though

⑤ I

09 Which word CANNOT be used for any of the blanks? 2점

U23_2A

> Derek looks _____ _____ he _____ a cold now. But he _____ healthy _____ to play basketball with us.

① enough ② if

③ has ④ as

⑤ is

10 Fill in the blanks to complete the sentence according to the conditions. 6점

U22_2B

★ 고난도

> · Condition 1 Without the life jacket과 같은 뜻으로 쓸 것
> · Condition 2 8단어로 쓸 것

→ _____ ,

we would have been in trouble.

11 다음 여행 광고지를 보고 주어진 질문에 대해 자신의 경우에 맞게 if절을 포함한 완전한 문장으로 답하시오. 5점

U22_1

👁 한눈에 쏙

Q: Which tourist attraction would you visit if you were in Jamaica now?

A: _____

_____

12 Fill in the blanks to translate the following. 6점

U22_2A

★ 고난도

> 내가 너를 거기서 봤다면, 인사를 했겠지. 근데 정말 널 못 봤다니까.

→ If I _____ _____ you there,

I _____ _____

_____ hi to you. But I'm telling you I

_____ _____ you.

13 우리말과 일치하도록 빈칸을 채우시오. 각 3점

U22_1A

👁 한눈에 쏙

> 내가 남은 모바일 데이터가 조금이라도 있다면 너에게 좀 줄 수 있을 텐데.

(1) If I _____ any mobile data left, I

_____ _____ you some.

(2) As I _____ _____

any mobile data left, I _____

_____ you any.

14 괄호 안의 단어를 재배열하여 빈칸 (A)에 들어갈 말을 쓰시오. 4점

U22_2A

> Your coffee would have tasted better _____(A)_____ too much sugar in it.
> (you, put, not, if, had)

(A) _____

15 U23_1B

과거에 이루지 못한 일에 대한 유감을 나타내도록 빈칸에 알맞은 말을 쓰시오. 4점

> Our city did not succeed at hosting the Winter Olympic Games.

→ I wish _____ at hosting the Winter Olympic Games.

16 U23_1B

다음은 I wish 가정법 문장 전환에 관한 동생 규진이와 누나 혜림이의 대화이다. 빈칸에 알맞은 말을 쓰시오. 각 3점

규진: 누나! I wish 가정법 과거완료가 과거 사실에 대한 유감을 표현하는거 맞아?

어. 내 동생 똑똑하네! I am sorry _____ 로 바꿔 쓸 수 있어.

규진: 그럼 _____ 는 어떻게 바꿔?

I'm sorry I deleted your folder. 인데... 음...니 폴더 지워서 미안해. 실수였어. ☹

혜림: _____

규진: _____

17 U23_2B

어법상 어색한 문장을 찾아 바르게 고치시오. 4점

ⓐ You're just acting as if you didn't see me there, aren't you?

ⓑ Karen acted as though she could afford to buy a mansion on the hill.

( ) _____ → _____

[18~19] Read the following and answer each question.

Karl Menninger was an American psychiatrist. He once gave a lecture on medical health and answered questions from the audience. Someone asked, "What would you advise a person to do if that person ⓐhad felt depressed?" Most people thought ⓑthat he would say, "Go to see a psychiatrist immediately," but he ⓒdidn't. To their surprise, Dr. Menninger replied, "Lock up your house, go across the railroad tracks, find somebody in need, and help that person. Focusing on other people's worries helps you ⓓforget your own." Dr. Menninger strongly believed that helping others ⓔare the best way to help oneself.

*psychiatrist: 정신과 의사

18 U22_1A+U05_GP

Among the underlined, which is grammatically <u>incorrect</u>? (Up to 3 answers) 4점

① ⓐ   ② ⓑ

③ ⓒ   ④ ⓓ

⑤ ⓔ

19 U22_1A

Summarize the paragraph by using the given letters. 5점

> If you felt d_____, helping others w_____ h_____ you out of your depression.

CHAPTER 12

특수 구문

24 강조, 생략

개념이해책
126쪽 함께 보기

■ 아래 표의 빈칸에 알맞은 내용을 써 넣으세요. >>> 정답 31쪽

① 강조 구문

동사 강조	1)_____/does/did+동사원형	He 2)_____ meet the actress yesterday.
명사 강조	the 3)_____+명사	She's the 4)_____ girl I've been looking for.
It ~ that 강조	It is/was+강조어+5)_____ ~	It was Mary 6)_____ got a perfect score.

② 생략

7)_____되는 어구	Some stars appear red, and others (8)_____) blue.
9)_____ 격 관계대명사	This is the book (10)_____) I bought yesterday.
11)_____ 격 관계대명사+12)_____ 동사	I read a novel (13)_____) written in English.
부사절에서 14)_____+15)_____ 동사	While (16)_____) walking on the street, I heard this song.
to부정사(17)_____ 부정사)	I can't save as much money as I want to (18)_____).
재귀대명사(19)_____ 용법)	He repaired the bike (20)_____).

Level 1 Test

>>> 정답 31쪽

A 밑줄 친 부분을 강조하는 문장으로 전환하시오.

1 Andy <u>delivered</u> the pizza 30 minutes ago.

→ Andy _____ _____ the pizza 30 minutes ago.

2 <u>Andy</u> delivered the pizza 30 minutes ago.

→ _____ _____ _____ delivered the pizza 30 minutes ago.

3 Andy delivered the pizza <u>30 minutes ago</u>.

→ _____ _____ _____ _____ _____ _____ Andy delivered the pizza.

B 다음 문장이 '강조 구문'인지 '가주어-진주어 구문'인지 구분하시오.

1 It is important that you keep your promise.

→ _____

2 It was her son that saved the woman.

→ _____

3 It was in the mall that my son lost his bag.

→ _____

4 Is it true that you're retiring soon?

→ _____

5 It is certain that he will succeed.

→ _____

VOCA deliver 배달하다 | keep one's promise 약속을 지키다 | retire 은퇴하다 | certain 확실한 | succeed 성공하다

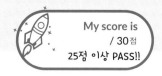

Level 2 Test

01 다음 중 밑줄 친 부분이 [보기]와 <u>다른</u> 의미로 쓰인 문장을 고르시오. 2점

> Economists <u>do</u> worry about declining birth rates.

① He'll <u>do</u> his best.
② She <u>does</u> like the violin.
③ He <u>did</u> go to the U.S. to study.
④ You <u>did</u> have a happy childhood.
⑤ Many foreigners <u>do</u> love Korean food.

02 다음 중 어법상 <u>어색한</u> 문장은? 2점

① It was I who saw an alien in my dream last night.
② It was in my dream where I saw an alien last night.
③ It was last night when I saw an alien in my dream.
④ It was saw that I an alien in my dream last night.
⑤ It was an alien that I saw in my dream last night.

03 다음을 밑줄 친 부분을 강조하는 문장으로 바꿀 때 쓰이지 <u>않는</u> 것은? 2점

> I ate <u>a peanut</u> on Thursday.

① It   ② was
③ what   ④ a peanut
⑤ on

04 다음 문장에서 생략할 수 있는 것은? 2점

> Can you lend me the suit that you bought yesterday?

① lend   ② me
③ that   ④ bought
⑤ yesterday

05 다음 대화의 내용에 따라 밑줄 친 부분을 강조하는 문장으로 만들 때, 빈칸에 알맞은 단어를 쓰시오. 4점
서술형

> A: Who discovered the Americas?
> B: <u>Columbus</u> discovered the Americas.

→ It _____ _____

_____ discovered the Americas.

06 빈칸에 강조하는 말을 넣어 문장을 완성하시오. 4점
서술형

> The _____ thought of meeting him makes me happy.

07 밑줄 친 부분을 바르게 고쳐 쓰시오. 4점
서술형

> In the 1800s, the prairies <u>do stretched</u> as far as the eye could see.

→ _____

08 다음 중 어법상 <u>어색한</u> 문장을 찾아 바르게 고치시오. 4점
서술형

> ⓐ When is driven at a fast speed, the car causes a few problems.
> ⓑ She didn't follow the rules as instructed.

(   ) _____ → _____

09 다음 문장에서 생략된 부분을 추가하여 문장 전체를 다시 쓰시오. 6점
서술형

> Perhaps love is like the ocean full of conflict.

→ _____

_____

VOCA economist 경제학자 | decline 줄어들다 | birth rate 출생률 | alien 외계인 | suit 정장 | discover 발견하다 | the Americas 남북 아메리카 | prairie 대초원 | cause 야기시키다 | follow a rule 규칙을 따르다 | instruct 교육시키다 | conflict 갈등

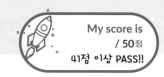

01 Choose ALL of the correct sentences. 3점

① It was yesterday when the prince saw a mummy in the pyramid.

② It was the prince who saw a mummy in the pyramid yesterday.

③ It was in the pyramid where the prince saw a mummy yesterday.

④ It was the prince whom saw a mummy in the pyramid yesterday.

⑤ It was a mummy what the prince saw in the pyramid yesterday.

02 Which underlined words can be omitted? 2점

ⓐ There are many teenagers who want to become stars themselves.

ⓑ You have to help yourself if you want to improve your ability.

ⓒ He went there by himself.

ⓓ Enjoy yourself at the party.

ⓔ I myself had a similar experience as a young girl.

① ⓐ, ⓔ ② ⓐ, ⓒ, ⓓ

③ ⓑ, ⓔ ④ ⓓ, ⓔ

⑤ ⓔ

03 Which underlined word has a different usage than the others? 2점

① A: He doesn't like vegetables, does he?
   B: Yes, he does like vegetables.

② A: Boni didn't solve the hard question.
   B: Yes, he did solve the question.

③ A: Hani didn't use a dictionary when she took the test.
   B: Yes, she did use one. I saw it myself.

④ A: I think you never worry about your health.
   B: That's not true. I do worry about my health.

⑤ A: Do you use your cell phone during classes?
   B: Yes, I do. I use it sometimes.

04 Which sentence has the same usage for the underlined word as in the given sentence? 2점

He did require that I pay the money.

① Why does he follow your plan?

② He didn't send the child on an errand.

③ Do you like sightseeing?

④ He doesn't want to save money, does he?

⑤ She thinks I don't like her, but I do like her.

05 Choose the best answer for the blank. 3점

A: Jenny keeps giving me the cold shoulder.
B: _____ jealousy that she's doing that. She is jealous that you won the contest.

① It is because ② She is because

③ Her it is ④ It is her

⑤ It is because of

06 Which sentence has a different usage for the underlined words than the others? 2점

① It is certain that he accepted Jesus Christ as his savior.

② It was on Sunday that we used to go fishing.

③ It was his strong will that made Tom succeed.

④ It was yesterday that I learned about Darwin's theory.

⑤ It is in my room that I usually study English.

07 Which underlined word CANNOT be omitted? 2점

① He went to the library and he studied.

② She made herself strong.

③ He doesn't skate these days, but he used to skate a lot.

④ Do you know the actors who are standing over there?

⑤ Can you understand the theory that the professor explained?

VOCA mummy 미라 | require 요구하다 | send ~ on an errand ~을 심부름 보내다 | sightseeing 관광 | give the cold shoulder 차갑게 대하다 | jealousy 질투 | jealous 시기하는 | savior 구세주, 구조자 | Darwin 다윈(진화론을 주장한 19세기 영국의 생물학자) | theory 이론

08 Which CANNOT make a grammatically correct sentence? 4점

① waves / did / see / . / huge / We / some
② not / on / sit / down / Do / the / . / bench
③ . / dress / do / You / pretty / that / look / in
④ She / does / be / he / wrong / that / . / thinks
⑤ a / did / find / I / online / shopping / good / . / site

Challenge! 주관식 서술형

09 Rearrange the given words to fill in blank (A) according to the conditions. 7점

| Is that a joke? ____(A)____ . |
| (teasing, believe, I, be, you, me) |
| · Condition 1   주어진 한 단어의 어형을 변화할 것 |
| · Condition 2   동사를 강조하도록 단어를 하나 추가할 것 |

(A) _____

10 Rearrange the given words according to the conditions to make a complete sentence. 7점

| do, told, it, when, to, people, do, what |
| · Condition 1   Do NOT change the given words. |
| · Condition 2   Start the sentence with a conjunction(접속사). |
| · Condition 3   Use a comma. |

→ _____

11 Fill in the blanks to complete the sentence that emphasizes the underlined part. 5점

| <u>Her family's generosity and care for the poor</u> made a great impact on young Mother Teresa. |

→ _____ _____ her family's

generosity and care for the poor

_____ made a great impact on

young Mother Teresa.

12 Find the sentence that has an error, and rewrite the sentence correctly. 5점

| ⓐ It was when that you last visited Mom? |
| ⓑ She did marry a truck driver. |

(   ) → _____

13 Look at the picture and translate the underlined sentence according to the conditions. 4점

| Mother: Didn't I tell you to close the door? |
| Daughter: Yes. You told me to close the door many times, 근데 제가 닫는 것을 잊어버렸어요. |
| · Condition 1   어휘 – but, forget |
| · Condition 2   4단어로 쓸 것 |

(A) _____

UNIT 25 도치

개념이해책 129쪽 함께 보기

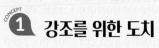
■ 아래 표의 빈칸에 알맞은 내용을 써 넣으세요. >>> 정답 32쪽

CONCEPT 1 강조를 위한 도치

장소 부사(구)가 문장 첫머리에 올 때	주어가 명사인 경우: 1)_____ +2)_____ +3)_____	There goes my career!
	주어가 대명사인 경우: 4)_____ +5)_____ +6)_____	There he stood like a statue.
부정어(구)가 문장 첫 머리에 올 때	be동사가 쓰인 경우: 7)_____ +8)_____ +9)_____	Seldom is he passionate about school.
	일반동사/조동사가 쓰인 경우: 10)_____ +11)_____ +12)_____ +본동사	Hardly did she answer directly. Never have I deceived anybody.

CONCEPT 2 어법상 도치

so/neither가 문장 첫머리에 올 경우	So+13)_____ /be동사+14)_____	A: I like the design of the suit. B: 15)_____. (= I like the design, too.) → 16)_____문에 대한 동의
	Neither+17)_____ /be동사+18)_____	A: I am not qualified to teach them. B: 19)_____. (= I am not qualified either.) → 20)_____문에 대한 동의
가정법에서 if의 생략	(If)+21)_____ +22)_____ ~, 주어+동사	If I were you, I wouldn't do that. → 23)_____, I wouldn't do that.

Level 1 Test

>>> 정답 32쪽

A 괄호 안의 지시대로 문장을 다시 쓰시오.

1 She is not only intelligent but also humble. (강조)

→ _____ but

also humble.

2 If he had arrived here 5 minutes earlier, he could have saved her life. (If 생략)

→ _____ 5 minutes

earlier, he could have saved her life.

3 The girls danced on the stage. (강조)

→ _____

B 밑줄 친 부분이 어색하면 바르게 고치시오.

1 Here our commuter bus comes now.

→ _____

2 Not a single word said she to him.

→ _____

3 Hardly has he enough money to study for a master's degree.

→ _____

4 Never have I thought about such a great thing.

→ _____

VOCA intelligent 총명한 | humble 겸손한 | commuter bus 통근 버스 | hardly 거의 ~하지 않다 | master's degree 석사 학위

01 빈칸에 알맞은 것을 고르시오. 2점

> Never _____ anything like this.

① have I done
② I have done
③ I haven't done
④ do I have done
⑤ I haven't done

02 밑줄 친 부분과 바꾸어 쓸 수 있는 것은? 2점

> Jini is interested in jazz-rock, and <u>Ian is interested in it, too.</u>

① so is Ian
② so has Ian
③ neither is Ian
④ neither has Ian
⑤ so does Ian

03 빈칸에 들어갈 말이 순서대로 짝지어진 것은? 3점

> • Sami can drive, and so _____ Philip.
> • Jane lives in L.A., and so _____ Peter.
> • You are never confident, and _____ am I.

① can – do – neither
② can – does – either
③ can – does – neither
④ does – does – neither
⑤ does – do – either

04 다음에 대해 바르게 설명한 학생을 <u>모두</u> 고르시오. 3점

> ⓐ There goes she.
> ⓑ On the top of the hill lives a few sheep.

① 현진: ⓐ There가 문장 앞으로 가서 주어와 동사가 도치된 문장으로 어법상 어색한 것이 없다.
② 동호: ⓐ there가 문장 앞에 있어도 대명사 주어일 때는 도치하지 않으므로 어색한 문장이다.
③ 은빛: ⓑ 도치된 올바른 문장이다.
④ 은일: ⓑ 주어가 복수이므로 lives가 아니라 live가 알맞다.
⑤ 건희: ⓐ a few sheep과 lives의 순서가 바뀌어야 한다.

05 밑줄 친 부분과 같은 의미의 말을 3단어로 쓰시오. 4점
서술형

> All of us enjoy the sounds of nature, and <u>composers enjoy the sounds of nature, too.</u>

→ _____

06 밑줄 친 부분을 어법에 맞게 고치시오. 4점
서술형

> <u>Not only did I met the actor</u>, but I also received his autograph.

→ _____

07 다음 대화에서 B가 A의 말에 동의하는 뜻이 되도록 빈칸 (A)에 알맞은 말을 쓰고, B의 응답과 같은 의미의 문장 2개를 쓰시오. 각 3점
서술형

> A: I can't play golf.
> B: I can't play golf (A) _____.

(1) _____ (2단어)
(2) _____ (3단어)

08 그림을 보고 조건에 맞게 영작하시오. 6점
서술형

> 나는 그렇게 빠른 소년은 결코 본 적이 없다.

• 조건 1 어휘 – such a fast boy, see, never
• 조건 2 현재완료로 쓸 것
• 조건 3 부정어를 문장 맨 앞에 쓸 것

→ _____

_____

VOCA be interested in ~에 흥미가 있다 | jazz-rock 재즈록(재즈와 록이 혼합된 음악) | confident 자신감 있는 | composer 작곡가 | receive 받다 |
autograph 사인

01 Choose ALL of the grammatically correct dialogs. 2점

① A: She had a good appetite.
　B: So had he.
② A: I haven't watched the film yet.
　B: Neither have I.
③ A: I'm happy to see you again.
　B: I'm happy either.
④ A: I had a good memory when I was little.
　B: So did I.
⑤ A: I wasn't disappointed with the results.
　B: I wasn't disappointed neither.

02 Choose the best answer for the blank. 2점

> A: I wasted too much time worrying about the project.
> B: _____.

① So did I
② So am I
③ So do I
④ So was I
⑤ So I did

03 Which sentence is grammatically correct? 2점

① I like music, and so do my brother.
② Molly has an e-book reader, and so has I.
③ He went to Phuket last year, and so does I.
④ Kate has been to Japan, and so has Emma.
⑤ Brad lives in Boston, and so do Tom.

04 Which sentence is grammatically correct? 2점

① There my weekend goes.
② There did he stand like a statue.
③ Seldom did she answered directly.
④ Never do I have deceived anybody.
⑤ At the airport, I lost my wallet.

05 Which sentence emphasizes the underlined word correctly? 2점

> I had <u>never</u> understood the appeal of skydiving before I actually tried it.

① I did have never understood the appeal of skydiving before I actually tried it.
② It was never that I had understood the appeal of skydiving before I actually tried it.
③ Never had I understood the appeal of skydiving before I actually tried it.
④ Never I had understood the appeal of skydiving before I actually tried it.
⑤ It was never that had I understood the appeal of skydiving before I actually tried it.

06 Which sentence has a <u>different</u> usage for the underlined word? 2점

① <u>There</u> is a puppy in my hand.
② <u>There</u> was a fire burning in the garage.
③ <u>There</u> lived a wise old man in town.
④ <u>There</u> I saw a glacier for the first time.
⑤ <u>There</u> has been heavy traffic on the road this morning.

VOCA appetite 식욕 | memory 기억력 | disappointed 실망한 | result 결과 | Phuket 푸켓(태국의 관광지) | statue 동상, 조각상 | seldom 좀처럼 ~ 않다 | deceive 속이다 | appeal 매력 | skydiving 스카이다이빙 | garage 차고 | glacier 빙하

07 Whose explanation is correct? (Find ALL.) 3점

> ⓐ Never she has been to Mexico.
> ⓑ Seldom is he passionate about school.

① 경수: ⓐ she has를 does she have로 바꿔야 한다.
② 유미: ⓐ she has를 has she로 바꾸어야 한다.
③ 은희: ⓐ 어법상 어색한 부분이 없다.
④ 이린: ⓑ 어법상 어색한 부분이 없다.
⑤ 경원: ⓑ Seldom is he를 He is seldom으로 바꿀 수 있다.

08 Which CANNOT make a grammatically correct sentence? 4점

① again / goes / There / she / .
② the / There / no / were / in / sky. / clouds
③ would / I / agree / Were / you, / not / . / I
④ visiting / Never / restaurant / I / again. / this / will
⑤ she / performance. / her / aware / Hardly / of / is

Challenge! 주관식 서술형

09 Write a sentence in 3 words to have the same meaning as the underlined sentence in the following dialog. 4점

> A: Never have I seen such a vivid rainbow.
> B: I haven't either.

→ _____

10 Write the proper words for the blanks. 각 3점

(1) Paul can drive, and so _____ Sam.

(2) Tom lives in New York, and so _____ Peter.

(3) You are late, and so _____ I.

11 Find the error and correct it. 4점

> No sooner he had walked through the door than he heard the phone ringing.

_____ → _____

12 Translate the sentence into English according to the conditions. 8점

> 그는 자신이 직면하고 있던 그 위험을 거의 깨닫지 못했다.
>
> · Words   little, realize, face
> · Condition 1   필요 시 어형 변화할 것
> · Condition 2   첫 번째 단어는 부정어로 쓸 것
> · Condition 3   마지막 단어는 현재분사로 쓸 것
> · Condition 4   주어진 단어를 포함하여 9단어로 쓸 것

(A) _____

13 Translate the underlined Korean according to the conditions. 6점

> 내가 부자라면, I would buy a Lamborghini .
>
> · Condition 1   가정법을 쓰되 if를 쓰지 말 것
> · Condition 2   어휘 – I, be, rich

→ _____ _____

_____ , I would buy a Lamborghini,

VOCA passionate 열정을 보이는 | vivid 선명한 | no sooner ~ than... ~하자마자 …하다 | Lamborghini 람보르기니(유명한 고급 자동차 브랜드)

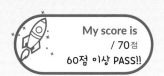
My score is
/ 70점
60점 이상 PASS!!

U24_1+GP

01 밑줄 친 'It ~ that'의 쓰임이 나머지 넷과 다른 것은? 3점

① It is strange <u>that</u> he never comes back here.
② It was yesterday <u>that</u> I met him at the library.
③ It was my dog Max <u>that</u> came to help me.
④ It is in the springtime <u>that</u> orange trees are beautiful.
⑤ It was this morning <u>that</u> I saw him jogging in the park.

U25_1

02 Which sentences are correct? 4점

ⓐ Around the building did some homeless people live.
ⓑ Hardly does she ever helps her mother.
ⓒ I did meet the world-famous architect.

① ⓐ
② ⓐ, ⓑ
③ ⓑ
④ ⓑ, ⓒ
⑤ ⓒ

U24_1

03 밑줄 친 단어가 [보기]와 같은 용법으로 사용된 것은? 2점

보기   They <u>do</u> become more mature.

① <u>Do</u> you like me?
② How are you <u>doing</u>?
③ You don't like apples, <u>do</u> you?
④ I have to <u>do</u> my homework.
⑤ She <u>did</u> love me in the past.

U24_2

04 Which is NOT proper for the blank? 3점

While _____, he began to fall asleep.

① there
② on the sofa
③ we were chatting
④ watching YouTube
⑤ talked on the phone

U24_1

05 다음을 강조 표현으로 바르게 전환한 것은? 2점

He broke his right leg yesterday.

① He did broke his right leg yesterday.
② It was him that broke his right leg yesterday.
③ It was yesterday that broke his right leg.
④ It was his right leg that he broke yesterday.
⑤ It was broke that he his right left yesterday.

U24_1

06 다음 문장을 바르게 설명하지 못한 것은? (정답 최대 3개) 2점

It was at the airport that I lost my suitcase.

① at the airport를 강조하고 있다.
② that이하가 문장의 진짜 주어이다.
③ that은 when으로 바꿔 쓸 수 있다.
④ that은 관계대명사와 같은 역할을 한다.
⑤ I lost my suitcase at the airport.가 원래 문장이다.

U24_2

07 다음 문장에서 생략할 수 있는 부분은? 2점

Mr. Park, who is my homeroom teacher, is very kind.

① Mr. Park
② who
③ who is
④ very
⑤ 없음

08 밑줄 친 부분과 바꾸어 쓸 수 있는 것은? 2점

> Mary has been looking forward to summer vacation, and <u>Ann has been looking forward to it, too.</u>

① so did Ann

② so has Ann

③ neither is Ann

④ neither has Ann

⑤ so does Ann

09 Whose explanation of the following sentences is correct? (Find ALL.) 3점

함정

> ⓐ Scarcely had the game started when it began to rain.
> ⓑ Never she has eaten a taco before.

① 재원: ⓐ 어법상 어색한 부분이 없다.

② 민희: ⓐ had → did로 바꾸어야 한다.

③ 혜성: ⓐ The game had scarcely started when ~으로 바꿀 수 있다.

④ 지호: ⓑ she has를 does she have로 바꾸어야 한다.

⑤ 원주: ⓑ 어법상 어색한 부분이 없다.

10 아래 문장의 밑줄 친 부분을 강조하고자 한다. 빈칸에 들어갈 단어들을 쓰시오. 4점

> <u>My father</u> came to help me yesterday.
> → 어제 나를 도와주러 오신 분은 바로 나의 아버지였다.

→ _____ _____ my father

_____ came to help me yesterday.

11 [보기]를 참고하여 빈칸에 알맞은 단어를 쓰시오. 4점

> I'm tall, and my sister is tall, too.
> → I'm tall, and so is my sister.
>
> Julia lives in Sydney, and Robert lives in Sydney, too.

→ Julia lives in Sydney, and _____

_____ _____.

12 동사를 강조하는 조동사를 빈칸에 쓰시오. (1단어) 3점

> He talks a lot.
> → 그는 정말 말을 많이 한다.

→ He _____ talk a lot.

13 Put the proper word in the blank for emphasis. 3점

> Continental drift is the _____ movement of the continents over the Earth's surface.

14 밑줄 친 부분에서 생략할 수 있는 말을 생략해서 쓰시오. 4점

> Seoul, <u>which is the largest city in Korea</u>, has several old palaces.

→ Seoul, _____, has

several old palaces.

15 다음 문장과 같은 의미가 되도록 7단어로 문장을 줄여 쓰시오. 5점

> If I were you, I wouldn't do that.

→ _____

16 Look at the picture and make a complete sentence according to the conditions. Use only the **necessary** words and rearrange them correctly. 6점

> · **Condition 1** 어휘 – on, the top, of the hill, stand, stands, does, do, an old castle
> · **Condition 2** 문장을 전치사로 시작하고 명사로 끝낼 것

→ _____

_____

17 조건에 맞게 우리말을 영작하시오. 8점

> 나는 그가 거짓말을 했다고 한 번도 생각한 적 없다.
>
> · **조건 1** 어휘 – think, tell a lie
> · **조건 2** never를 문장 앞에 쓸 것
> · **조건 3** 시제를 유의해서 사용할 것
> · **조건 4** 9단어로 쓸 것

→ _____

_____

[18~19] Read the following and answer each question.

> Lou took a deep breath. He began ⓐ<u>to walk</u> into the cold, dark cave. Inside it, everything was silent. Here and there, bones were lying on the floor. "We have to go further in," said Carmen. "I know," said Lou. "But stay ⓑ<u>closely</u> behind me. Do not say a word." They walked deeper into the cave. Before long, they ⓒ<u>reached</u> a rock with an X on it. The air felt different. Suddenly, a strange cry came to their ears from out of nowhere. Out of the shadows ⓓ<u>flying</u> a dark figure. It moved by them quickly and ⓔ<u>was disappeared</u> into the shadows. (A)<u>They could hardly move at all.</u>

18 Which of the following correction is correct? (3 answers) 4점

① ⓐ to walk → walking
② ⓑ closely → close
③ ⓒ reached → reached at
④ ⓓ flying → flew
⑤ ⓔ was disappeared → disappeared

19 Complete the sentence below to make the sentence have the same meaning as the underlined sentence (A). 6점

→ Hardly _____.

불규칙 동사 변화표

불규칙 동사도 외우는 방법이 있다!

1 A – A – A 형태 동일

★표시는 필수 기본 동사들

원형	뜻	과거	과거분사
broadcast	방송하다	broadcast	broadcast
bet	돈을 걸다	bet	bet
burst	파열하다	burst	burst
cast	던지다	cast	cast
cost	비용이 들다	cost	cost
*cut	자르다	cut	cut
forecast	예고하다	forecast	forecast
*hit	치다	hit	hit
hurt	아프게 하다	hurt	hurt
let	~하게 하다	let	let
*put	놓다	put	put
quit	~을 그만두다	quit	quit
*read	읽다	read [red]	read [red]
rid	~을 제거하다	rid	rid
set	놓다	set	set
shed	흘리다	shed	shed
shut	닫다	shut	shut
spit	침을 뱉다	spit	spit
split	쪼개다	split	split
spread	펴다	spread	spread
thrust	찌르다	thrust	thrust
upset	뒤엎다	upset	upset

2 A – A – A' 과거분사만 살짝 바뀜

원형	뜻	과거	과거분사
beat	때리다, 이기다	beat	beaten

3 A – B – A 과거형에서 모음만 바뀜

원형	뜻	과거	과거분사
*come	오다	came	come
*become	되다	became	become
*run	달리다	ran	run

4 A – B – A' 과거형은 모음 변화, 과거분사형은 원형에 –n 붙임

원형	뜻	과거	과거분사
arise [əráiz]	(일이) 일어나다	arose [əróuz]	arisen [ərizn]
*be (am, is, are)	~이다	was, were	been
blow	불다	blew [blu:]	blown [bloun]
*do, does	하다	did	done
draw	당기다, 그리다	drew [dru:]	drawn [drɔ:n]
*drive	운전하다	drove [drouv]	driven [drivn]
*eat	먹다	ate	eaten
fall	떨어지다	fell	fallen
forbid	금지하다	forbade	forbidden
forgive	용서하다	forgave	forgiven
forsake	그만두다, 저버리다	forsook	forsaken
*give	주다	gave [geiv]	given [givn]
*go	가다	went [went]	gone [gɔ:n]
*grow	자라다	grew [gru:]	grown [groun]
*know	알다	knew [nju:]	known [noun]
ride	(차, 말 등을) 타다	rode [roud]	ridden [ridn]
rise	일어서다	rose [rouz]	risen [rizn]
*see	보다	saw [sɔ:]	seen [si:n]
shake	흔들다	shook [ʃuk]	shaken [ʃeikn]
show	보여주다, 보이다	showed	shown, showed
sow [sou]	(씨를) 뿌리다	sowed [soud]	sown [soun]
strive	노력하다	strove [strouv]	striven [strivn]
*take	잡다	took [tuk]	taken [teikn]
thrive	번영하다	throve [θrouv], thrived	thriven [θrivn], thrived
*throw	던지다	threw [θru:]	thrown [θroun]
withdraw	물러나다	withdrew [wiðdrú:]	withdrawn [wiðdrɔ́:n]
*write	쓰다	wrote [rout]	written [ritn]

5 A – B – B 원형에 –t 붙임

원형	뜻	과거	과거분사
bend	구부리다	bent	bent
*build	세우다	built	built
burn	태우다	burnt, burned	burnt, burned
deal	다루다	dealt [delt]	dealt
dwell	거주하다, 살다	dwelt, dwelled	dwelt, dwelled
lend	빌려주다	lent	lent
mean	의미하다	meant [ment]	meant
*send	보내다	sent	sent
smell	냄새 맡다, 냄새가 나다	smelt, smelled	smelt, smelled

원형		과거	과거분사
spend	소비하다	spent	spent
spoil	망쳐놓다	spoilt, spoiled	spoilt, spoiled

6 A – B – B 원형의 자음 + ought/aught

원형	뜻	과거	과거분사
*bring	가져오다	brought [brɔːt]	brought
*buy	사다	bought [bɔːt]	bought
*catch	잡다	caught [kɔːt]	caught
*fight	싸우다	fought [fɔːt]	fought
seek	찾다	sought [sɔːt]	sought
*teach	가르치다	taught [tɔːt]	taught
*think	생각하다	thought [θɔːt]	thought

7 A – B – B 원형의 자음 + ound

원형	뜻	과거	과거분사
bind	묶다	bound [baund]	bound
*find	발견하다	found [faund]	found

8 A – B – B 원형의 모음이 하나로 줄고 + t

원형	뜻	과거	과거분사
creep	기다, 포복하다	crept [krept]	crept
*feel	느끼다	felt	felt
*keep	유지하다	kept	kept
kneel [niːl]	무릎 꿇다, 굴복하다	knelt [nelt]	knelt
*leave	떠나다	left	left
*lose [luːz]	잃다	lost [lɔːst]	lost
*sleep	자다	slept	slept
sweep	쓸다	swept [swept]	swept

9 A – B – B 원형의 모음이 하나로 줄어듦

원형	뜻	과거	과거분사
feed	먹이다	fed [fed]	fed
*meet	만나다	met [met]	met
shoot [ʃuːt]	쏘다	shot [ʃɑt]	shot

10 A – B – B y를 i로 바꾸고 -d를 붙임

원형	뜻	과거	과거분사
lay	두다	laid [leid]	laid
*pay	지불하다	paid [peid]	paid
*say	말하다	said [sed]	said

11 A – B – B 원형에서 모음만 바뀜

원형	뜻	과거	과거분사
behold	~를 보다	beheld	beheld
bleed	피를 흘리다	bled	bled
breed	기르다	bred	bred
cling	달라붙다	clung	clung
dig	파다	dug [dʌg]	dug
fling	내던지다	flung	flung
hang	걸다	hung	hung
*hold	잡다, 손에 들다	held	held
lead	이끌다	led	led
shine	빛나다	shone [ʃoun]	shone
*sit	앉다	sat [sæt]	sat
spin	(실을) 잣다	spun [spʌn]	spun
*stand	서다	stood [stud]	stood
stick	찌르다	stuck	stuck
sting	쏘다	stung	stung
strike	때리다	struck [strʌk]	struck
*win	이기다	won [wʌn]	won
wind [waind]	감다	wound [waund]	wound
withhold	보류하다	withheld	withheld

12 A – B – B 모음 변화, 끝에 -d 붙임

원형	뜻	과거	과거분사
flee	도망치다	fled [fled]	fled
*have, has	가지다	had	had
*hear [hiər]	듣다	heard [həːrd]	heard
*make	만들다	made	made
*sell	팔다	sold	sold
slide	미끄러지다	slid	slid
*tell	말하다	told	told

13 A – B – B' 모음 변화, 과거형 + n

원형	뜻	과거	과거분사
awake [əwéik]	깨다	awoke [əwóuk]	awoken [əwoukn]
*bear [bɛər]	낳다	bore [bɔər]	born [bɔːrn]
bite	물다	bit [bit]	bitten [bitn]
*break	깨뜨리다	broke [brouk]	broken [broukn]
*choose	고르다	chose [tʃouz]	chosen [tʃouzn]
*forget	잊다	forgot [fərgát]	forgotten [fərgátn]
freeze	얼음이 얼다	froze [frouz]	frozen [frouzn]
*get	얻다	got [gat]	gotten [gatn]
*hide	감추다	hid [hid]	hidden [hidn]
*speak	말하다	spoke [spouk]	spoken [spoukn]
steal	훔치다	stole [stoul]	stolen [stouln]
swear	맹세하다	swore [swɔər]	sworn [swɔːrn]
tear [tɛər]	찢다	tore [tɔər]	torn [tɔːrn]
tread [tred]	걷다, 짓밟다	trod [trad]	trodden [tradn]
wake	깨다	woke	woken
*wear	입다	wore [wɔər]	worn [wɔːrn]

14 A – B – C

원형	뜻	과거	과거분사
*begin	시작하다	began [bigǽn]	begun [bigʌ́n]
*drink	마시다	drank [dræŋk]	drunk [drʌŋk]
*fly	날다	flew [fluː]	flown [floun]
lie	가로눕다	lay [lei]	lain [lein]
cf. lie (규칙 변화)	거짓말하다	lied	lied
*ring	울리다	rang [ræŋ]	rung [rʌŋ]
shrink	줄어들다	shrank [ʃræŋk]	shrunk [ʃrʌŋk]
*sing	노래하다	sang [sæŋ]	sung [sʌŋ]
sink	가라앉다	sank [sæŋk]	sunk [sʌŋk]
spring	튀다	sprang [spræŋ]	sprung [sprʌŋ]
*swim	수영하다	swam [swæm]	swum [swʌm]

15 조동사

원형	뜻	과거
*must	~해야 한다	(had to)
*can	~할 수 있다	could [cud]
*may	~해도 좋다	might [mait]
shall	~할 것이다	should [ʃud]
*will	~할 것이다	would [wud]

16 뜻에 따라 활용이 달라지는 불규칙 동사

원형	뜻	과거	과거분사
bear	참다	bore	borne
	낳다	bore	born
bid	명령하다	bade	bidden
	말하다	bid	bid
hang	걸다	hung	hung
	교수형에 처하다	hanged	hanged

17 혼동하기 쉬운 불규칙 동사와 규칙 동사

원형	뜻	과거	과거분사
bind	묶다	bound [baund]	bound
bound [baund]	되튀다	bounded	bounded
fall	떨어지다, 쓰러지다	fell	fallen
fell	쓰러뜨리다	felled	felled
find	발견하다	found [faund]	found
found [faund]	세우다, 창립하다	founded	founded
fly	날다	flew [fluː]	flown [floun]
flow	흐르다	flowed	flowed
lie	눕다	lay	lain
lay	눕히다, 낳다	laid	laid
see	보다	saw	seen
saw [sɔː]	톱질하다	sawed [sɔːd]	sawed, sawn [sɔːn]
sew [sou]	바느질하다	sewed [soud]	sewed, sewn [soun]
sit	앉다	sat	sat
set	두다	set	set
wind	감다	wound [waund]	wound
wound [wuːnd]	상처를 입히다	wounded	wounded
welcome	환영하다	welcomed	welcomed
overcome	이겨내다, 극복하다	overcame	overcome

MEMO

MEMO

MEMO

신영주

2급 외국어 정교사 자격증, UCSD TESOL취득(국제영어교사 교육자격증, University of California)
(전) EBSi 온라인 강사, 대치 시대인재, 이강학원 강사
(현) 프라우드 세븐 어학원 원장, 리딩타운 원장
저서: 체크체크, 올백(천재교육), 투탑 영어(디딤돌), Grammar 콕, VOCA콕(꿈을담는틀), 중학 영문법 클리어(동아) 등 다수의 교재 공저

이건희

쥬기스(http://jugis.co.kr) 대표
저서: 맨처음 수능 시리즈 – 맨처음 수능 영문법, 맨처음 수능 영어(기본, 실력, 독해, 완성)
　　　 내공 시리즈 – 내공 중학영문법, 내공 중학 영어구문, 내공 중학영어듣기 모의고사 20회
　　　 체크체크(천재교육), Grammar In(비상교육) 외 다수
instagram@gunee27

최신개정판

내신공략 중학영문법 3 문제풀이책

지은이 신영주, 이건희
펴낸이 정규도
펴낸곳 (주)다락원

개정판 1쇄 발행 2021년 3월 15일
개정판 6쇄 발행 2024년 9월 20일

편집 김민주, 서정아
디자인 구수정
조판 블랙엔화이트
영문 감수 Michael A. Putlack, Mark Holden
삽화 김진용

다락원 경기도 파주시 문발로 211
내용문의: (02)736-2031 내선 532
구입문의: (02)736-2031 내선 250~252
Fax: (02)732-2037
출판등록 1977년 9월 16일 제406-2008-000007호

ISBN 978-89-277-0894-0 54740
　　　978-89-277-0888-9 54740(set)

http://www.darakwon.co.kr

다락원 홈페이지를 방문하시면 상세한 출판 정보와 함께 동영상 강좌,
MP3 자료 등 다양한 어학 정보를 얻으실 수 있습니다.

내신공략
신공략

중학영문법

신영주 ✦ 이건희 지음

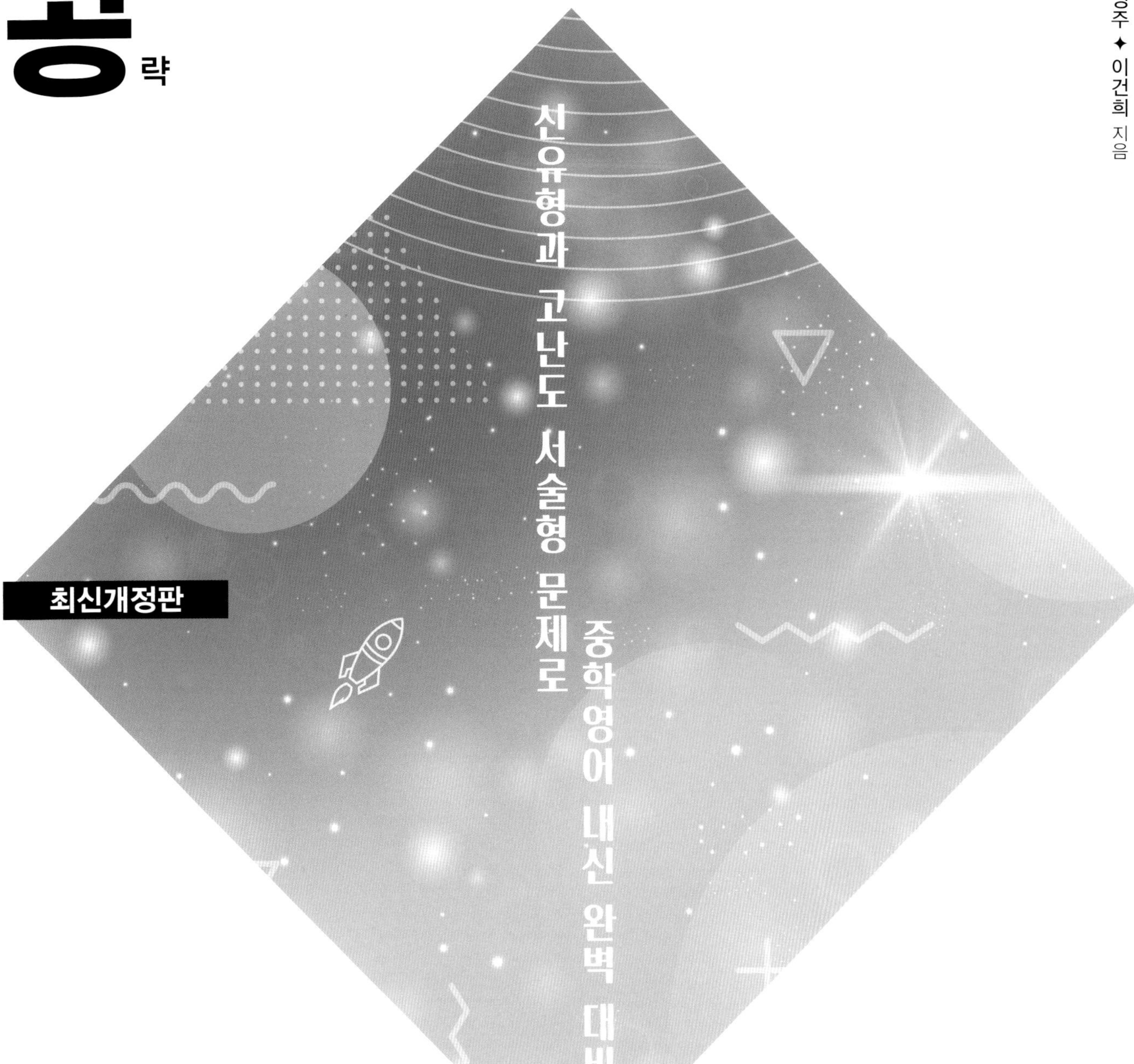

최신개정판

신유형과 고난도 서술형 문제로 중학영어 내신 완벽 대비

문제풀이책

정답 및 해설

3

🔷 DARAKWON

내신공략 중학영문법

문제풀이책 3
정답 및 해설

CHAPTER 01
문장의 구조

UNIT 01 주어, 목적어, 주격 보어

1) 명사
2) 명사구
3) the＋형용사
4) 의문사＋to부정사
5) 명사절
6) 명사류
7) 형용사류

Level 1 Test
p. 12

A 1 Playing 또는 To play 2 Laziness
　3 to keep 4 good
　5 to listen

B 1 where to study 2 if I had
　3 that she told the truth

Level 2 Test
p. 13

01 ② 02 ③
03 ③ 04 ①
05 The fruit has turned hard.
06 where she lives
07 I don't think that she told a lie.
08 what he is looking for

》》 해설
01 동사의 목적어로 형용사는 올 수 없다.
02 주격 보어로는 형용사류 또는 명사류가 와야 하고 동사는 올 수 없다.
03 주어는 명사류만 될 수 있다. ⓐ Kind → Kindness ⓑ The strong = Strong people(복수 명사)이므로 동사는 endure가 알맞다. ⓓ That 대신에 목적어를 포함한 관계대명사 What이 알맞다.
04 ①은 관계대명사이고, 나머지는 문장을 명사절로 만들어주는 접속사 that이다.
05 2형식 동사 turn(~하게 되다, 변하다) 다음에 오는 주격 보어로 형용사 hard가 알맞다.
06 목적어로 의문사절이 올 때는 '의문사 주어＋동사'의 순서이다.
07 she told a lie라는 문장을 명사절로 만드는 접속사 that을 쓴다. that절은 동사 think의 목적어 역할을 한다.
08 불완전한 문장을 '~하는 것'이라는 의미의 주어나 보어로 만들 수 있는 what절로 써야 5단어로 문장을 완성할 수 있다.

Level 3 Test
p. 14

01 ② 02 ③
03 ④ ⑤ 04 ① ② ③
05 ④ 06 ② ③ ④
07 ④ 08 ②

09 ① ⑤
10 He is fond of drinking Coke.
11 if[whether] he was happy then
12 To listen to[Listening to] / falling
13 it is illegal to eat peanuts in church

》》 해설
01 ② 문장을 주어로 만들어 줄 수 있는 접속사 that이 필요하다. ⑤는 believe 뒤에 접속사 that이 생략된 것으로 가능하다.
02 All of my money was used to buy a birthday present[gift] for my sister.로 영작할 수 있다. money는 단수이므로 단수 동사 was가 알맞다.
03 ④와 ⑤는 It ~ that 강조 용법이고, 나머지와 주어진 문장은 가주어-진주어 구문이다.
04 ①은 to부정사가 주어, ②는 가주어-진주어 구문, ③은 동명사가 주어이다.
05 문장의 주어는 the film이고, 다음에 온 that은 목적격 관계대명사이므로 주어 역할을 하는 the film 앞의 That은 필요 없다.
06 ② to help → helping ③ eat → to eat ④ to look for → looking for
07 ④는 관계대명사이고, 나머지는 명사절을 만드는 접속사 that이다.
08 ⓑ sadly → sad ⓒ is → is that (또는 I will → to) ⓔ sleep → asleep
09 ① 주어는 복수인 The men이다. ⑤ keep은 형용사 보어를 취한다.
10 전치사 of의 목적어로 동명사 drinking이 알맞다.
11 문장을 목적절로 연결할 때 의문사가 없으면 if[whether]를 쓴다.
12 첫 번째 빈칸은 listen을 주어로 만들기 위해 to부정사나 동명사 형태로 쓰고, 두 번째 빈칸은 leaves를 수식하는 현재분사 falling이 적절하다.
13 to eat peanuts in church is illegal에서 주어 자리에 가주어 it을 쓰고 to부정사구는 문장 끝으로 보낸다.

UNIT 02 목적격 보어

1) make
2) elect
3) name
4) keep
5) find
6) 현재분사
7) make
8) have
9) let
10) see
11) hear
12) to부정사
13) help
14) 능동
15) 수동

Level 1 Test
p. 16

A 1 look 2 Chatterbox
　3 sleepy 4 to go out

B 1 she → her
　2 to rise → rise 또는 rising
　3 repair → repaired
　4 standing → stand 또는 to stand

C 1 called him a troublemaker
　2 leaves the door open

3   found the safe empty
4   help me count the money

Level 2 Test
p. 17

01 ①   02 ④
03 ② ③   04 ② ③ ④
05 made / feel   06 let
07 The man had his new house built.
08 The girl helped the blind man cross the road.

≫ 해설

01 「make+목적어+형용사」 구문으로, 목적어 다음에 부사는 올 수 없다. (① sadly → sad)
02 목적격 보어로 동사원형이 올 수 있는 동사는 사역동사, 지각동사, 그리고 help동사이다. get은 to부정사를 써야 한다.
03 ① the patient는 목적어이다. ④ 목적격 보어 to smoke 앞에 부정어로 not을 쓸 수 있다. ⑤ advise는 목적격 보어로 to부정사가 온다.
04 ⓐ ask동사는 to부정사를 목적격 보어로 취한다. ⓑ 지각동사 see는 동사원형이나 -ing를 목적격 보어로 취한다. ⓒ help동사는 목적격 보어로 동사원형과 to부정사 둘 다 취하므로 changing → change 또는 to change로 바뀌어야 한다.
05 「make+목적어+동사원형」 구문이다. 과거 시제이므로 made가 되어야 함에 유의한다.
06 목적어 다음에 동사원형이 오므로 사역동사가 와야 한다. 허락을 나타내는 사역동사로는 let이 가장 적절하다.
07 사역동사 have 다음에 목적어(his new house)와 목적격 보어(build)의 관계가 수동이므로 과거분사 built가 알맞다.
08 준사역동사 help는 목적격 보어로 동사원형이나 to부정사가 올 수 있다. 주어진 표현에는 to가 없으므로 동사원형을 쓴다.

Level 3 Test
p. 18

01 ②   02 ② ③ ⑤
03 ③   04 ① ③
05 ①   06 ①
07 ⑤   08 ②
09 ⑤   10 ④
11 We kept the room warm.
12 have your cavity filled
13 We saw John smiling[smile] at a tall girl yesterday.
14 told me not to waste any money

≫ 해설

01 「make동사는 목적격 보어로 형용사나 동사원형 둘 다 취할 수 있다.
02 목적격 보어로 동사원형이 올 수 있는 동사는 사역동사, 지각동사, help동사이다. ask와 want는 to부정사를 써야 한다.
03 ③ allow는 목적격 보어로 to부정사를 취한다. 나머지는 동사원형을 쓸 수 있다. 의미상 go동사가 어울린다.
04 지각동사는 목적격 보어로 동사원형이나 현재분사를 취한다.
05 목적어(your hair)와 목적격 보어(do)의 관계가 수동이므로 과거분사 done이 알맞다.
06 지각동사 see는 목적격 보어로 bark나 barking이 온다.
07 모두 「have+목적어+과거분사」 구문이다. 목적어와 목적격 보어가

수동의 관계이다. ⑤는 make가 아니라 made가 되어야 한다. (나는 열쇠를 잃어버려서 하나를 더 만들어지게 했다.)
08 ⓑ 그녀의 차가 세차되는 수동의 관계이므로 과거분사 washed가 알맞다.
09 ⑤ make는 목적격 보어로 부사가 아닌 형용사를 취하므로 specially가 아니라 special이 필요하다. (→ What made the day so special to you?) ① She helped me make the bed. ② He had his watch stolen last night. ③ You must keep your password safe. ④ Sam advised her to leave London.
10 make는 목적격 보어를 취할 때 명사, 형용사, 동사원형이 온다. ⓐ sadly → sad ⓒ felt → feel ⓓ going → go ⓕ to tell → tell
11 「주어+동사(kept)+목적어(the room)+목적격 보어(warm)」 순서로 쓴다.
12 「have+목적어+과거분사」 구문이다. 목적어와 목적격 보어의 관계가 수동이므로 과거분사를 쓴다.
13 지각동사는 목적격 보어로 동사원형이나 현재분사를 취한다.
14 tell동사는 목적격 보어로 to부정사를 취하며, to부정사의 부정은 앞에 not을 붙인다.

Review Test
p. 20

01 ④   02 ①
03 ⑤   04 ⑤
05 ③   06 ③
07 ③   08 ①
09 where to start
10 The party is getting noisy.
11 if[whether] she really likes me
12 It is true that he was born in Jamaica.
13 made my dad feel better
14 felt my face turning red
15 coolly → cool / close → closed
16 I saw my tablet computer fall and break.
17 ② ⑤
18 Getting some good rest will help your tired eyes work properly again.

≫ 해설

01 의문사절이 주어로 쓰인 문장이다. matter는 '문제가 되다' 라는 뜻의 일반동사이다. 의문사절은 3인칭 단수 취급하므로 doesn't matter가 맞다.
02 2형식 동사 remain의 주격 보어로 현재분사 missing이 알맞다. remain은 진행형으로 쓸 수 없으므로 ⑤는 오답이다.
03 의문사절이 목적절로 쓰일 때 어순은 「의문사+주어+동사」의 순서이다.
04 ⓔ 완전한 문장을 목적절로 이끄는 접속사가 필요하다. (what → that)
05 ③ She made me angry. 목적격 보어로 angrily부사는 형용사형 angry 로 써야 알맞다. ① I enjoyed riding a motor kickboard. ② I don't know when to start. ④ My dad got me to separate the trash. ⑤ Jane helped me to complete the assignment.
06 I heard my name called.로 영작할 수 있다. 나의 이름이 '불려지는' 수동의 관계이므로 목적격 보어 자리에는 과거분사 called가 알맞다.

07 「let＋목적어＋동사원형」 구문으로 going은 go가 되어야 한다.

08 ⓐ keep동사 다음에 주격 보어로 형용사가 와야 한다. (silently → silent) ⓒ the gift를 선행사로 하는 관계사가 필요하다. (what → that)

09 「의문사＋to부정사」가 목적어로 쓰인 문장이다.

10 get동사는 주격 보어로 형용사를 취한다. (noise: 소음 / noisy: 시끄러운)

11 문장을 목적절로 연결할 때 의문사가 없으면 if[whether]를 접속사로 쓴다.

12 he was born in Jamaica 문장을 that절로 만들어 진주어로 문장 끝에 쓰고, 가주어 It을 문장 앞에 써서 표현한다.

13 「사역동사(made)＋목적어(my dad)＋목적격 보어(feel better)」 순서로 쓴다.

14 지각동사 feel이 목적격 보어로 진행의 의미를 강조하는 현재분사 turning을 취하고 있다. 'turn＋형용사'는 '～해지다'의 뜻으로 쓰인다.

15 keep동사는 목적격 보어로 형용사 cool을 취한다. / 창문이 닫혀지는 수동의 관계이므로 과거분사 closed가 알맞다.

16 fall(떨어지다)과 break(깨지다)는 자동사로 쓰이므로 그대로 동사원형으로 써서 see의 목적격 보어 역할을 할 수 있다.

17 ⓑ 진주어는 가주어 It이 있어야 한다. to부정사의 부사적 용법(목적)으로 사용되었다. ⓔ There is 구문의 주어로 쓰였다.

18 푹 쉬는 것은 get some good rest인데 주어 자리이고 단어 수에 맞게 Getting some good rest로 쓰고, 술어 동사인 will help를 쓴 후, 목적어가 '당신의 피곤한 눈'이므로 본문에서 tired를 찾아 your tired eyes를 쓴 후 「help＋목적어＋(to)＋동사원형」 구문을 이용하여 to를 빼고 work properly again으로 쓰면 된다.

[17~18]

> 사람들이 믿는 것과는 달리, 낮은 빛에서 책을 읽는 것은 눈을 손상시키지 않는다. 당신이 어둠 속에서 책을 읽을 때, 당신은 글자에 집중하기 위해 눈을 부분적으로 감은 채 무언가를 보는 경향이 있다. 희미한 빛은 눈의 집중을 어렵게 하며 눈 주위에 통증을 유발하고 단기적인 눈의 피로를 유발할 수 있다. 그러나 어둠 속에서 책을 읽는 것이 눈에 장기적인 해를 끼친다는 과학적 증거는 없다. <u>푹 쉬는 것은 당신의 피곤한 눈이 제대로 다시 활동하는 것을 도울 것이다.</u>

• 어휘 · contrary to ～와는 달리 | low 낮은 | damage 손상시키다 | be likely to ～하는 경향이 있다, ～하기 쉽다 | focus on ～에 집중하다 | cause 유발하다 | pain 고통 | short-term 단기의 | evidence 증거 | long-term 장기의 | harm 해 | properly 제대로, 적절히

CHAPTER 02
to부정사

UNIT 03 용법, 의미상의 주어, 부정

1) 명사적	2) 주어	3) 목적어
4) 보어	5) 형용사적	6) 명사
7) 대명사	8) 부사적	9) 목적
10) 원인	11) 근거	12) 결과
13) 형용사	14) 일반	15) for
16) 성품	17) of	18) not
19) never		

Level 1 Test
p. 24

A 1 명사적 용법　　　2 부사적 용법(목적)
　 3 형용사적 용법

B 1 for　　　2 of

C 1 not to play　　　2 어색한 곳 없음
　 3 never to take off　　　4 not to pollute

Level 2 Test
p. 25

01 ⑤　　　　　　02 ③
03 ③　　　　　　04 ③
05 I will try not to be late tomorrow.
06 for him to stop crying
07 (1) of Andy　 (2) for us
08 I wanted to / I didn't have enough time

》》 해설

01 [보기]와 ⑤는 부사적 용법 중 감정의 원인을 나타낸다. ①~④는 명사적 용법이다.

02 일반 형용사가 오는 경우 to부정사의 의미상의 주어는 'for＋목적격'으로 쓴다.

03 not이 to climb을 부정하고 있으므로 ③이 적절하다.

04 It was careless of me not to lock[have locked] the door.로 영작할 수 있다. careless는 성품 형용사이므로 of를 쓴다.

05 'try＋to부정사'는 '～하려고 노력하다'이고, to부정사의 부정은 'not to＋동사원형'으로 쓴다.

06 일반 형용사인 경우 'for＋목적격'으로 쓰며, 대명사이므로 him으로 쓰고, stop＋-ing는 '～하는 것을 멈추다'이다.

07 성품 형용사인 경우는 to부정사의 의미상의 주어를 'of＋목적격'으로, 일반 형용사인 경우는 'for＋목적격'으로 표현한다. mean은 '야비한'이란 뜻의 성품 형용사이다.

08 I wanted to (see the pyramids), but I didn't have enough time.에서 반복어구를 생략하고 재배열하면 된다.

Level 3 Test
p. 26

01 ① ②　　　　　　　02 ④ ⑤
03 ③　　　　　　　　04 ⑤
05 ④　　　　　　　　06 ⑤
07 ②　　　　　　　　08 ②
09 can live to be 200 years old
10 for him to carry
11 must be angry to say
12 ⓐ 엄마는 나에게 지하실 문을 열지 말라고 말씀하셨다.

≫ 해설
01 [보기]와 ①, ②는 목적을 나타내는 부사적 용법이고, ③은 형용사적 용법, ④, ⑤는 명사적 용법이다.
02 ・「kind(성품 형용사)+of+목적격+to부정사」이므로 빈칸에는 of 가 들어가야 한다.
　　・「important(일반 형용사)+for+목적격+to부정사」이므로 빈칸 에는 for와 to가 들어가야 한다.
03 She told me not to eat her ice cream.으로 영작할 수 있다.
04 write paper가아니라 write on paper이므로 전치사 on을 써야 한다.
05 ④ 성품 형용사가 있을 경우 to부정사의 의미상의 주어로 'of+목적 격'을 쓴다. 나머지는 일반 형용사가 쓰였으므로 for가 알맞다.
06 사진을 찍지 말라는 것은 to부정사(to take pictures)를 부정하므로 The actor asked us not to take pictures of him.으로 영작할 수 있다.
07 'for+목적격'이 왔으므로 성품 형용사 ⓓ, ⓔ는 올 수 없다.
08 ② ask는 목적격 보어로 to부정사를 취한다. (→ He asked her not to eat his snacks.) ① It's not safe to drink the water. ③ It's important for us to help others. ④ She didn't have anything to write with. ⑤ Why did you want me to meet here?
09 살아서 200살이 된다는 부사적 용법 중 '결과'로 쓰면 된다.
10 일반 형용사인 경우 to부정사의 의미상의 주어는 'for+목적격'을 쓴 다. (그가 자전거로 그 벽돌을 다 나르는 것은 힘들어 보인다.)
11 to부정사의 부사적 용법 중 판단의 근거를 이용해서 표현하면 된다. 확실한 추측을 나타내는 조동사는 must이다.
12 '문을 열지 말라'고 했으므로 to open을 부정하는 것을 찾고 해석하 면 된다.

UNIT 04 시제, 독립부정사, 대부정사

1) to+동사원형　　　　　2) to have+p.p.
3) to be sure　　　　　　4) to begin with
5) to tell (you) the truth
6) to be honest[frank] (with you)
7) to be brief
8) to make matters[things] worse
9) sad to say　　　　　　10) strange to say
11) so to speak
12) not to mention (= needless to say)
13) 동사　　　　　　　　14) to

Level 1 Test
p. 28

A　1　To be frank　　　　2　To tell the truth
　　3　not to mention

B　1　seems / she is interested
　　2　appeared to be

C　1　stand up　　　　　2　wear it[my dress]

Level 2 Test
p. 29

01 ① ④　　　　　　　02 ④
03 ⑤　　　　　　　　04 ④
05 to have finished writing the novel
06 to speak / sweet / salty taste
07 I tried to
08 to caught → to have caught

≫ 해설
01 that절과 주절의 시제가 같을 때는 It seems that S V 또는 S seems to ~로 표현할 수 있다.
02 to be brief는 독립부정사로 '간단히 말하면'의 뜻이다.
03 to 이하 동일어구는 생략할 수 있다.
04 길을 잃어버린 것이 먼저이므로 주절보다 앞선 시제로 써서 It seemed that he had lost his way. (= He seemed to have lost his way.)로 쓰면 된다.
05 주절의 시제보다 먼저 일어났으므로 완료부정사(to have+p.p.) 형 태로 쓰면 된다.
06 so로 시작하는 '말하자면'은 so to speak로, 영영풀이는 '입 안에서 어떤 물질로부터 얻어지는 감각'으로 taste(맛)를 쓰면 된다.
07 I tried to get a ticket.에서 중복되는 어구를 제외하고 쓰면 된다.
08 주절의 시제보다 앞선 시제이므로 완료부정사(to have+p.p.)로 써 야 한다.

Level 3 Test
p. 30

01 ④　　　　　　　　02 ③
03 ③　　　　　　　　04 ④
05 ①　　　　　　　　06 ④
07 ④　　　　　　　　08 ② ⑤
09 (1) 기태　(2) briefly　(3) brief
10 attend the meeting
11 doesn't seem / the employee works hard
12 Needless to say, we attracted a lot of attention.
13 "Sorry" seems that it is → It seems that "sorry" is (위에서 5째 줄) / It seems that the boys lost → It seemed that the boys had lost (마지막 문장)

≫ 해설
01 단순부정사이므로 주절의 시제와 같은 시제가 와야 한다.
02 to begin with: 우선
03 ③은 대부정사의 to이고, 나머지는 전치사이다.
04 ⓑ에서 It seems that S+V 구조로 써야 하며, 주절은 과거인데 that절에 현재완료가 올 수 없고, 파리로 간 것이 먼저이므로 had gone으로 써야 한다.

05 독립부정사는 문장 전체를 수식하며, that은 shirt를 수식하는 지시형용사이다.

06 ④의 go는 주절의 go를 반복해서 쓴 것이므로 생략해서 대부정사로 만들 수 있다.

07 ⓐ와 ⓑ 둘 다 내용상 본동사보다 앞선 시제이므로 완료부정사 형태로 써야 한다.

08 ② She → It ⑤ had → have

09 '간단히 말해서'는 to be brief인데 맞는 것으로 채점했으므로 기태가 틀렸다. ⓐ는 이상이 없고, ⓑ는 make인데 making으로 썼으므로 미라와 정성이는 바르게 채점했다.

10 to부정사구에서 반복어구는 생략할 수 있다.

11 부정문의 경우는 It doesn't seem that ~으로 전환한다.

12 '두말할 나위 없이'는 needless to say나 not to mention으로 표현할 수 있는데, 선택지에 not이 없으므로 needless to say로 문장을 시작하면 된다.

13 It seems that S+V로 쓴다. / 주어진 문장의 주절이 과거이고 지도를 잃어버린 것이 더 전에 일어난 일이므로 It seemed that을 쓰고 lost를 had lost로 써야 한다.

Review Test

p. 32

01 ②	02 ⑤
03 ④	04 ④
05 ⑤	06 ②
07 ⑤	08 ④
09 ②	10 ②

11 The actor woke up to find himself a superstar.

12 I didn't mean to (yell at you).

13 you don't want to

14 not to worry

15 appeared / the kids had gotten lost

16 ⓐ to be → to have been (또는 seems → seemed)

17 to be sure

18 W R O N G

19 It was cruel of my sister to have deleted my secret folder.

20 (1) It seems / have rained
    (2) It seems / it rained

21 ③

22 (A) to do (B) answer

≫ 해설

01 [보기]와 ②는 진주어로 쓰인 명사적 용법이다. ① ③ 형용사적 용법 ④ ⑤ 부사적 용법

02 'of+목적격'이 왔으므로 일반 형용사(hard, necessary, important, possible)는 들어갈 수 없다.

03 「tell+목적어+to부정사」에서 to부정사의 부정은 「not to+동사원형」이다.

04 ④ I'd like to have dinner with you tonight에서 공통어구만을 빼야 하므로 대부정사를 사용해서 like to로 써야 한다.

05 ⓐ write with ⓑ drink ⓒ sit on ⓓ read ⓔ wear

06 to부정사의 주체가 주어이므로 for me를 삭제해야 한다.

07 부정문의 경우 It doesn't seem ~으로 쓰고, 완료부정사이므로 It doesn't seem that he had a plan then.으로 쓴다.

08 not to mention(~은 말할 것도 없이)이 문맥상 적절하다.

09 형용사를 수식하는 부사적 용법의 to부정사가 알맞다. (네 손 글씨는 읽기 어려워.)

10 ⓑ for → of ⓔ has been → was (when young이라고 과거를 나타내는 부사구가 있으므로 현재완료는 쓸 수 없다.)

11 부사적 용법의 결과로 표현할 수 있다.

12 to부정사에서 to를 제외한 반복되는 어구는 생략할 수 있다.

13 to wear that windbreaker에서 반복어구(wear that windbreaker)를 빼고 대부정사로 표현하면 된다.

14 to부정사의 부정은 「not to+동사원형」으로 표현한다.

15 완료부정사가 왔으므로 주절의 시제보다 앞선 시제이다. 따라서 주절은 과거 시제로 쓰고 that절은 과거완료로 써야 한다.

16 yesterday라고 나와 있으므로 주절의 시제보다 앞선 시제이다. 따라서 완료부정사로 표현해야 한다. 또는 주절의 시제를 과거로 쓴다.

17 유의어로 보아 '확실히'라는 독립부정사의 표현이 적절하다.

18 ⓑ는 형용사적 용법이고 나머지는 부사적 용법(목적)이다. 따라서 ⓐ, ⓒ, ⓓ, ⓔ의 첫 글자인 G, N, O, W를 적절히 빈칸에 넣어 단어를 완성하면 된다.

19 [보기]와 주어진 문장 모두 성품 형용사라 'of+목적격'으로 써야 한다. (누나가 내 비밀 폴더를 지운 것은 잔인했다.)

20 주절은 현재이고 비가 온 것은 과거이므로 완료부정사를 이용하여 쓰고, 이를 It seems that 구문으로 전환하면 된다. (1)에서 It은 비인칭 주어이다.

21 ⓑ 내용상 옷을 바닥에 놓은 것이므로 laid로 고쳐야 한다. '놓다'의 동사 변화는 lay-laid-laid이다. (cf. 눕다: lie-lay-lain) ⓒ 「find+목적어+목적격 보어」 구문에서 목적어와 목적격 보어가 능동이므로 sleeping이 적절하다. ⓓ 완료부정사는 주절의 시제보다 앞선 시제일 때 사용한다. 여기서는 주절의 시제보다 앞선 시제가 아니므로 to see로 고쳐야 한다.

22 (A) 빨래를 하기 위해서 아래층으로 내려간 것이므로 부사적 용법의 목적 표현으로 to do laundry가 적절하다. (B) Lindsay가 전화를 받지 않아서 부모님이 돌아온 것으로 answer가 적절하다. (요약문 해석: Lindsay는 빨래를 하기 위해 아래층으로 내려갔을 때 지하실에 갇혔다. 그녀가 전화를 받지 않아서 그녀의 부모님은 다음 날 돌아오셨다.)

[21~22]

Lindsay는 끔찍한 주말을 보냈다. 그녀의 부모님은 그녀의 숙모를 방문하기 위해 오타와로 갔지만, 그녀는 집에 머물렀다. 지난 토요일, 그녀는 빨래를 하기 위해 지하실로 내려갔다. 그녀는 위층으로 다시 갔지만, 문이 잠겨 있었다! 다행히 Lindsay는 약간의 먹을 것을 발견했다. 지하실에는 여분의 식료품이 있었다. 그녀는 세탁물에서 옷을 꺼내 바닥에 놓고 그것들 위에서 잤다. 일요일 이른 아침에 그녀의 부모님은 집에 왔고 그녀가 지하실에서 자고 있는 것을 발견했다. 그녀의 아빠는 말했다. "어젯밤에 우리는 모든 것이 괜찮은지 알아보기 위해 너에게 전화했지만, 너는 전화를 받지 않았단다. 그래서 우리는 되도록 빨리 돌아왔어. 네가 괜찮아서 안심이다."

• 어휘 awful 끔찍한 | basement 지하실 | laundry 빨래, 세탁물 | fortunately 다행히 | extra 여분의 | grocery 식료품 | lie 눕다(lie-lay-lain), 거짓말하다(lie-lied-lied) | relieved 안심한, 안도한

CHAPTER 03

동명사

UNIT 05 용법, 의미상의 주어, 부정

1) 주어   2) 보어   3) 동사
4) 전치사   5) 소유   6) 목적
7) 목적   8) not   9) never

Level 1 Test
p. 36

A   1   Being 또는 To be   2   driving
     3   writing   4   riding

B   1   his 또는 him   2   어색한 곳 없음
     3   My

C   1   not learning   2   not saying

Level 2 Test
p. 37

01 ②   02 ③
03 ③   04 ④
05 skate → skating
06 She didn't like them having
07 He always complains about not having time to study.
08 Laughing a lot is good for our health.

≫ 해설
01 선택지 중에서 주어가 될 수 있는 것은 동명사이다.
02 동명사의 의미상의 주어가 목적격이 가능한 경우는 목적어 자리인 경우이므로, 주어 자리인 첫 번째 빈칸에는 소유격 His가 맞다. 두 번째 빈칸은 절의 주어 자리이므로 주격 I로 써야 한다.
03 부정하고 있는 것은 동명사이므로 not+-ing로 써야 한다.
04 ④는 주어로 쓰인 동명사이고, 주어진 문장과 나머지는 동사 또는 전치사의 목적어로 쓰인 동명사이다.
05 skate도 enjoy의 목적어이므로 skating으로 써야 한다.
06 '그녀는 그들이 그녀의 집에서 파티를 하는 것을 좋아하지 않았다'의 의미로 영작하면 된다. 동명사의 의미상의 주어로 they가 아닌 them을 써야 하는 것에 주의한다.
07 빈도부사(always)는 일반동사 앞에 쓰고, 동명사의 부정은 동명사(having) 앞에 not을 쓴다.
08 '웃는 것'은 To laugh 또는 Laughing으로 표현할 수 있으나 조건1에 맞도록 동명사로 쓴다. 동명사의 주어가 일반인인 경우는 쓰지 않는다.

Level 3 Test
p. 38

01 ④   02 ⑤
03 ③   04 ② ③
05 ④   06 ① ② ③ ④

07 ① ⑤   08 ②
09 ④
10 Don't eat food before washing your hands.
11 My mom[mother] was angry about my not telling the truth.
12 ⓑ to go → going
13 You → Your

≫ 해설
01 주어진 문장과 ④는 보어로 쓰인 동명사이다. ① ③ 주어 ② 목적어 ⑤ 전치사의 목적어
02 동명사(winning)의 의미상의 주어는 her son's이다.
03 주어가 동명사(Swimming)이므로 단수 취급해야 한다.
04 ②와 ③은 주어로 쓰인 동명사이고, 나머지는 목적어로 쓰인 동명사이다.
05 She considered not cycling up the mountain.으로 영작할 수 있다.
06 ①~④ 동명사의 의미상의 주어가 목적어 자리이면 소유격과 목적격 모두 가능하다. ⑤ 부정대명사는 목적격으로 쓴다.
07 ① he → him[his] ⑤ to send → sending
08 ⓐ C ⓑ I (having not → not having) ⓒ I (are → is) ⓓ I (go → going)이므로 바른 표기는 ⓐ C와 ⓓ I이다.
09 ④ chance는 불가산명사로 쓰였으므로 few를 little로, the bus가 of의 의미상의 주어이므로 to be를 being으로, lately는 '최근에'라는 뜻으로 '늦은'이란 뜻의 late로 고쳐야 한다. ① 어색한 것 없음 ② to be → being ③ to give → giving ⑤ dislike → dislikes, to keep → keeping
10 부정 명령문이므로 Don't로 시작하고, before가 전치사로 사용되었으므로 그 뒤에는 동명사(washing)를 쓰면 된다.
11 목적어 자리에 사용된 동명사의 의미상의 주어로 목적격을 쓸 수 있으나 조건2에 맞게 my로 써야 하며, 동명사의 부정은 not+-ing이다.
12 go가 전치사의 목적어이므로 to부정사가 아니라 동명사로 써야 한다.
13 주어 자리에 사용된 의미상의 주어는 소유격으로 써야 한다.

UNIT 06 동명사, 현재분사, to부정사

1) 명사   2) 용도
3) 진행형   4) 동작
5) 동명사   6) to부정사
7) 둘 다   8) ~하자마자
9) ~하지 않을 수 없다   10) 계속 ~하다
11) ~하러 가다   12) ~하기를 고대하다
13) ~하는 게 어때?   14) ~하는 것에 익숙하다
15) ~할 가치가 있다   16) ~하는 것과 거리가 멀다
17) ~하는 것은 불가능하다   18) ~하느라 바쁘다
19) ~하고 싶다   20) ~해봐야 소용없다
21) ~하느라 시간[돈]을 쓰다[낭비하다]
22) ~에 싫증이 나다   23) ~하는 데 어려움을 겪다

Level 1 Test
p. 40

A 1 solving, 동명사   2 singing, 현재분사

B 1 finished   2 give up
    3 enjoy

C 1 laugh   2 walking
    3 following   4 어색한 곳 없음

Level 2 Test
p. 41

01 ⑤   02 ②
03 ②   04 ⑤
05 he tried drinking some warm milk
06 ⓐ to meet → meeting
07 have trouble[difficulty] studying
08 spent / buying

》》 해설

01 ⑤는 couple을 꾸며주는 현재분사이고, 나머지는 동명사이다.

02 목적어가 동명사(watching)이므로 to부정사를 목적어로 취하는 ⓔ 와 ⓕ는 적절하지 않다.

03 be worth+-ing는 '~할 만한 가치가 있다'이고, start는 to부정사와 동명사 모두 목적어로 취하므로 이상이 없다.

04 'stop to+동사원형'은 '~하기 위해 하던 것을 멈추다'이므로 stop smoking으로 써야 금연한다는 의미가 된다.

05 try+-ing는 '시험 삼아 ~해보다'이고, 긍정문에는 some을 쓴다.

06 그를 전에 본 기억이 안 나므로 remember+-ing로 써서 '~한 것을 기억하다'로 표현해야 한다.

07 '~하는 데 어려움을 겪다'라는 표현으로는 have difficulty[trouble, a hard time]+-ing가 있는데, 단어 수에 맞도록 하려면 difficulty나 trouble을 쓰면 된다.

08 「spend+목적어+-ing」(~하는 데 …을 소비하다)의 구조로 쓰면 된다.

Level 3 Test
p. 42

01 ②   02 ⑤
03 ②   04 ②
05 ③   06 ③
07 ① ③ ④   08 ④
09 ③   10 ④
11 He decided to keep (on) learning Pilates.
12 (1) sleeping 또는 to sleep   (2) sleeping   (3) to sleep
13 climbing up without
14 ⓑ be → being

》》 해설

01 ②의 reading은 진행을 나타내는 현재분사이다.

02 Rob is not used[accustomed] to using chopsticks.로 영작할 수 있다.

03 ⓐ see → seeing ⓔ try → trying (spend+목적어+-ing)

04 be about to+동사원형: 막 ~하려고 하다 / stop+-ing는 '~ 하던 것을 그만두다'이다.

05 be healthy(건강하다)가 that절의 주어가 되어야 하므로 'being

healthy ~'로 고쳐야 한다.

06 ⓐ는 진행으로 쓰인 현재분사이고, ⓑ는 용도, 목적을 나타내는 동명 사이다.

07 ① to fish → fishing ③ to write → writing ④ to visit → visiting

08 주어진 문장과 ⓓ는 동명사이고, 나머지는 현재분사이다.

09 ⓐ I didn't expect to see you here. (expect+to부정사: seeing → to see) ⓑ She avoided answering my questions. (avoid+-ing: to answer → answering) ⓒ The snow continued falling until dark. ⓓ Would you like to make a donation? (would like+to부정사: making → to make) ⓔ They agreed to reserve two tickets for us.

10 첫 번째 빈칸에는 과거의 한 시점에 시작해서 지금까지 비 또는 눈이 오고 있으므로 현재완료 시제가, 두 번째 빈칸에는 앞으로도 그럴거나 그렇지 않을 것이라는 미래 시제가 와야 한다.

11 decide는 to부정사를, keep (on)은 동명사를 목적어로 취한다.

12 (1) like는 동명사나 to부정사를 목적어로 취한다.
    (2) dislike는 동명사만 목적으로 취한다.
    (3) would like는 to부정사만 목적어로 취한다.

13 고양이가 Simba 없이 혼자 산 위에 올라온 것으로, '고양이는 Simba 없이 산을 오른 것을 후회한다'라는 의미의 표현이 적절하다.
regret+-ing는 '~한 것을 후회하다'라는 표현이다.

14 cannot help+-ing는 '~하지 않을 수 없다'의 의미로 사용된다.

Review Test
p. 44

01 ②   02 ② ④ ⑤
03 ③   04 ⑤
05 ②   06 ③
07 ④   08 ④
09 ②
10 My sister had a hard time getting over 100,000 points
11 ⓐ not your → your not
12 I couldn't understand his[him] not joining the team.
13 He is not ashamed of smoking
14 Having not → Not having
15 On hearing / father('s) passing away
16 P L E A S E
17 cutting → cut (답변의 첫째 줄과 마지막 줄)
18 ② ③ ④
19 asking a parent or a sibling for advice

》》 해설

01 ⓐ의 sleeping은 용도, 목적을 나타내는 동명사이고, ⓑ의 sleeping 은 진행형에 사용된 현재분사이다.

02 전치사(on) 다음에는 동명사를 써야 하며, 이 문장에서 의미상의 주어 는 생략할 수 없고, 소유격 his 또는 목적격 him 둘 다 가능하다.

03 주어진 문장과 ③은 보어로 쓰인 동명사이다. ①은 주어, ②는 전치사 의 목적어, ④와 ⑤는 동사의 목적어로 쓰인 동명사이다.

04 Miu appears[seems] to be happy about not going to school today.로 영작할 수 있다.

05 동명사의 부정은 not[never]+-ing로 나타낸다. (didn't → not)

06 try+-ing는 '시험 삼아 ~해보다'이므로 ③이 적절하다.

07 'forget+to부정사'는 '~할 것을 잊다'이므로 ④가 적절하다.

08 There is no use+-ing는 '~하는 것이 소용없다'이고, be worth+
-ing는 '~할 만한 가치가 있다'의 관용적 표현이다.

09 ⓐ to find → finding ⓒ cry → crying ⓔ to 삭제

10 'have a hard time+-ing'는 '~하는 데 어려움을 겪다'이므로 get을
getting으로 고쳐 쓰면 된다.

11 의미상의 주어를 먼저 쓰고, 부정어를 다음에 써야 한다.

12 동명사의 의미상의 주어는 소유격 또는 목적격으로 하고, 부정은 not
을 동명사 앞에 쓴다.

13 남자가 버스 정류장에서 담배 피는 것을 수치스러워하지 않는 그림으
로, not은 본동사 is를 부정해야 한다.

14 동명사의 부정은 동명사 앞에 not을 쓴다.

15 on+-ing는 '~하자마자'라는 의미의 동명사의 관용적 표현이다.

16 ⓓ와 ⓔ는 진행형으로 쓰인 현재분사이므로 나머지의 첫 글자인 A, E,
P, S를 적절히 넣으면 된다.

17 be used to+-ing는 '~하는 데 익숙하다'이고, 'be used to+동사
원형'은 '~하는 데 사용되다'이다.

18 ② 집(Home)이 간주되는 것이므로 수동형인 considered로 바르게
고쳤다. ③ 접속사 that절에서 주어 역할을 해야 하므로 동명사인
having으로 바르게 고쳤다. ④ 주어가 Teenagers이므로 복수 동사
인 are로 바르게 고쳤다.

19 「ask A for B」는 'A에게 B를 요청하다'의 의미로 주어 자리이므로
asking을 먼저 쓰고 목적어인 a parent or a sibling을 쓴 후 for
advice로 쓰면 된다.

[18~19]

십대들이 집 밖에서 해야 할 많은 일들이 있다. 집은 더 이상
즐거움의 중심으로 간주되지 않는다. 하지만, 그들은 집 밖에서
흥미진진한 생활을 하는 것이 가족 관계가 중요하지 않다는 것을
의미하지 않는다는 것을 명심해야 한다. 해결해야 할 문제가 있을
때, 부모님이나 형제자매에게 조언을 요청하는 것은 그들이 해야
할 필요가 있는 것이다. 가족 구성원과 가까운 관계가 있는 십대
들은 운이 좋다. 왜냐하면 그들은 어떤 조언을 위해서 너무 멀리
갈 필요가 없기 때문이다.

• 어휘 • consider 간주하다 | entertainment 즐거움, 오락 | keep in mind 명
심하다 | unimportant 중요하지 않은 | solve 해결하다 | ask A for B A에게 B
를 요청하다

UNIT 07 단순 시제, 현재완료 시제

1) 습관
2) 진리
3) 사실
4) 의지
5) 시간·조건
6) if
7) 왕래·발착
8) 막 ~했다
9) just
10) already
11) yet
12) ~한 적이 있다
13) ever
14) ~해 오고 있다
15) for
16) since
17) ~해버렸다(그래서 지금은 …하다)

Level 1 Test
p. 48

A 1 does
   2 do
   3 get
   4 has read
   5 did you leave
   6 been

B 1 has seen → saw
   2 been → gone
   3 ago 삭제 (또는 for → since)
   4 will get → get

Level 2 Test
p. 49

01 ②
02 ④
03 ④
04 ② ⑤
05 ridden / rode
06 written
07 since
08 The weather has been sunny for four days.

≫ 해설

01 ②는 현재완료의 '계속' 용법이고, 나머지는 모두 '경험'을 나타내는 용
법이다.

02 현재완료(have/has+p.p.)로 질문했으므로, 대답은 have를 써서 해
야 하는데 내용상 부정의 대답이 알맞다.

03 ⓐ의 when, ⓑ의 ago, ⓓ의 'in+연도', ⓔ의 yesterday는 현재완료
와 같이 쓰일 수 없고 과거 시제와 함께 써야 한다.

04 현재완료는 과거 부사와 쓰일 수 없으므로 the other day를 before
로 바꾸거나, 과거 부사를 그대로 쓰려면 have been을 단순 과거 시
제로 바꾸어야 한다.

05 A의 말에는 현재완료 시제가 쓰였으므로 괄호 안에는 ride의 과거분
사 ridden이 들어가야 한다. B의 말에는 '제주도에 갔을 때'라는 과거
시점이 있으므로 단순 과거 rode로 쓴다. (ride – rode – ridden)

06 프로그램을 만든 것은 이미 완료된 일이므로, 현재완료(have/has+
p.p.)를 쓴다. 따라서 write의 과거분사 written이 알맞다. (나는
Jane이에요. 제 아버지는 컴퓨터 프로그래머예요. 전 아주 어릴 때부
터 컴퓨터에 관심이 있었어요. 저는 이미 몇 개의 프로그램을 만들었
어요.)

07 현재완료 시제와 과거 시점을 연결해 주는 since(~이래로)가 알맞다.

08 4일 동안 날씨가 맑았다는 것을 표현하도록 for 다음에 숫자 기간을 쓰고 시제는 현재완료를 쓴다.

Level 3 Test

p. 50

01 ④	02 ④
03 ③	04 ①
05 ④	06 ④
07 ③	08 ① ④

09 has fought → fought

10 has been interested in / since

11 We haven't received the parcel yet.

12 (1) Yuki hasn't[has not] met Lee Minho.
   (2) Yuki has been to Gyeongju.

≫ 해설

01 왕래·발착 동사는 미래 부사구와 함께 쓰여 현재 시제로 가까운 미래를 나타낼 수 있다.

02 • just(이제 막) 또는 already(이미)가 들어갈 수 있다.
   • 부정문으로 yet(아직)이 알맞다.

03 조건의 부사절에서는 현재 시제가 미래를 대신한다. ③은 미래를, 나머지는 현재를 나타낸다.

04 주어진 문장은 현재완료의 경험 용법이다. ①은 경험, ②와 ③은 완료, ④는 계속, ⑤는 결과 용법이다.

05 when절이 목적절(명사절)로 쓰이면 미래를 나타낼 때 미래 시제를 써야 한다.

06 내용상 독일어를 완전히 익히지 못했다는 것이 자연스러우므로 '아직 ~하지 않았다'라는 의미가 되도록 현재완료 부정문(have not+p.p.)이 알맞다.

07 ⓐ did → has ⓑ will rain → rains ⓒ for → since

08 ① 현재완료는 의문사 when과 함께 쓸 수 없다. (→ When did he got out of prison?) ④ 과거 부사구 In 2018이 있으므로 과거형으로 쓴다. (→ In 2018, they moved to a new house.) ② I haven't seen him since yesterday. ③ Have you ever used this app before? ⑤ She has worked hard to support her family.

09 고인이 된 인물에 대해서는 현재완료 시제를 쓸 수 없다. 과거 시제로 써야 한다.

10 과거의 상태가 현재까지 이어지므로 현재완료를 쓰며, since 다음에는 '주어+과거 동사'가 온다.

11 현재완료 부정문에서 줄임말 haven't+p.p.를 써야 6단어에 맞출 수 있다. 부정문에서 '아직'은 yet으로 나타낸다.

12 경험은 현재완료로 쓴다. 이민호는 만나지 못했고 경주는 가 본 적이 있으므로 각각 부정과 긍정으로 쓰면 된다. has been to는 '가본 적이 있다'이고 has gone to는 '가버렸다'이므로 경험을 나타내는 표현으로는 has been to가 알맞다.

UNIT 08 과거완료 시제, 진행 시제

1) 완료	2) 막 ~했었다
3) 경험	4) ~한 적이 있었다
5) 계속	6) ~해 오고 있었다
7) 결과	8) ~해버렸었다
9) am/are/is+-ing	10) was/were+-ing
11) have/has been+-ing	12) had been+-ing
13) is writing	14) wrote
15) was writing	16) will write
17) will be writing	18) has written
19) has been writing	20) had written
21) had been writing	22) will have written
23) will have been writing	

Level 1 Test

p. 52

A

1 had been		2 had had
3 has spent		4 had seen
5 had worn		

B

1 was having		2 had been chatting
3 has been talking		

Level 2 Test

p. 53

01 ⑤	02 ⑤
03 ①	04 ⑤

05 had spent

06 has been raining

07 (A) had already done his math homework
   (B) hadn't written a diary entry

≫ 해설

01 과거(found)를 기준으로 그 이전의 일은 과거완료(had+p.p.)로 나타낸다.

02 주절의 시제가 과거(couldn't see)이므로 안경을 망가뜨린 그 이전의 상황은 과거완료여야 한다. (미나는 안경을 망가뜨려서 아무것도 잘 볼 수 없었다.)

03 과거 어느 시점부터 현재까지 계속되는 일은 현재완료 진행(have been+-ing)을 쓴다. (A: 이건 뭐니? B: 미국 역사에 관한 책이야. 나는 그것을 지난달부터 읽고 있어.)

04 ⓔ since 뒤에는 과거 시점이, for 뒤에는 기간이 온다.

05 과거보다 이전에 일어난 일이므로 과거완료를 쓴다. 과거완료의 형태는 had+p.p.이고 spend의 과거분사는 spent이다.

06 과거에 시작된 동작이 현재까지 계속되고 있을 때는 '~해 오고 있는 중이다'라는 의미의 현재완료 진행(have/has been+-ing)을 쓴다.

07 (A) 엄마가 온 과거 시점 이전에 수학 숙제를 했으므로 과거완료 긍정문(had+p.p.)이 알맞다.
   (B) 엄마가 온 과거 시점 이전에 일기를 쓰지 않았으므로 과거완료 부정문(had not+p.p.)이 알맞다.

Level 3 Test

p. 54

01 ②　　　　　　　　　02 ①
03 ②　　　　　　　　　04 ②
05 ⑤　　　　　　　　　06 ④
07 ①　　　　　　　　　08 ②
09 ②
10 had finished
11 She failed the test because she had never studied.
12 had been waiting

≫ 해설

01 belong과 같이 소유를 나타내는 동사는 진행형으로 쓰지 않는다.

02 과거(remembered)를 기준으로 그보다 더 먼저 일어났던 일이므로, 과거완료 had said가 알맞다.

03 체스를 해본 적이 없다는 것이 이모를 만난 과거보다 더 이전의 일이므로 과거완료 시제를 써야 한다. 말한 것은 단순 과거 사실이므로 과거 시제로 쓴다.

04 ⓑ 동아리에 가입하기 이전의 과거를 가리키므로 과거완료를 쓴다. (haven't known → hadn't known) ⓒ 현재완료 진행형 have been studying이 알맞다.

05 병원에 간 과거보다 먼저 아팠던 것이므로 과거완료를 쓴다.

06 ⓑ 나가기 전에 확인한 것이므로 과거완료를 써야 한다.

07 지원한 것이 과거이고, 그 전부터 계속 연습해 오고 있었던 것이므로 과거완료 진행형으로 써야 한다.

08 ② 최근에 피곤하게 느껴 왔다는 내용으로 현재완료 진행형(have been feeling)이 되어야 하는데 been이 없다. (→ Recently, I have been feeling really tired.) ① What have you been doing? ② He called her office, but she'd already left. ③ We have visited Philadelphia several times. ④ When the police arrived, the thief had run away.

09 ⓒ 현재까지 기다리고 있는 중이므로 현재완료 진행형인 have been waiting으로 고쳐야 한다. ⓔ 현재완료 시제는 적절하나 nobody는 단수 취급하므로 has taken으로 고쳐야 한다.

10 아빠가 오기 전에 숙제를 이미 끝낸 상태이므로 과거완료가 되어야 한다. (나는 어제 저녁 8시에 숙제를 하기 시작했다. 나는 그것을 9시에 끝마쳤다. 아빠는 9시 30분에 집에 오셨다. 아빠가 집에 오셨을 때, 나는 숙제를 이미 끝마쳤다.)

11 공부를 하지 않은 것이 시험에 떨어진 것보다 먼저 발생한 것이므로 과거완료를 쓴다.

12 팬들은 콘서트가 시작하기 이전부터 계속 기다리고 있었으므로 과거완료에 진행의 의미를 더한 과거완료 진행형을 쓰는 것이 알맞다. (그 콘서트는 오후 3시에 시작하기로 계획되었지만, 몇몇 팬들은 오전 6시부터 모습을 나타내기 시작했다. 오후 1시에는 약 2천 명의 팬들이 모여서 뜨거운 여름 태양 아래에서 기다렸다. 콘서트가 시작될 무렵에는 많은 팬들이 약 7~8시간 동안 줄을 서 있었다.)

Review Test

p. 56

01 ②　　　　　　　　　02 ①
03 ②⑤　　　　　　　　04 ④
05 ④　　　　　　　　　06 ③
07 ④　　　　　　　　　08 ④
09 ⓐ am understanding → understand
10 (A) get　(B) will get

11 We will have arrived at the historic site by the time the sun sets.
12 He built his house with the wood he had cut down.
13 have been reading
14 Have you ever been to London before?
15 had been
16 had been playing / came
17 ②
18 that I had been pursuing

≫ 해설

01 ② since(~ 이래로) 대신에 for(~ 동안)를 쓰는 것이 알맞다. ③ ④ 불변의 진리나 사실은 주절이 과거여도 항상 현재를 쓴다.

02 현재의 동작이나 상태는 현재 시제(look)로 쓴다. / 과거 부사 last night과 함께 과거 시제(prepared)를 쓴다. / 미래의 일은 미래 시제(will)로 쓴다.

03 ⓐ 의문사 when은 단순 시제와 함께 쓰일 수 있다. ⓑ when이 '~할 때'라는 의미의 접속사일 때 시간의 부사절에서는 현재 시제가 미래를 나타낸다.

04 ④ 과거 부사 ago는 과거 시제와 쓰여야 한다. (→ arrived)

05 두 시간 전에 시작된 동작이 현재까지 계속되고 있으므로 현재완료 진행을 쓴다. 주어가 he이므로 has를 쓴 ④가 알맞다.

06 과거완료의 '완료' 용법이 되어야 한다. already는 '완료'를 나타내는 부사이다. (신 선생님은 그 영화를 이미 보았기 때문에 우리와 함께 극장에 가고 싶어 하지 않았다.)

07 핸드폰을 먼저 잃어버렸기 때문에 과거완료를 쓴다.

08 ⓐ는 계속, ⓑ와 ⓕ는 경험, ⓒ와 ⓔ는 완료, ⓓ는 결과의 용법이다.

09 ⓐ 인식 동사 understand는 진행형으로 쓰지 않는다. ⓑ have가 '먹다'의 의미로 쓰일 때는 진행형으로 쓸 수 있다.

10 (A) 접속사 when(~할 때)이 이끄는 시간 부사절에서는 현재 시제가 미래를 뜻한다.
(B) when절이 명사절로 쓰일 때는 미래를 나타낼 때 미래 시제를 써야 한다.

11 해가 질 즈음은 미래로, 지금부터 해서 미래에 완료되는 동작은 미래완료 시제(will have + p.p.)를 쓴다. by the time 다음에는 현재형이 미래의 뜻을 나타낸다.

12 나무를 자른 것이 집을 짓기 전의 일이므로 과거완료를 쓰고, 집을 지은 것은 과거 시제로 나타낸다. 단어 수에 맞게 목적격 관계대명사를 생략한다.

13 30분 전에 시작된 동작이 현재까지 계속되고 있으므로, 현재완료 진행(have been + -ing)을 써서 '~해 오고 있는 중이다'를 표현한다.

14 have gone to(~로 가버리고 없다)는 주로 3인칭 주어와 함께 쓴다. have been to(~에 갔다 왔다)는 2인칭 주어 you와 함께 쓰일 수 있다.

15 과거보다 이전에 일어난 일을 나타낼 때 과거완료를 쓴다. (27살 때, 그는 자신이 학생이었던 학교에서 교사가 되었다.)

16 어머니가 온 과거보다 더 이전부터 계속 게임을 하고 있는 중이었으므로, 과거완료 진행형(had been + -ing)을 쓴다.

17 ⓑ (that) I used가 관계사절이고 주어가 the password이므로 시제에 맞게 became 또는 had become으로 고쳐야 한다. ⓒ 대과거부터 과거까지 동작이 계속 진행된 것이므로 have가 아니라 had로 고쳐야 한다. ⓔ 사역동사 made의 목적격 보어이므로 feel로 고쳐야 한다.

18 비밀번호를 바꿨던 것(과거)보다 목표를 추구해 온 것이 더 먼저 일어났으므로 과거완료 진행형(had been + -ing) 형태로 쓰면 된다.

나는 매일 내 컴퓨터에 비밀번호를 친다. 나는 인스턴트 메시지를 계속 확인한다. 어느 날, 나는 내가 그것을 반복해서 이용해 왔기 때문에, 내가 사용하는 비밀번호가 나의 일부가 되었음을 깨달았다. 나의 비밀번호는 'struckhimout11'이었는데, 내가 비록 누군가를 의도적으로 삼진을 잡는 것에 대해서 항상 생각하지 않았음에도, 나는 야구가 내가 가장 좋아하는 활동이라고 생각하게 되었다. 그것은 내가 살아 있음을 느끼게 해주는 것이었고, 그것은 내가 가장 즐기는 것이었다. 나중에, 나는 내 비밀번호를 내가 <u>추구해 온 목표</u>로 바꿨다. 그것은 나에게 매일 나의 꿈을 기억나게 해주는 것이 되었다.

• 어휘 • instant message 인스턴트 메시지, 쪽지 | realize 깨닫다, 실현하다 | repeatedly 반복해서 | intentionally 의도적으로 | later on 나중에 | goal 목표 | pursue 추구하다 | remind A of B A에게 B를 기억나게 하다

CHAPTER 05
조동사

UNIT 09 조동사(1)

1) be able to
2) 허락
3) may
4) may not
5) can
6) cannot
7) be going to
8) be not going to
9) have/has to
10) don't/doesn't need to
11) ~일 리가 없다
12) ought to
13) ought not to
14) ~하지 않을 수 없다
15) ~하는 것이 당연하다
16) 아무리 ~해도 지나치지 않다
17) …할 때마다 꼭 ~하게 된다
18) ~하는 편이 낫다
19) B 하기보다는 A 하는 편이 낫다
20) suggest
21) insist

Level 1 Test
p. 60

A 1 don't have to
2 have to
3 ought not to

B 1 couldn't help laughing
2 may well
3 cannot[can't] be

Level 2 Test
p. 61

01 ③
02 ②
03 ② ④ ⑤
04 ③

05 He can't[cannot] be a fraud.
06 I won't make a speech in public.
07 (1) He was so angry that he couldn't help shouting.
　(2) He was so angry that he couldn't (help) but shout.
08 It was natural that she be thirsty after running.

》》 해설
01 [보기]와 ③은 추측, ①, ④, ⑤는 가능, ②는 허락을 나타낸다.
02 '~할 필요 없다'는 don't have to로 쓴다.
03 cannot help + -ing = cannot (help) but + 동사원형: ~하지 않을 수 없다
04 ⓑ back then은 과거이므로 have to를 had to로 써야 한다. ⓔ must 다음에 동사원형이 와야 하므로 형용사 afraid 앞에 be를 붙여야 한다.
05 강한 추측 must be(~임에 틀림없다)의 부정은 can't[cannot] be(~일 리가 없다)이다.
06 '~하지 않겠다'는 미래의 부정형은 will not인데, 단어 수를 맞추기 위해서는 줄임말 won't로 써야 한다.
07 cannot help + -ing = cannot (help) but + 동사원형: ~하지 않을 수 없다
08 natural이 있는 문장의 that절 다음에는 '(should)+동사원형'이 와야 한다. 조건에 맞도록 should를 생략하고 동사원형을 쓰면 된다.

Level 3 Test
p. 62

01 ③
02 ②
03 ④
04 ③
05 ①
06 ③
07 ③
08 ④
09 ③
10 must
11 He insisted that I (should) accept his proposal, but I declined.
12 I may as well sleep as watch TV.
13 Parents might well love their children.

》》 해설
01 ③은 '~해도 좋다'는 허락을 나타내고, 나머지는 '~일지도 모른다'는 추측을 나타낸다.
02 • 공손한 표현의 could
　• '~할 수 없었다'는 의미의 can의 부정 과거형 couldn't
03 허락을 묻는 질문 May I ~?에 대한 대답으로는 may와 can 둘 다 가능하다. won't(~하지 않을 것이다)라고 대답하는 것은 어색하다.
04 ⓒ ago가 사용된 과거 시제이므로 has to를 had to로 써야 한다. ⓓ ought to의 부정은 ought not to이다. ⓔ 주어가 3인칭 단수 He이므로 doesn't have to로 바꾸어야 알맞다.
05 급하게 결정하지 말고, 시간을 갖고 문제에 대처하라는 의미이므로 'must not + 동사원형(~해서는 안 된다)'을 쓴다.
06 '~할 필요가 없다'라는 불필요의 의미는 don't have[need] to 또는 need not으로 나타낸다.
07 「suggest, insist, ask + that + 주어 + (should) + 동사원형」
　(ⓐ seeks → (should) seek ⓑ ⓒ is → (should) be)

08 주절에 natural이 있는 문장의 that절에는 '(should)+동사원형'이 와야 한다.

09 '~임에 틀림없다'는 must (be), '~일 리가 없다'는 can't (be)로 표현한다.

10 첫 번째 must는 '~임에 틀림없다'는 강한 추측을 나타내고, 두 번째 must not은 '~해서는 안 된다'는 금지를 나타낸다.

11 insist동사가 있는 문장의 that절 다음에는 '(should)+동사원형'이 와야 한다.

12 may[might] as well A(동사원형) as B: B 하기보다는 A 하는 편이 낫다

13 may[might] well+동사원형: ~하는 것이 당연하다

UNIT 10 조동사(2)

1) ~하고 싶다
2) ~하고 싶지 않다
3) ~하는 것이 좋겠다
4) ~하지 않는 것이 좋겠다
5) ~하는 것이 낫겠다
6) ~하지 않는 것이 낫겠다
7) ~하곤 했다
8) 예전에 ~이었다
9) ~하곤 하지 않았다[예전에 ~이지 않았다]
10) ~하곤 했다
11) should
12) should not
13) may[might]
14) may[might] not
15) must
16) cannot

Level 1 Test
p. 64

A 1 had better take   2 used to sleep
   3 would like to trust

B 1 should have listened   2 must have been
   3 cannot have been   4 might have been

Level 2 Test
p. 65

01 ④   02 ①
03 ⑤   04 ②
05 assemble → assembling
06 I would not like to see you become a musician.
07 She must have been innocent.
08 used to be in shape

≫ 해설

01 would like to+동사원형: ~하고 싶다

02 멋있어 보이고 싶다는 말에 머리 색깔을 바꾸는 것이 좋겠고 그러면 세련되어 보일 것이라고 조언하는 것이 자연스러우므로 'had better+동사원형'(~하는 게 좋겠다)과 'will+동사원형'(~할 것이다)이 적절하다.

03 might는 may의 과거형으로, might[may] have+p.p.는 '~했을지도 모른다'라는 의미이다.

04 ⓐ ought to not → ought not to ⓓ practice → practiced (must have+p.p.: ~였음에 틀림없다)

05 '그는 레고 블록들 조립하는 데 익숙하다'라는 뜻이다. (be used to+

-ing: ~하는 데 익숙하다 / be used to+동사원형: ~하기 위해 사용되다)

06 would like to의 부정문은 'would not like to+동사원형'(~ 하고 싶지 않다)이다.

07 과거 사실에 대한 강한 추측의 의미를 나타내는 must have+p.p.(~였음에 틀림없다)를 쓰면 된다.

08 'used to+동사원형'(~하곤 했다)은 과거에 그랬는데 지금은 더 이상 그렇지 않은 것을 의미한다.

Level 3 Test
p. 66

01 ③   02 ④
03 ①   04 ⑤
05 ④   06 ①
07 ②   08 ②
09 ⑤
10 can't[cannot] have
11 would like to
12 is certain / were attacked
13 Nuclear energy is used to produce electricity.
14 should have been more careful

≫ 해설

01 • have to의 과거형 had to(~해야 했다)가 알맞다.
   • 충고를 나타내는 had better(~하는 게 좋겠다)가 알맞다.

02 'used to+동사원형' 또는 'would+동사원형'은 과거의 습관을 나타낸다.

03 오디션에 합격하지 못했다는 소식을 들었을 때의 반응으로 '연습을 더 많이 했어야 했다'고 말하는 것이 자연스럽다. (should have+p.p.: ~했어야 했다)

04 ⑤ would rather A than B(B 하느니 차라리 A 하는 게 낫다)에서 A와 B는 동사원형으로 써야 한다. (→ read)

05 be used to+-ing: ~하는 데 익숙하다

06 should have+p.p.(~했어야 했다)는 이루지 못한 과거의 일에 대한 후회를 나타낸다.

07 'Ethan은 파티에 대해 잊어버렸음에 틀림없다. 그는 오겠다고 했는데 오지 않았다.'라는 의미가 되어야 자연스러우므로 과거에 대한 강한 추측을 나타내는 must have+p.p.(~였음에 틀림없다)를 쓴다.

08 ⓐ 조동사는 나란히 쓸 수 없다. (will must → will have to) ⓑ must have+p.p.(~했음에 틀림없다)를 써야 한다. (be → been) ⓒ can have+p.p.는 쓰이지 않는다. cannot have+p.p.(~했을 리 없다)만 쓰인다. (can → cannot)

09 '~하지 말았어야 했는데'는 shouldn't[should not] have+p.p.로 쓴다. I shouldn't have yelled[shouted] at you yesterday. I apologize (to you). (또는 I'm[I am] sorry.)로 영작할 수 있다.

10 A의 비행기가 6시간이나 지연되어 A가 항공사에 만족했을 리가 없으므로 can't[cannot] have p.p.를 이용한다.

11 want to = would like to: ~하고 싶다

12 과거 사실에 대한 강한 추측이므로 is certain(확실한)과 과거 동사 were attacked가 알맞다. (그들은 적에 의해 공격 당했음에 틀림없다.)

13 '원자력은 전력 생산에 사용된다.'는 뜻으로 「be used to+동사원형」(~하기 위해 사용되다)으로 써야 한다. be used to+-ing는 '~하는 데 익숙하다'라는 의미이다.

14 여자가 음료를 쏟은 남자에게 '더 조심했어야지'라고 말하는 것이 자연스럽다. (should have+p.p.: ~했어야 했다)

Review Test
p. 68

p. 68

01 ③ ⑤   02 ②
03 ①   04 ③
05 ⑤   06 ②
07 ① ③   08 ② ⑤
09 must
10 ought to not → ought not to
11 I would like to donate all my money to charity.
12 cannot[can't] help
13 There didn't use[used not] to be a stationery store on the corner.
14 I would rather fail than cheat on the test.
15 ⓐ is → (should) be
16 It is important that he should drink water before every meal.
17 ① ②
18 the sound must have reached them through the water

》》 해설

01 borrow(빌리다)를 써서 요청을 의미하는 Can I borrow ~?는 lend(빌려주다)를 써서 Will[Would, Can, Could] you lend ~?로 바꿀 수 있다. '나에게' 빌려주는 것이므로 to me를 쓴다.
02 컴퓨터가 문서를 자동으로 저장하니 저장할 필요가 없다는 의미이므로 'don't have to+동사원형'(~할 필요 없다)이 알맞다.
03 ⓐ had better not 다음에 동사원형이 와야 하므로 to interrupt는 interrupt가 되어야 알맞다.
04 may[might] well+동사원형: ~하는 것이 당연하다
05 may not, must not, should not, ought not to: ~하면 안 된다
06 cannot have+p.p.: ~했을 리가 없다
07 He may[might] have admitted his mistake.로 영작할 수 있다.
08 ⓐ 조동사는 나란히 쓸 수 없다. ⓒ should have+p.p.: ~했어야 했다
09 첫 번째 must는 '~임에 틀림없다'는 강한 추측을 나타내고, 두 번째 must not은 '~해서는 안 된다'는 금지를 나타낸다.
10 ought to의 부정형은 ought not to이다.
11 would like to+동사원형: ~하고 싶다
12 cannot[can't] help+-ing: ~하지 않을 수 없다
13 과거의 상태를 나타내는 there used to be의 부정문은 there didn't use to be 또는 there used not to be이다. (~이 원래 없었는데 지금 있다)
14 would rather+동사원형(A)+than+동사원형(B): B 하느니 차라리 A 하겠다
15 insist의 목적어 역할을 하는 that절에는 '(should)+동사원형'이 와야 한다. (ⓐ 그녀는 그 죄수가 감옥에서 석방되어야 한다고 주장했다. ⓑ 그녀는 지난 여름에 하와이에서 즐거운 시간을 보냈음에 틀림없다. 그녀는 다시 그곳에 가기를 원한다.)
16 important가 있는 문장의 that절에는 '(should)+동사원형'이 와야 한다. 단어 수를 맞추도록 should를 쓴다.
17 ① reach는 타동사로 to를 삭제해야 한다. ② 선행사가 있으므로 which 또는 that으로 고쳐야 한다. ③ fish는 단·복수 동일형이고 여

기서는 them이 적절하다. ④ listen의 주체가 An American Indian 이므로 적절하다. ⑤ 내용상 소리가 도달할 수 있다는 '능력, 가능'을 나타내므로 can은 적절하다.
18 '~이었음에 틀림없다'는 must have+p.p.로 표현하고 '도달하다'는 지문의 reach를 이용하면 된다.

[17~18]

> 일반적으로, 소리는 공기를 통해 귀에 도달한다. 하지만 공기는 소리가 이동하는 유일한 매개체는 아니다. 시끄러운 소음은 물고기를 놀라게 하고 그것들이 재빠르게 도망치게 한다. 그래서 우리는 소리가 물을 통해서 그것들에게 도달했었음에 틀림없다고 결론을 내린다. 아메리카 인디언은 먼 거리의 발소리를 듣기 위해 땅에 귀를 댄다. 왜냐하면 그런 소리들은 땅을 통해 이동할 때 상대적으로 깨끗하기(잘 들리기) 때문이다. 긴 나무로 된 탁자의 한쪽 끝에서 톡톡 두드리는 소리는 귀를 탁자에 대고 있으면 다른 한 쪽 끝에서 확실히 들릴 수 있다. 따라서 우리는 소리가 고체, 액체 또는 기체에 의해 귀에 도달할 수 있다는 것을 안다.

• 어휘 • generally 일반적으로 | medium 매개체 | draw a conclusion 결론을 내리다 | comparatively 상대적으로 | tapping 톡톡 두드리기 | solid 고체 | liquid 액체 | gas 기체

CHAPTER 06
수동태

UNIT
11 조동사, 진행형, 완료형의 수동태

1) be   2) p.p.   3) be
4) p.p.   5) be   6) p.p.
7) being   8) am/is/are   9) was/were
10) been   11) have/has   12) had

Level 1 Test
p. 72

p. 72

A 1 was beaten   2 is held
  3 was worn   4 was rung
  5 threw   6 is being put

B 1 will be sold by my father
  2 aren't playing football
  3 Many boxes have been carried
  4 The furniture was being moved

Level 2 Test
p. 73

p. 73

01 ① ②   02 ④

05 was the Internet invented
06 The flowers are being watered by your kid.
07 A confirmation message will be sent to you.
08 ⓐ A lot of musicals have been composed by him.

》》 해설

01 My brother wrote this fan fiction.의 능동태 문장으로 전환할 수 있다.
02 현재완료의 수동태는 have (not) been+p.p.이다.
03 A picture of him is being taken by her.로 전환할 수 있다.
04 과거완료 수동태는 had been+p.p.이므로 had been completely destroyed로 써야 한다.
05 주어(A group of researchers and scientists at ARPA) 뒤의 invented the Internet을 수동태로 전환한 후(The Internet was invented,) 제목에 맞도록 의문문으로 바꾸어 빈칸을 채우면 된다.
06 진행형의 수동태는 「be동사+being+p.p.」이다.
07 조동사의 수동태는 「조동사+be+p.p.」이다. send A to B는 'A를 B에게 보내다'의 의미이다. will 대신 be going to를 써도 되나 주어진 단어에 going밖에 없으므로 쓸 수 없다.
08 능동태는 현재완료(have+p.p.)가 사용된 ⓐ이다. 현재완료의 수동태는 have/has been+p.p. 형태로 쓴다.

Level 3 Test
p. 74

01 ③   02 ③
03 ④   04 ② ⑤
05 ④   06 ④
07 ②   08 ⑤
09 ⑤
10 has been given
11 The championship has been won by their team.
12 The vet was combing the pony's tail.
13 (1) isn't[is not] liked by
   (2) The villagers don't[do not] like her.
14 Are you being stalked?

》》 해설

01 주어가 동작을 받으므로 수동태가 적절하며, You mother should be told about this problem.의 의문문이다.
02 질문이 현재 진행형이므로 대답도 현재 진행형으로 해야 한다. 진행형의 수동태는 「be동사+being+p.p.」이다.
03 ⓒ 주어가 the party이므로 의문문의 수동태로 써야 한다. ⓐ와 ⓑ는 올바른 수동태 문장이다.
04 The harp was being played by a young Asian boy.로 바꿀 수 있다.
05 The race is going to be canceled because of the rain.으로 영작할 수 있다.
06 They[People] have built a new hotel in the city.의 수동태에서 'by+행위자'를 생략한 문장이다.
07 주어진 수동태 문장에서 불분명한 'by+행위자'가 생략된 것이다. by Monday에서 by는 전치사(~까지)이다.
08 ⓒ finished → be finished ⓔ has suggested → has been suggested

09 ⑤ 진행형의 수동태는 be being+p.p.이므로 is가 필요하다. (→ His painting is being exhibited at the gallery.) ① The carpets have been sold out since this morning. ② The present hasn't been opened yet. ③ Is dinner being prepared by the chef? ④ The castle was built in the 16th century.
10 주어가 The house이고 동사가 give이므로, 수동태 has been given으로 써야 한다.
11 현재완료의 수동태는 have been+p.p.이므로 been을 더하고 won으로 쓴다.
12 was being+p.p.의 형태로 보아 과거 진행형의 수동태임을 알 수 있으므로 능동태도 과거 진행형으로 쓴다.
13 (1)은 주어가 She이고 수동태이므로 isn't[is not] liked by 형태로 쓰고, (2)는 능동태이고 주어가 복수이므로 don't[do not] like 형태로 쓴다.
14 Is someone stalking you? → Someone is stalking you. → You are being stalked (by someone).의 의문문을 만들면 된다.

UNIT 12 여러 가지 수동태

1) 명사/형용사   2) 명사/형용사
3) 명사/형용사   4) to부정사
5) to부정사   6) to부정사
7) 동사원형   8) 동사원형
9) to+동사원형   10) 동사원형/-ing
11) 동사원형/-ing   12) to+동사원형/-ing
13) 나머지 동사구   14) to V

Level 1 Test
p. 76

A 1 was found innocent   2 was told / to leave
   3 is said to be

B 1 어색한 곳 없음   2 was woken up by me
   3 어색한 곳 없음   4 is believed

Level 2 Test
p. 77

01 ⑤   02 ④
03 ⑤   04 ④
05 He is called J for short.
06 is being made fun of by
07 The ground was felt shaking in the area.
08 with

》》 해설

01 목적어 the walls를 수동태의 주어로 써야 한다.
02 지각동사(saw)가 사용된 문장을 수동태로 전환할 때는 목적격 보어에 to를 써서 The monster was seen to come back to him (by the kid).으로 전환한다.
03 ① 주어진 문장의 that절은 목적절이다. ② ⓐ were → was ③ ⓑ의 by them은 일반인 행위자로 생략 가능하다. ④ ⓒ said → was said

04 동사구는 한 덩어리로 인식해서 수동태로 전환한다.

05 We call him J for short.에서 목적격 보어를 주어로 하여 잘못 전환한 것이다.

06 동사구를 수동태로 전환할 때는 전치사에 주의하고, 진행형의 수동태로 be being+p.p. 형태로 쓴다.

07 지각동사가 수동태가 될 때 목적격 보어는 'to+동사원형' 또는 현재분사를 쓰는데 조건에서 8단어로 쓰라고 했으므로 shaking으로 쓰면 된다.

08 ⓐ be filled with: ~로 가득하다 ⓑ be satisfied with: ~에 만족하다 ⓒ be crowded with: ~로 붐비다

Level 3 Test
p. 78

01 ⑤	02 ②
03 ②	04 ④
05 ④	06 ② ⑤
07 ②	08 ⑤
09 ⑤	

10 The singer is said to be planning a comeback.

11 I was asked to sing over and over by the captain.

12 ⓒ am made → was made ① 능동태 → 수동태

13 say that / runs

14 ⓐ many people → by many people

》》 해설

01 「keep+목적어+목적격 보어」와 조동사가 합쳐진 수동태로 「주어(the kitchen)+조동사+be+p.p.+목적격 보어」 형태로 쓰면 된다.

02 사역동사 make가 있는 문장의 수동태는 to를 써서 I was made to wear this stupid hat by my mom.으로 전환할 수 있다.

03 It is believed that the chief has magical powers. 또는 The chief is believed to have magical powers.로 전환할 수 있다.

04 목적격 보어가 to부정사인 5형식의 수동태로 He was expected to answer the questions.로 재배열할 수 있다.

05 ⓐ는 Somebody made a dress for Lynn.(또는 Somebody made Lynn a dress.)의 수동태이고, ⓑ는 물리적 변화이므로 of가 와야 한다.

06 ② the manager → by the manager ⑤ has → has been

07 ⓐ be covered with: ~로 덮여 있다 ⓑ be surprised by[at]: ~에 놀라다 ⓒ be known for: ~로 유명하다

08 ⓐ ask동사의 수동태로 keep이 to keep으로 되어야 한다. ⓑ 시험 결과가 보내지는 것이므로 수동태 will be sent가 되어야 한다.

09 ⑤ 「make+목적어+목적격 보어」의 수동태 구문으로 목적격 보어는 부사가 아니라 형용사여야 한다. (→ Some people are made happy by rain.) ① She has been called a spy. ② He was brought up in Arizona. ③ Everybody was told to be quiet. ④ My daughters have planted orange trees.

10 They say that the singer is planning a comeback.의 수동태인 It is said that the singer is planning a comeback.에서 that절의 주어를 문장의 주어로 전환한 것이다.

11 사역동사 have의 수동태는 유사한 의미의 「be asked to+동사원형」으로 쓴다.

12 ⓒ be+p.p.에서 인칭과 수는 수동태의 주어에, 시제는 능동태의 동사에 일치시킨다. ① 수동태로 문장 전환을 하므로 능동태가 아니라 수동태이다.

13 It is said by them that Lucy runs the biggest restaurant in town. → That Lucy runs the biggest restaurant in town is said (by them). → They say that ~ 으로 전환하면 된다.

14 ⓐ는 Many people have looked up to the scholar.의 수동태이고 ⓑ는 They laughed at the new employee.의 수동태이다.

Review Test
p. 80

01 ③	02 ②
03 ③	04 ⑤
05 ②	06 ① ④
07 ④	08 ②

09 He was elected mayor of Seoul by its residents.

10 ⓐ recording → recorded

11 not allowed to date

12 The house is not going to be sold by him.

13 brought up → was brought up

14 Her dresses were made of the most expensive cloth.

15 (1) is said that this image of Buddha is over 700 years old
    (2) is said to be over 700 years old

16 was asked to vacuum the carpets by Jia

17 how it was made and where it came from

18 ④ ⑤

》》 해설

01 ought to도 조동사이므로 「조동사+be+p.p.」의 형태인 ought to be shared로 써야 한다.

02 내용상 방이 막 청소되었고 현재 깨끗하므로 현재완료 수동태가 적절하다.

03 ⓐ는 has와 by가, ⓑ는 will과 with가 들어간다.

04 목적격 보어(Izzy)는 수동태의 주어가 될 수 없으므로 목적어(our dog)를 주어로 해서 Our dog was named Izzy by my grandfather 로 전환한다.

05 You call this what in English. → This is called what in English (by you).를 의문문으로 바꾸면 된다.

06 ① 사역동사의 수동태이므로 stand → to stand ④ 진행형의 수동태이므로 cleaning → cleaned

07 훌륭한 아이디어가 재사용된 것이므로 수동태 has been reused로 써야 한다.

08 ⓒ make → to make 또는 making ⓔ estimating → estimated

09 명사(mayor)가 목적격 보어로 쓰인 5형식의 수동태이다. 목적격 보어 mayor를 주어로 해서 수동태로 전환할 수 없음에 유의한다.

10 ⓐ 진행형의 수동태는 be being+p.p.이므로 recorded로 써야 한다.

11 사역동사 let의 수동태는 「be allowed to+동사원형」으로 만든다.

12 「be (not) going to+동사원형」의 수동태는 be (not) going to be+p.p.이다.

13 bring up(기르다)과 같은 동사구는 한 덩어리로 인식하여 수동태로 전환한다.

14 주어가 her dresses로 제품이 앞에 왔으므로 물리적 변화를 나타내는 「be made of+재료」를 사용한다.

15 (1) that절을 목적어로 전환한 뒤 가주어-진주어 구문으로 만든다.
    (2) that절의 주어를 문장의 주어로 해서 전환한다.

16 사역동사 have의 수동태는 「be asked to+동사원형」으로 전환한다.

17 간접의문문이며 그것이 만들어진 것이므로 수동태이다. 따라서 시제에 맞게 was를 추가하고 어순에 맞게 how it was made and where it came from으로 쓰면 된다.

18 ⓐ 동물의 뼈나 가죽이 '사용되었다'이므로 수동형이며 be동사가 필요하므로 was used로 고쳐야 한다. ⓑ is가 술어동사이고 이의 주어가 필요하므로 Pick을 Picking 또는 To pick으로 고쳐야 한다. ⓒ very는 원급을 수식하므로 much, still, even, far, a lot, yet와 같은 단어로 고쳐야 한다.

[17~18]

집으로 가져갈 기념품을 선택하기 전에, 그것이 어떻게 만들어졌고 어디서 왔는지 신중히 생각해 보아라. 만약 동물의 뼈나 가죽이 그것을 만드는 데 사용되었다면, 그것을 선반 위에 그냥 두어라. 자연에서 바로 기념품을 집어오는 것은 좋은 생각이 아니다. 야생화는 당신의 책상 위에서보다 야생에서 훨씬 더 아름답다. 대신에, 당신이 방문한 장소에 부정적인 영향을 끼치지 않는 것을 골라라. 지역 주민들에 의해 만들어진 그림이나 공예품은 좋은 예이다.

• 어휘 • souvenir 기념품 | think over 신중히 생각하다 | skin 가죽, 피부 | shelf 선반 | wild flower 야생화 | the wild 야생 | pick out 고르다 | negative 부정적인 | effect 영향, 효과 | local 지역의

CHAPTER 07
관계사

UNIT 13 관계대명사의 역할과 용법

1) who
2) who(m)
3) whose
4) which
5) which
6) that
7) that
8) 뒤
9) comma(,)
10) 접속사
11) 소유
12) 계속적
13) 전치사
14) 최상급
15) thing
16) which
17) that

Level 1 Test
p. 84

A 1 who(m) 또는 that
　 2 which 또는 that
　 3 whom
　 4 what

B 1 what
　 2 that
　 3 that
　 4 what

Level 2 Test
p. 85

01 ② ③ ⑤
02 ② ③ ④

03 ①
04 ① ⑤
05 that
06 Chopin's nocturnes are the classical music pieces which[that] I often listen to.
07 What scared me was his huge dog.

>>> 해설

01 ② ③ 선행사가 사람이고 반복되는 명사가 목적격이면 who(m)과 that 모두 가능하다. ⑤ 목적격 관계대명사는 생략할 수 있다. ④ 전치사 다음에 that을 쓸 수 없다.

02 ②는 명사절을 이끄는 접속사 that이고 ③, ④는 의문사이다.

03 주어 Justin 다음에 '접속사＋주어'가 계속적 용법의 who로 바뀐다.

04 ② ④ 목적격 관계대명사 that ③ 접속사 that ① 소유격 whose가 필요하다. ⑤ 전치사 앞에 that을 쓸 수 없다. (→ whom)

05 • 선행사가 최상급이므로 관계대명사는 주로 that을 쓴다.
　 • 목적절을 이끄는 접속사 that이다.

06 선행사 the classical music pieces가 뒤의 문장에서 목적어 역할을 하므로 관계대명사는 which나 that을 쓴다. 「주어＋동사＋선행사＋관계대명사＋주어＋동사 ～」의 어순으로 쓴다.

07 선행사 the thing을 포함한 관계대명사 what을 넣어야 7단어로 문장을 완성할 수 있다.

Level 3 Test
p. 86

01 ②
02 ③
03 ④
04 ②
05 ① ⑤
06 ①
07 ③ ④ ⑤
08 ①
09 ①
10 What you said made her cry.
11 The shoes which I lent to Judy are my sister's.
12 and it
13 (1) that[which]　(2) what
14 What he made in the kitchen was

>>> 해설

01 • 사물이 선행사일 때 목적격 관계대명사로 which나 that이 알맞다.
　 • 사람이 선행사일 때 목적격 관계대명사로 who(m)이나 that이 알맞다.

02 선행사를 포함한 관계대명사로 '～한 것'이라고 해석되는 what이 알맞다.

03 ④ 내용상 말다툼하는 일이 거의 일어나지 않는다는 뜻이므로 앞 문장 전체를 가리키는 which가 알맞다.

04 • 간접의문문을 이끄는 의문사 what이 적절하다. (그는 내가 무엇을 가장 무서워하는지 물었다.)
　 • 선행사 something을 꾸며주는 관계사절을 이끄는 관계대명사 that이 들어가야 한다. (나는 나의 인생을 더 멋지게 만들 수 있는 새로운 어떤 것을 시도해 볼 것이다.)

05 ① went 다음에 전치사 to가 있어야 관계사 which로 연결될 수 있다. ⑤ 소유격 관계대명사는 「whose＋명사」 또는 「명사＋of which」로 쓴다. which the sleeves → whose sleeves 또는 the sleeves of which

06 that은 앞에 전치사가 있으면 쓸 수 없다.

07 주어진 문장과 ③, ④, ⑤는 주격 관계대명사이고, ①은 It ～ that 강조 용법, ②는 목적절을 이끄는 접속사이다.

08 ① 「the very + 명사」 다음에 관계대명사 that이 와야 하고, 나머지는 선행사가 포함된 관계대명사 what이 알맞다.

08 ① 「the very + 명사」 다음에 관계대명사 that이 와야 하고, 나머지는 선행사가 포함된 관계대명사 what이 알맞다.

09 ① that을 what으로 고쳐야 한다. (→ I don't understand what you said.) ② know the man who is sitting next to you. ③ Choose the character whose name you like. ④ She goes to the school which her father went to. ⑤ The musician who wrote the song is Mexican.

10 선행사가 없으므로 what을, 사역동사 made가 있으므로 목적격 보어에 동사원형을 쓴다.

11 주어가 복수(The shoes)이므로 동사 is는 are가 되어야 한다.

12 계속적 용법의 which는 '접속사 + 대명사'로 바꿀 수 있다. 여기서 which는 앞 문장 전체를 가리킨다.

13 (1) 선행사가 -thing일 때 관계사는 that을 주로 쓴다. (which도 가능) (2) 선행사를 포함한 관계대명사 what이 알맞다.

14 선행사 the thing을 포함한 관계대명사 what을 넣어야 7단어로 쓸 수 있다.

UNIT 14 관계부사, 관계사의 생략

1) where 2) when 3) why
4) how 5) 목적 6) 목적
7) 목적 8) 주 9) be
10) 관계부사

Level 1 Test
p. 88

A 1 which 2 why
   3 when 4 where
   5 How

B 1 how
   2 (1) which[that] / at (2) at (3) where (4) where

Level 2 Test
p. 89

01 ③ 02 ① ③
03 ④ 04 ②
05 He found a bug which[that] was crawling up his leg.
06 ⓐ I will introduce the man (whom[that]) I share my office with. ⓒ This is the furniture (which[that]) you should get rid of. (또는 This is the furniture of which you should get rid.)
07 Nobody knows the reason why she made such a decision.
08 how she would persuade him

》》 해설
01 첫 번째와 세 번째는 앞에 있는 선행사가 뒤 문장에서 부사 역할을 하므로 차례대로 관계부사 when, why가 알맞고, 두 번째는 목적격 관계대명사 that이나 which가 알맞다.
02 ① 주격 관계대명사는 생략할 수 없다. ③ 전치사 바로 뒤의 관계대명사는 생략할 수 없다. ② ④ 목적격 관계대명사는 생략할 수 있다. ⑤

「주격 관계대명사 + be동사」는 같이 생략 가능하다.
03 전치사 on이 있을 때는 목적격 관계대명사 which를 붙여 써야 하고, 전치사 on을 문장 뒤에 쓸 때는 관계대명사 which나 that을 생략할 수 있다. on which는 where로 바꾸어 쓸 수 있다.
04 ⓐ ⓒ 관계부사 when, where 다음에 전치사 on이나 in은 필요 없다.
05 현재분사 앞에 「주격 관계대명사 + be동사」가 생략되어 있다.
06 ⓐ 앞에 the man이 있으므로 목적격 관계대명사 whom이나 that이 알맞고, 이때 생략이 가능하다. ⓒ 전치사 of가 있을 때는 목적격 관계대명사 which를 써야 하고, 전치사 of를 문장 뒤에 쓸 때는 목적격 관계대명사 which나 that을 생략할 수 있다.
07 이유를 나타내는 선행사 the reason과 관계부사 why는 같이 쓸 수도 있고 둘 중 하나를 생략할 수도 있다. 10단어에 맞추려면 같이 써야 한다.
08 단어 수에 맞게 방법을 나타내는 관계부사 how를 써서 연결한다.

Level 3 Test
p. 90

01 ② 02 ④
03 ③ 04 ③
05 ③ 06 ③
07 ⑤ 08 ④
09 ② ④
10 why / that
11 This is the ice cream I am fond of.
12 He has just gotten a package which[that] was sent by his parents.
13 where he is waiting is crowded with people

》》 해설
01 선행사가 시간(the day)이며 뒤의 문장에서 on the day로 부사 역할을 하므로 관계부사 when이 적절하다.
02 ④ 전치사 바로 뒤의 관계대명사는 생략할 수 없다.
03 ③ 앞에 시간을 의미하는 말이 없고 '~할 때'라고 해석되는 접속사이다. 나머지는 시간을 나타내는 선행사와 함께 쓰인 관계부사이다.
04 선행사 the restaurant가 뒤의 문장에서 in the restaurant로 부사 역할을 하므로 계속적 용법의 관계부사 where가 알맞다.
05 ⓒ 선행사 places가 뒤의 문장에서 목적어 역할을 하므로 where는 which[that]가 되어야 알맞다.
06 ③ 주격 관계대명사는 생략할 수 없다.
07 앞에 있는 선행사가 뒤의 문장에서 부사 역할을 하므로 차례대로 관계부사 when, where가 알맞다.
08 ⓑ museum이 you can see ~에서 in the museum으로 부사 역할을 하므로 관계부사 where 또는 in which가 알맞다.
09 ② on when → on 삭제 또는 on which ④ the way 또는 how 삭제
10 첫 번째 빈칸은 the reason이 뒤의 문장에서 for the reason으로 부사 역할을 하므로 why가 알맞고, 두 번째 빈칸은 be동사의 보어절을 이끄는 접속사 that이 알맞다.
11 목적격 관계대명사를 생략하려면 전치사가 문장 뒤로 가야 한다.
12 과거분사(sent)가 뒤에서 앞에 있는 명사를 꾸며줄 때는 「주격 관계대명사 + be동사」가 생략된 것이다.
13 the platform이 뒤의 문장에서 장소 부사 역할을 하므로 관계부사 where로 연결한다.

UNIT 15 복합관계사

1) who(m)ever
2) anyone who(m)
3) no matter who(m)
4) whichever
5) anything that
6) no matter which
7) whatever
8) anything that
9) no matter what
10) whenever
11) at any time when
12) no matter when
13) wherever
14) at any place where
15) no matter where
16) however
17) no matter how

Level 1 Test
p. 92

A 1 whatever 2 Anyone who
   3 However 4 Whenever

B 1 whatever 2 However
   3 Whenever 4 wherever

Level 2 Test
p. 93

01 ④ 02 ①
03 ① ⑤ 04 ③
05 No matter what your idea is
06 (1) However (2) No matter how
07 Whatever
08 Ask who(m)ever you know.

》》 해설

01 '너의 계획이 무엇이든'이라는 의미가 되어야 하므로 ④의 what을 whatever로 고쳐야 한다.

02 '～할 때는 언제든지'라는 뜻으로 시간의 부사절을 이끄는 whenever가 들어가는 것이 자연스럽다. can't help+-ing는 '～하지 않을 수 없다'는 뜻이다. (그녀는 시내에 갈 때마다 옷을 사지 않을 수 없다.)

03 주어진 문장에서 Whoever (= Anyone who)는 명사절에 쓰였고 '누구든지'라는 의미의 복합관계대명사이다. (나의 집을 방문하기를 원하는 사람은 누구든 먼저 전화해야 한다.)

04 ③ whoever가 한 문장 안에 쓰였으므로 명사절을 이끄는 복합관계대명사이고, anyone who로 바꿔 쓸 수 있다. no matter who는 양보의 부사절에 쓰인다.

05 양보의 부사절을 이끄는 no matter what(무엇이든) 다음에 '주어+동사'의 어순이다. (A: 저 사람들을 돕는 방법에 대해 어떤 생각이 있니? B: 아니, 없어. 너의 생각이 무엇이든 나는 그것에 동의할게.)

06 however (= no matter how): 아무리 ～할지라도

07 no matter what (= whatever): 무엇이든 (그의 의견이 무엇이든, 나는 더 이상 신경 쓰지 않아.)

08 '누구에게나'는 who(m)ever를 이용한다. 이때 who(m)ever(목적격)는 everyone who(m)이라는 뜻으로 know의 목적어 역할을 한다.

Level 3 Test
p. 94

01 ④ 02 ① ②
03 ② 04 ① ③
05 ③ 06 ①
07 ③ 08 ① ④
09 Put whatever you want in your shopping cart.
10 Whatever
11 No matter how
12 Do whatever makes you happy.
13 (1) At any time when (2) Whenever

》》 해설

01 '어디서 ～하든지'의 뜻이 되어야 하므로 whatever는 wherever가 되어야 한다.

02 선행사가 장소인 the town과 the place이므로 관계부사 where가 알맞다. where는 in which로 바꿀 수 있다.

03 '무슨 일이 생기더라도'의 의미가 알맞다. ⓔ의 even if는 '비록 ～일지라도'라는 양보의 뜻이다.

04 명사절을 이끄는 복합관계대명사로 whatever (= anything that)가 알맞다. no matter what은 양보의 부사절을 이끌며 '무엇을 ～할지라도'의 뜻이다.

05 Wherever[No matter where] he is, I'll find him.으로 영작할 수 있다. Wherever[No matter where] he is는 양보의 부사절로, 장소의 부사절을 이끄는 at any place where와는 다른 의미이다.

06 '무엇이[무엇을] ～할지라도'라는 의미의 whatever는 no matter what과 바꾸어 쓸 수 있다. (그것[그 시간]이 무엇일지라도, 매일 그것을 지키는 것이 중요하다.)

07 ⓑ whatever → what ⓓ How → However[No matter how]

08 ① '무엇일지라도'이므로 what을 whatever로 고쳐야 한다. ④ '어디를 가든지'이므로 Whatever를 Wherever로 고쳐야 한다.

09 put A in B 구문과 '무엇이든지'에 해당하는 복합관계대명사 whatever를 이용한다.

10 no matter what (= whatever): 무엇이든 (네가 무엇을 하든 난 네 편이다.)

11 양보의 부사절을 이끄는 복합관계부사 however는 no matter how와 바꿔 쓸 수 있다. (네가 아무리 능숙하다고 해도, 안전 규칙을 무시해서는 안 된다.)

12 '～한 것은 무엇이든지'라고 해석되는 복합관계대명사 whatever를 쓴다.

13 every time은 '～할 때마다'의 뜻으로, 시간 부사절을 이끄는 복합관계부사 whenever (= at any time when)와 같은 뜻이다. (난 가끔 너무 피곤해서 기자로서의 일을 그만두고 싶어진다. 이렇게 느낄 때마다 난 내가 어렸을 적에 가졌던 꿈에 대해 생각해 본다. 내 꿈은 훌륭한 기자가 되어 퓰리처상을 타는 것이었다.)

[02~03]

리히터 척도 7.2강도의 지진이 내가 사는 마을[도시]에 일어났다. 지진이 강타하고 난 후, 나는 나의 아들의 유치원으로 달려갔다. 내가 거기에 도착했을 때 건물은 완전히 파괴되어 있었다. 그것은 끔찍해 보였지만 나는 내가 아들에게 말했던 약속을 계속 기억했다. "무슨 일이 생겨도 나는 너를 위해 그곳에 있을 것이다." 나는 나의 아들의 교실이 있었던 곳을 알았고, 그곳으로 갔다.

01 ④ ⑤
02 ⑤
03 ①
04 ② ⑤
05 ③
06 ⑤
07 ②
08 ① ③
09 what
10 some unique flowers
11 (1) They bought a couch whose price was reasonable.
(2) They bought a couch(,) the price of which was reasonable.
12 how he runs the restaurant
13 No matter how good you are
14 (1) when (2) where
15 You can use whatever[whichever] is available.
16 where
17 ⑤
18 Whatever the reason is

≫ 해설

01 ① ② 주격 관계대명사 that ③ 접속사 that ④ 소유격 whose가 들어가야 한다. ⑤ 전치사 바로 뒤에 that을 쓸 수 없다.

02 ⑤는 '무엇'이라고 해석되는 의문사이고 나머지는 '~하는 것'이라고 해석되는 관계대명사이다.

03 them은 반복되는 명사 all the things를 나타내므로 없애야 한다.

04 ② 주격 관계대명사는 생략할 수 없다. ⑤ 전치사 바로 뒤의 관계대명사는 생략할 수 없다.

05 ⓑ 주격이므로 who가 알맞다. (whom → who[that]) ⓒ 주어가 the man이므로 동사는 is가 와야 한다. (are → is) ⓔ 주어가 the girl이므로 동사는 looks가 알맞다. (look → looks)

06 「선행사+주격 관계대명사+be동사+분사구/형용사구」에서 '주격 관계대명사+be동사'는 흔히 생략된다. 여기서는 who were가 생략된 것으로 보면 living은 ⑤의 위치가 알맞다.

07 선행사가 장소(the house)이므로 in which는 장소의 관계부사 where로 바꿀 수 있다. (이것은 내 사촌이 살고 있는 집이다.)

08 양보의 부사절을 이끄는 whatever(= no matter what)가 적절하다.

09 두 문장을 연결하며 앞 문장의 목적어와 뒤 문장의 주어 역할을 동시에 하는 것은 관계대명사 what(= the thing which)이다.

10 계속적 용법의 관계대명사는 '접속사+대명사'로 바꿀 수 있다. which는 앞에 나온 some unique flowers를 가리키며 뒤의 문장에서 목적격으로 쓰였다.

11 소유격 관계대명사는 「명사+of which」나 「whose+명사」의 순서로 쓴다.

12 방법을 나타내는 관계부사는 how이며, the way와 함께 쓰이지 않는다. 5단어로 써야 하므로 how로만 답할 수 있다.

13 6단어여야 하므로 however 대신 no matter how가 필요하고, be동사 are의 보어가 되어야 하므로 내용상 good을 선택하면 된다. well이 형용사이면 '건강한'이란 뜻으로 어울리지 않는다. (네가 아무리 좋을지라도[잘할지라도] 사람들은 자신들의 기분과 필요에 의해서 너를 판단할 것이다.)

14 (1) 선행사가 the days이므로 시간을 나타내는 관계부사 when이 필요하다. (우리 부모님들은 그들이 어렸을 때를 기억할 필요가 있다.)
(2) 선행사가 the park이므로 장소를 나타내는 관계부사 where가 필요하다. (여기는 내가 남자친구를 처음 만났던 공원이다.)

15 '무엇이든'이라는 의미의 복합관계사 whatever[whichever]가 알맞다.

16 도표에서 수치를 나타내는 지점은 뒤의 문장에서 at the point라는 장소 부사의 역할을 한다. 따라서 장소를 나타내는 관계부사 where가 적절하다. (1번 수치에서 균형 상태는 E 지점이다. 거기서 공급 곡선과 수요 곡선이 만난다.)

17 ⓔ 선행사가 복수 명사이고 주격이므로 whom을 who[that]로, disagrees를 disagree로 고쳐야 하고, ⓒ 선행사가 복수 명사이므로 is를 are로 고쳐야 한다. 나머지는 이상이 없다.

18 '무엇일지라도'는 whatever로 표현한다.

[17~18]

> 어떤 연구도 웃음과 통증 감소 사이의 명확한 관련성이 있다는 것을 보여주지 않았다. 하지만, 많은 환자들은 실컷 웃은 후에 고통이 감소했다고 말한다. 어떤 의사들은 그 감소가 피 속에서 생성되는 화학 물질에 관련되어 있을 수도 있다고 주장한다. 또는 단지 그 환자들의 근육이 더 이완되었기 때문에, 또는 그들이 그 순간에 통증을 잊었기 때문에 그 환자들은 더 적은 통증을 느낄 수도 있다. <u>그 이유가 무엇일지라도</u>, '광대는 아스피린과 같다'라는 말에 동의를 하지 않는 사람은 많지 않다.

• 어휘 • relationship 관련성, 관계 | reduction 감소 | decrease 감소하다; 감소 | good laugh 실컷 웃기 | chemical 화학 물질 | relaxed 이완된, 느긋한 | disagree 동의하지 않다

CHAPTER 08
비교 구문

UNIT 16 비교 변화, 원급 이용 비교 구문

1) better
2) best
3) worse
4) worst
5) more
6) most
7) less
8) least
9) later
10) latest
11) latter
12) last
13) farther
14) farthest
15) further
16) furthest
17) senior
18) junior
19) superior
20) inferior
21) prefer
22) B보다는 차라리 A 하겠다
23) ~보다는 오히려
24) ~을 제외하고
25) least
26) most
27) last
28) A는 B만큼 ~하다

29) A는 B만큼 ~하지 않다(=B가 A보다 더 ~하다)
30) 가능한 한 ~한/하게   31) A는 B보다 …배 ~하다

Level 1 Test
p. 100

A 1 junior to   2 prefer / to
   3 superior to

B 1 less / is not   2 as happy as I could
   3 taller than

Level 2 Test
p. 101

01 ③   02 ① ② ④
03 ① ⑤   04 ③
05 good → well
06 sleep twice as much as people
07 hung on to the iron bar as long as she could
08 ⓐ She is junior to me.
   ⓑ I would rather die than surrender.

》》해설
01 ⓐ than 앞에 비교급 easier가 필요하다. ⓑ of 앞에 최상급 the kindest가 알맞다. ⓒ '거리가 먼'이라는 의미일 때는 비교급 farther를 쓴다.
02 주어진 문장은 틀린 부분이 없으며, possible은 「she(주어)+could(can의 과거형)」으로 바꾸어 쓸 수 있다.
03 ① superior는 than 대신에 to를 쓴다. ⑤ slender는 원급이므로 비교급 slenderer 또는 more slender가 되어야 한다.
04 ⓐ me → my hair 또는 mine (비교 대상이 her hair이므로 동일하게 써야 한다.) ⓓ less cuter → cuter 또는 less cute ⓔ possibly → possible
05 play the instrument well이 '그 악기를 잘 연주하다'라는 의미로, good을 부사형 well로 바꾸어야 한다.
06 '배수사+as+원급+as'와 셀 수 없는 '많이'라는 부사 much를 쓰면 된다.
07 as+원급+as+주어+can/could: 가능한 한 ~한/하게 / 과거 시제이므로 could를 쓴다.
08 ⓐ junior는 비교할 때 than 대신 to를 쓴다. (junior to: ~보다 직급[학년]이 낮은) ⓑ would rather A than B: B보다 A 하는 것이 낫다

Level 3 Test
p. 102

01 ④   02 ① ② ③
03 ②   04 ② ④
05 ③ ④   06 ①
07 ②   08 ③ ⑤
09 ③
10 inferior to
11 Technology has made children less creative than they were in the past.
12 (1) twice as well[much] as   (2) worst[least]
13 (1) She tried to laugh as much as possible.
   (2) She tried to laugh as much as she could.

》》해설
01 ⓒ 원급 앞에 배수 표현이 오고, 비교 대상은 My bag이므로 문장 끝에는 Jane이 아니라 Jane's가 와야 한다.
02 ① 과거이므로 can → could ② as ~ as 동등 비교에는 원급 large를 쓴다. ③ worse는 bad의 비교급으로 more를 쓰지 않는다.
03 • superior 뒤에 to를 쓴다.
   • your coat와 비교 대상이 같아야 하므로 소유대명사 mine을 써야 한다.
   • the 다음에 순서를 나타내는 최상급 last가 알맞다. (유제품은 마지막 통로에 있습니다.)
04 '가능한 한 ~한/하게'는 「as+원급+as possible」 또는 「as+원급+as+주어+can[could]」로 표현하며, danced를 수식하는 부사가 필요하다.
05 ③ 스키 장갑과 골프 장갑이 서로 바뀌어야 한다. '골프 장갑이 스키 장갑만큼 비싸지 않다'가 알맞다. ④ 권투 장갑과 야구 장갑이 서로 바뀌어야 한다. '야구 장갑이 권투 장갑보다 덜 비싸다'가 알맞다.
06 senior to: ~보다 직급[학년]이 높은 (그는 나보다 어리지만 회사에서 나보다 직급이 높다.)
07 prefer A to B: B보다 A를 더 좋아하다 (than → to)
08 ③과 ⑤는 내가 더 빨리 대답했다는 것이고, 나머지는 네가 더 빨리 대답했다는 의미이다.
09 ③ 'less ~ than…'은 열등 비교이다. 따라서 thicker가 아니고 원급 thick이 필요하다. (→ This sweater is less thick than that one.) ① She feels superior to her neighbors. ② Make your decision as soon as possible. ④ He did twice as much work as his brother. ⑤ Good looks are not as important as kindness.
10 worse than = inferior to: ~보다 못한
11 열등 비교는 「less+원급+than」으로 표현하므로 as를 than으로 고치고, 「make+목적어+목적격 보어」 구문으로 쓰이므로 creatively는 creative로 고쳐야 한다.
12 (1) 2배 팔린다는 것을 나타내기 위해 「배수사+as+원급+as」를 쓴다. (일요일에는 영화 표가 수요일보다 2배 잘[많이] 팔린다.)
   (2) 가장 안[적게] 팔린다는 것을 나타낼 때는 worst 또는 least를 쓴다. (영화 표가 목요일에 가장 안[적게] 팔린다.)
13 as much as possible = as much as she could(가능한 한 많이)로 나타낸다. 시제가 과거이므로 tried와 일치시킨 she could가 알맞다.

UNIT 17 비교급, 최상급 구문

1) A는 B보다 더 ~하다
2) ~하면 할수록, 점점 더 …하다   3) 점점 더 ~한/하게 되다
4) 둘 중에 더 ~한   5) ~ 때문에 그만큼 더 …한
6) 가장 ~한 … 중 하나   7) ~번째로 …한
8) A는 가장 ~한 …이다
9) A는 다른 어떤 …보다 더 ~하다
10) A는 다른 모든 …보다 더 ~하다
11) A보다 더 ~한 것은 없다   12) A만큼 ~한 것은 없다
13) A보다 더 ~한 것은 없다

Level 1 Test
p. 104

A 1 more delicious than　　2 No other
3 larger than

B 1 the funniest　　2 the more particular
3 There is nothing more precious

Level 2 Test
p. 105

01 ⑤　　　　　　　　　02 ②
03 ③④　　　　　　　　04 ④
05 The less / the higher
06 ⓐ woman → women
07 (1) Nothing is more important than family.
　　(2) Nothing is as important as family.
08 This painting is the more abstract of the two.

≫≫ 해설

01 ⑤ 다이아몬드가 다른 모든 보석만큼 투명하다는 뜻이다. 주어진 문장과 ①~④는 모두 다이아몬드가 보석 중에서 가장 투명하다는 최상급의 의미이다.

02 even은 비교급 앞에서 '훨씬'이라는 강조의 뜻이다. a lot, still, much, far도 마찬가지로 비교급을 강조하는 표현이다. very는 원급을 강조한다. (그의 설명은 나를 훨씬 더 혼란스럽게 만들었다.)

03 ⓐ 비교급 more의 수식은 so가 아니라 much, even, still, far, a lot이 와야 한다. ⓑ serious의 비교급은 more serious이고 강조의 much는 비교급 앞에 올 수 있다.

04 The earlier you start, the sooner you will arrive[get] there.로 영작할 수 있다. 원급 soon 대신 비교급 sooner가 사용되어야 한다.

05 접속사 as는 '~할수록, ~함에 따라, ~ 때문에' 등의 뜻으로 쓰인다. 「the+비교급 ~, the+비교급…」은 '~할수록 더 …해지다'라는 의미이다. (공급이 적어짐에 따라 가격은 더욱 높이 상승한다.)

06 「one of the+최상급+복수 명사」가 되어야 알맞다.

07 부정 주어+비교급 = 부정 주어+원급 = 최상급 (가족보다 더 중요한 것은 없다.)

08 the+비교급+of the two: 둘 중에 더 ~한

Level 3 Test
p. 106

01 ②⑤　　　　　　　　02 ④
03 ③　　　　　　　　　04 ③
05 ②　　　　　　　　　06 ③
07 ③　　　　　　　　　08 ①③④
09 Busan is the second largest city in South Korea.
10 The higher / the lower
11 Five times more
12 growing bigger and bigger

≫≫ 해설

01 The+비교급+주어+동사 ~, the+비교급+주어+동사… = As+주어+동사+비교급 ~, 주어+동사+비교급…: ~하면 할수록, 점점 더 …하다

02 ④ more 대신에 less가 와야 알맞다.

03 ⓐ one of the+최상급+복수 명사: 가장 ~한 … 중 하나 (actress → actresses) ⓑ 비교급+and+비교급: 점점 더 ~한 ⓒ the+비

교급, the+비교급: ~하면 할수록 더욱 ~한 (As cheaper → The cheaper) ⓓ (all) the+비교급+because: ~하기 때문에 더 …한

04 ③ 두 번째로 판매가 적은 해는 2008년이다.

05 ⓐ -ful로 끝나므로 more colorful이다. ⓒ high(높은; 높이)의 비교급은 higher이고, highly(매우)의 비교급은 more highly이다.

06 the+비교급+of the two: 둘 중에서 더 ~한

07 ③ 「one of the+최상급+복수 명사」로 쓰이므로 thing이 아닌 things가 필요하다. (→ One of the most important things in life is hope.) ① Nothing is more precious than freedom. ② Things are getting more and more expensive. ④ The more you know, the less you need to say. ⑤ Saudi Arabia produces more oil than any other country.

08 ② ⓐ '너보다 소중한 것은 없다' ⑤ ⓑ → As people have more, they want more.

09 「the+서수+최상급」 표현으로 larger를 largest로 바꾸고, 도시 이름으로 시작한다.

10 The+비교급+주어+동사 ~, the+비교급+주어+동사: ~ 하면 할수록 더욱 …하다 (가격이 높으면 높을수록 수요는 더 낮아진다.)

11 「배수사+원급/비교급」으로 표현한다.

12 grow+비교급+and+비교급: 점점 더 ~하게 되다 (전자책 판매량이 점점 더 커지고 있다.)

Review Test
p. 108

01 ①　　　　　　　　　02 ③
03 ①　　　　　　　　　04 ②
05 ⑤　　　　　　　　　06 ④
07 ①②　　　　　　　　08 ④
09 (1) I sat down as low as I could to hide.
　　(2) I sat down as low as possible to hide.
10 as flat as
11 becoming more and more serious
12 is the wider of the two
13 Food is not as important as books
14 The harder / the better
15 less popular than any other food
16 (1) less popular than　(2) more popular than
17 ②
18 there was nothing more valuable than intelligence

≫≫ 해설

01 A ~ not as[so]+원급+as B = B ~ 비교급+than A: A는 B만큼 ~하지 않다 = B가 A보다 더 ~하다

02 ③ prefer A to B: B보다 A를 더 좋아하다

03 「the+비교급, the+비교급」은 '~하면 할수록 더 …하다'의 뜻이므로, 접속사 as를 써서 바꾸면 ①과 같은 뜻이 된다. (가격이 낮아질수록, 사람들은 더 많이 살 것이다. 가격이 높아질수록 사람들은 더 적게 살 것이다.)

04 최상급+of+복수 명사: ~ 중에 가장 …하다

05 비교급 앞에 쓰인 much, even, still, far, a lot은 '훨씬'이라는 뜻으로 강조를 위해 쓰인다. (사고는 훨씬 더 심각할 뻔 했다. 다행히 아무도 다치지 않았다.)

06 ① There is nothing I like more than ~은 '~보다 내가 더 좋아하는 것은 없다'라는 뜻으로 가장 좋아하는 것을 말할 때 쓰는 표현이

다. ④는 '나는 다른 것만큼 달리기를 좋아한다'는 의미이다.

07 ① metals → metal ② → Mary reads as many books as Jane.

08 ⓑ can → could ⓒ more and more cold → colder and colder ⓓ more worse → worse ⓔ she is → she does

09 as+원급+as possible = as+원급+as+주어+can/could: 가능한 한 ~한/하게 (나는 숨으려고 가능한 한 낮게 앉았다.)

10 as+원급+as~: ~처럼 …한 (flat: 평평한, 납작한)

11 become/get/grow+비교급+and+비교급: 점점 더 ~해지다 / is가 있으므로 진행형으로 becoming이 알맞다. / more serious and more serious가 아니라 more and more serious 로 쓰는 것에 주의한다.

12 「the+비교급+of the two」(둘 중에서 더 ~한) 구문이다. wide의 비교급은 wider이다.

13 비교급을 동등 비교의 부정문으로 바꾸는 문제이다. (B ~ 비교급+than A = A ~ not as[so] 원급+as+B: A는 B만큼 ~하지 않다)

14 '~하면 할수록 더 …하다'라는 뜻의 「the+비교급, the+비교급」 구문이다. 그러므로 비교급이 들어가야 한다.

15 the most와 상반되는 '가장 ~하지 않은'의 의미로 the least를 쓴다. 「비교급+than any other+단수 명사」는 최상급의 의미를 나타낸다.

16 (1) 열등 비교 less than: ~보다 덜 …한
   (2) 우등 비교 more than: ~보다 더 …한

17 ⓑ 완전한 구조의 문장이 이어지므로 접속사 that으로 고쳐야 한다. ⓒ 「one of the+최상급+복수 명사」로 쓰이므로 things로 고쳐야 한다.

18 'there+be동사' 구문과 비교급 구문을 이용하여 완성한다.

[17~18]

Clara가 어렸을 때, 그녀의 선생님인 David Mills는 자신의 학생들에게 우유를 많이 마시라고 권하곤 했다. 왜 그런지 모르겠지만, 그는 우유가 지능을 향상시킨다고 믿었다. 그에게, <u>지능보다 더 가치 있는 것은 없었다.</u> 가끔 Clara는 그에게 묻곤 했다. "Mills 선생님, 지능이 뭐예요?" 매번, 그는 다른 방식으로 대답하곤 했다. "지능은 네 여동생의 첫 단어지." "지능은 인생에서 가장 위대한 것들 중 하나지." 또는 "지능은 오늘 아침 네가 도덕 시간에 물어본 질문이란다." 선생님의 대답은 그녀를 미치게 만들곤 했지만, 20년이 지난 지금, 그녀는 Mills 선생님이 그렇게 말했던 이유에 대해 생각해보는 것이 재미있다고 생각한다.

• 어휘 • encourage 권하다, 격려하다 | pupil 학생 | somehow 왜 그런지 (모르겠지만) | enhance 향상시키다 | valuable 가치 있는 | intelligence 지능 | ethics 도덕, 윤리 | response 대답, 반응 | drive ~ crazy ~을 미치게 하다

CHAPTER 09
분사

UNIT 18 분사

1) -ing	2) 형용사
3) 진행	4) -ed
5) 형용사	6) 완료
7) 수동	8) 지루하게 하는
9) 지루해하는	10) 흥분시키는
11) 흥분한	12) 놀라게 하는
13) 놀란	14) 충격을 주는
15) 충격을 받은	16) 실망시키는
17) 실망한	18) 만족시키는
19) 만족한	20) 기쁘게 하는
21) 기쁜	22) 짜증나게 하는
23) 짜증 난	24) 관심을 갖게 하는
25) 관심 있는	26) 놀라운
27) 놀란	28) 감동적인
29) 감동 받은	30) 무섭게 하는
31) 무서워하는	32) 명사
33) 보어	34) 진행
35) 목적어	

Level 1 Test
p. 112

A 1 boring   2 hidden
   3 written   4 crying
   5 interesting

B 1 build → built   2 run → running
   3 spoken → speaking   4 writing → written

Level 2 Test
p. 113

01 ②   02 ③
03 ⑤   04 ②

05 Look at the kites flying in the sky.
06 She gave a piece of candy to the crying child.
07 surprising → surprised
08 (1) tiring   (2) tired

》》 해설

01 '떨어진 나뭇잎'이므로 빈칸에 알맞은 것은 fall의 과거분사 fallen이다.

02 주어진 문장과 ③은 현재분사이고, ①, ②, ④, ⑤는 동명사이다.

03 영작하면 I know the man standing in line.이 된다. 따라서 쓸 수 없는 말은 stood이다.

04 ⓐ left → leaving ⓓ disappointed → disappointing

05 '하늘에서 날고 있는 연들'이므로 현재분사로 쓴다.

06 아이가 울고 있는 것이므로 능동의 의미를 갖는 현재분사 crying으로 수식한다. 분사가 혼자 명사를 수식할 때는 형용사처럼 앞에서 수식한다.

07 주어인 She가 감사 카드에 의해 놀란 것이므로 수동의 의미를 갖는 과거분사 surprised가 되어야 한다.

08 (1) 클래식 공연이 '피곤하게 한' 것이므로 능동의 의미를 갖는 현재분사 tiring이 알맞다.
   (2) 클래식 공연 때문에 주어인 I가 '피곤해진' 것이므로 수동의 의미를 갖는 과거분사 tired가 알맞다.

Level 3 Test
p. 114

01 ②　　　　　　　　　　02 ③
03 ⑤　　　　　　　　　　04 ③⑤
05 ④　　　　　　　　　　06 ②
07 ③　　　　　　　　　　08 ④
09 ②
10 The singer surrounded by his fans seems annoyed.
11 damaging → damaged
12 I'm afraid of barking dogs.
13 boring / bored
14 are excited about[by]

≫ 해설

01 'Dorothy라는 이름의 한 좋은 이웃이 있다.'라는 의미이므로 빈칸에는 수동의 의미를 나타내는 과거분사 named(이름 지어진)가 알맞다.

02 '구르는 돌에는 이끼가 끼지 않는다.'라는 의미이므로 빈칸에는 rolling이 알맞다.

03 • '물에 빠진 사람은 지푸라기라도 잡는다.'라는 뜻이므로 빈칸에는 drowning이 알맞다.
   • '엎질러진 우유를 보고 울지 마라.'라는 뜻이므로 빈칸에는 과거분사인 spilled가 알맞다.

04 ③ satisfying → satisfied ⑤ confused → confusing

05 책은 영어로 쓰여진 것이므로 writing은 과거분사 written으로 고쳐야 한다.

06 ② 현재분사 ①③④⑤ 동명사

07 ⓒ bending → bent ⓓ publishing → published

08 '잠자고 있는 사자'이므로 현재분사인 sleeping을 사용해서 Don't wake a sleeping lion.이라고 한다.

09 ② a bird가 앉아 있는 주체이므로 sat이 아니라 sitting이 필요하다. (→ I saw a bird sitting on my window.) ① Everybody was moved by his speech. ③ The girl walking her dog waved at me. ④ The speed of the truck was frightening. ⑤ She likes music composed by Beethoven.

10 singer가 둘러싸인 것으로 surrounded로, seem은 본동사이므로 seems로, 가수가 짜증 나진 것이므로 annoyed로 변형해서 완성하면 된다.

11 지붕이 폭풍우로 망가진 것이므로 damaging은 damaged가 되어야 한다.

12 '짖고 있는'이라는 진행의 의미를 갖는 현재분사 barking이 명사(dogs) 앞에서 수식하도록 배열한다.

13 강의는 '지루하게 하는' 것이므로 능동의 현재분사 boring을 쓰고, 학생들은 '지루해진' 것이므로 수동의 과거분사 bored를 쓴다.

14 사람들이 불꽃놀이에 '흥분한' 것이므로 수동의 과거분사 excited를 쓴다. be excited 뒤에는 전치사 about이나 by가 온다.

UNIT 19 분사구문

1) 시간	2) 이유	3) 조건
4) 양보	5) 동시 동작	6) 연속 동작
7) 주어	8) 주절	9) 비인칭
10) 주어	11) 일반인	12) 능동
13) 수동		

Level 1 Test
p. 116

A　1　ⓑ　　　　　　　　2　ⓐ
　　3　ⓓ　　　　　　　　4　ⓒ

B　1　Not having received　2　Having found
　　3　with the engine running

Level 2 Test
p. 117

01 ②　　　　　　　　　　02 ③
03 ②　　　　　　　　　　04 ①
05 playing soccer
06 Because[As, Since] the last subway had already left
07 with his legs crossed
08 (Being) Satisfied with the results

≫ 해설

01 주절의 주어와 분사구문의 주체가 같은 부정의 분사구문은 'not+-ing'로 표현한다.

02 부사절이 주절(과거)보다 앞선 시제(had+p.p.)이므로 'having+p.p.' 형태로 써야 한다.

03 부사절을 이용하여 If we judge from his uniform, he must be a policeman[police officer]. 또는 비인칭 독립분사구문으로 Judging from his uniform, ~로 영작할 수 있다.

04 ⓒ Knowing not → Not knowing ⓓ Having losing → Having lost

05 접속사를 지우고, 주어도 같으므로 지우고 전환하면 being playing soccer가 되는데 빈칸이 두 개이므로 being도 생략해야 한다.

06 형태(having already left)로 보아 완료 분사구문이며, 주어(The last subway)가 남아 있으므로 이유의 접속사를 덧붙여 부사절로 전환하면 된다.

07 「with+목적어+분사」에서 다리가 꼬여지는 수동의 의미이므로 with his legs crossed로 쓰면 된다.

08 be satisfied with가 '~에 만족하다'의 뜻이며, Because[As, Since] she was satisfied with the results의 분사구문은 (Being) Satisfied with the results이다.

Level 3 Test
p. 118

01 ①③　　　　　　　　　02 ②
03 ④　　　　　　　　　　04 ③⑤
05 ②　　　　　　　　　　06 ②
07 ③　　　　　　　　　　08 ⑤
09 Strictly speaking, your answer is not correct[right].

10 ⓐ Taken → Having taken
11 Not having met her before
12 having been stolen

≫ 해설

01 분사구문의 주어가 없는 것으로 보아, 주절에는 주절의 행위와 '다락방에 들어가는 것'(entering the attic)을 둘 다 할 수 있는 주어가 와야 한다. ④의 a black cat은 자고 있는 동시에 다락방에 들어갈 수 없으므로 적절하지 않다.

02 독립분사구문으로 주어를 써야 한다. (날씨가 맑아서 우리는 드라이브를 했다.)

03 ⓐ Playing ⓑ Not feeling ⓒ Running ⓓ Changing ⓔ Riding

04 관용적으로 쓰이는 비인칭 독립분사구문으로 ②는 Strictly speaking으로, ⑤는 Roughly speaking으로 써야 한다.

05 아파서 누워 있던 사실이 주절보다 먼저 일어났으므로 완료 분사구문으로 써야 한다. 즉, Because[As, Since] she had been sick ∼의 분사구문으로 Having been sick ∼으로 써야 한다.

06 ① Though → Because[As, Since] ③ As → Though ④ has not → doesn't have ⑤ unable → was unable

07 ⓑ Praising → Praised ⓒ Having not → Not having ⓓ Written → It[The note] being written

08 ⑤ 아기가 홀로 남겨진 것이므로 leaving이 아니라 left가 필요하다. (→ Left alone, the baby began to cry.) When the baby was left alone ∼의 분사구문이다. ① Frankly speaking, you are wrong. ② Being sick, she stayed at home. ③ She kept talking with her eyes blinking. ④ Not having any money, he skipped lunch.

09 조건 1과 조건 2에 부합하는 것은 분사구문이며, '엄격히 말해서'는 비인칭 독립분사구문으로 Strictly speaking으로 표현할 수 있다.

10 버스를 탄 것이 먼저이고 능동이므로 완료 분사구문 형태인 Having taken으로 써야 한다.

11 Because[As, Since] he had not met her before를 분사구문으로 고쳐 쓰면 조건에 맞는 답안이 된다.

12 Because[As, Since] my bike was stolen yesterday의 분사구문으로 시제가 앞선 완료 분사구문이면서 주어가 다른 독립분사구문으로 써야 한다.

Review Test

p. 120

01 ⑤	02 ④
03 ②	04 ③
05 ①	06 ②
07 ④	08 ④
09 ② ⑤	10 ④

11 He got on the waiting bus.
12 wounded / were carried
13 I was amazed by his success.
14 Animated movies made in Korea are very interesting.
15 with her dog sitting on her lap
16 (A) Opening (B) covered (C) fallen
17 ⓑ Being our dinner → Our dinner being
18 (1번) 같은 → 다른 / (마지막 예문) being → having been
19 ④
20 Experiencing success in achieving your goals

≫ 해설

01 '깨진 창문'이므로 빈칸에는 과거분사 broken이 알맞다.

02 '호수에서 수영하는 많은 백조들'이라는 뜻이므로 swum은 swimming이 되어야 한다.

03 ② 동명사 ① ③ ④ ⑤ 현재분사

04 She is wearing blue jeans made in Indonesia.로 영작할 수 있다. 인도네시아에서 만들어진 것이므로 과거분사 made를 써야 한다.

05 첫 번째는 질문이 선생님을 '당황하게 한' 것이므로 현재분사를 쓰고, 두 번째는 질문에 의해 선생님이 당황한 것이므로 과거분사를 쓴다.

06 각각 Because[As, Since] I didn't know what to say와 Because[As, Since] he lives in Mexico의 분사구문으로 ②가 적절하다.

07 ④ as he thought ∼의 분사구문으로 thought를 thinking으로 써야 하고 그 앞에 콤마를 써야 한다. ③은 while he was eating a hamburger의 분사구문으로 옳다.

08 ④는 knowing이 적절하며 나머지는 Being[being]이 알맞다.

09 Because[As, Since] I was confused의 분사구문으로 Being confused가 옳으며, 「ask+목적어+to+동사원형」으로 쓰므로 to explain으로 써야 한다.

10 '어젯밤에 늦게 잠자리에 들어서 나는 오늘 아침에 늦잠을 자고 싶었다.'라는 의미가 되어야 자연스럽다. 잠자리에 든 것이 앞선 시제이므로 완료 분사구문 형태로 쓴다. 의미상 not은 쓰지 않아야 한다.

11 버스가 '기다리고 있었던' 것이므로 능동과 진행의 의미를 갖는 현재분사 waiting이 명사(bus) 앞에서 수식하는 구조로 배열한다.

12 첫 번째 빈칸에는 '부상당한'이라는 수동의 의미를 나타내는 과거분사 wounded가 들어가야 하고, 두 번째 빈칸에는 문장의 본동사로서 수동태 과거형이 사용되어야 한다.

13 '(사람이) 놀란'이라고 할 때는 과거분사 amazed를 쓴다.

14 '한국에서 만든'이라는 의미의 분사구 made in Korea가 명사(animated movies) 뒤에서 수식하는 구조이다. 주어는 복수 명사인 animated movies이므로 be동사 are를 쓴다.

15 「with+목적어+분사」 순으로 쓰면 된다. (Jamila는 그녀의 강아지가 무릎 위에 앉아 있는 상태로 인터넷 서핑을 하고 있었다.)

16 (A) As[When] she opened the window의 분사구문이다.
   (B) 주체와 수동의 관계이므로 과거분사를 써야 한다.
   (C) '쓰러진' 나무라는 의미로 완료의 의미를 갖는 과거분사 fallen이 적절하다.

17 As[After] our dinner was over의 분사구문으로, 주어가 다르므로 Our dinner being over로 써야 맞다.

18 부사절의 주어와 주절의 주어가 다른 경우에 전환할 때이다. / 예문에서 부사절이 앞선 시제이므로 완료 분사구문(having+p.p.)으로 써야 한다.

19 ④ 흐름에 맞는 접속사 If와, 주절의 주어 you 그리고 시제에 맞게 fail을 써서 부사절로 전환할 수 있다. ① 명사가 목적어로 왔으므로 전치사 during이 적절하고 접속사 while은 어울리지 않는다. ② gain과 병렬 구조를 이루므로 grow는 옳은 표현이다. ③ 「감각동사+형용사」로 사용되므로 happy는 옳은 표현이다. ⑤ Knowing은 주어 자리이므로 현재분사가 아니라 동명사로 쓰였다.

20 주절의 주어와 같으므로 접속사와 주어를 지우고 동사에 -ing를 붙여서 분사구문으로 전환하면 된다.

진정한 성공은 그 과정에서 많은 작은 성공으로 구성되어 있다. 청소년기 동안 성공을 경험하는 것은 네가 자신감을 얻고 한 개인으로서 성장하는 데 도움이 된다. 네가 목표를 달성하는 데 성공을 경험할 때, 너는 자신을 행복하게 느끼기 시작할 것이다. 너는 새로운 목표를 설정하고 새로운 것들을 시도하고 싶어 할 것이다. 그러나 네가 목표에 이르지 못하는 때가 있을 수도 있다. 만약 목표를 이루는 데 실패한다면, 무엇이 잘못되었는지 밝혀내려고 애써라. 네가 왜 실패했고, 그 실패로부터 배운 것을 아는 것은 네가 다음 번에 성공할 가능성을 향상시켜 줄 것이다.

• 어휘 • consist of ~로 구성되다 | along the way 그 과정에서 | adolescence 청소년기 | gain 얻다 | confidence 자신감 | individual 개인 | achieve 달성하다 | feel like -ing ~하고 싶다 | find out 알아내다 | failure 실패 | improve 향상시키다

CHAPTER 10
접속사

UNIT 20 등위 접속사, 상관 접속사, 종속 접속사

1) and
2) but
3) or
4) both A and B
5) either A or B
6) not A but B
7) neither A nor B
8) not only
9) but also
10) as well as
11) that[That]
12) whether[Whether]
13) if

Level 1 Test
p. 124

A 1 and
   2 can't
   3 or
   4 but
   5 eating fruit
   6 if

B 1 either → neither (또는 nor → or)
   2 that → if 또는 whether
   3 if → that
   4 are → is

Level 2 Test
p. 125

01 ④
02 ⑤
03 ④
04 ①
05 Not only / but also / are
06 The plan has both merits and demerits.
07 ⓐ that → if[whether] ⓑ or → but

08 It is natural that a warmhearted person should be loved by everyone.

》》 해설

01 ④ not only A but also B는 B에 동사를 일치시킨다. (play → plays)

02 you have made the right decision은 think의 목적어 역할을 하므로 목적절을 이끌 수 있는 접속사 that이 필요하다.

03 ⓒ 주어가 3인칭 단수이므로 중간에 상관 접속사가 있어도 동사는 주어에 일치시킨다. (smoke nor drink → smokes nor drinks)
ⓓ them이 복수이므로 동사는 are이다. (is → are)

04 not only A but also B = B as well as A: A뿐만 아니라 B도 (그는 스위스뿐만 아니라 체코에도 다녀온 적이 있다.)

05 not only A but also B에서 동사는 B에 일치시킨다.

06 both A and B(A와 B 둘 다)를 쓰면 된다.

07 ⓐ if[whether]: ~인지 (아닌지) ⓑ not A but B: A가 아니라 B

08 that절이 주어로 쓰이는 경우 주어 자리에 가주어 it을 쓰고 that절을 문장 뒤로 보낼 수 있다.

Level 3 Test
p. 126

01 ②
02 ② ⑤
03 ②
04 ② ⑤
05 ②
06 ② ⑤
07 ⑤
08 ③
09 ⑤
10 Whether or not we will go to Iceland depends on the cost.
11 that
12 as well as
13 Neither Bill nor Sue was able to solve
14 The knight wonders if the princess will defeat the dragon.

》》 해설

01 ⓐ neither A nor B는 B에 수를 일치시키므로 am은 is가 되어야 한다. ⓒ B as well as A는 B에 수를 일치시키므로 cherish는 cherishes가 되어야 한다.

02 ⓐ or ⓑ and ⓒ but ⓓ or ⓔ but

03 ② 관계대명사 ① ③ ④ ⑤ 명사절을 이끄는 접속사

04 '~인지 아닌지'는 if 또는 whether를 쓰며, whether만 or not과 붙여 쓸 수 있다. ② 접속사를 쓰지 않아도 되나 우리말과 일치하지 않는다.

05 B as well as A는 B에 수 일치하므로 ②에는 am이 들어가야 하고 나머지에는 are가 들어가야 한다.

06 ② ⑤ 접속사 ① 지시대명사 ③ 관계대명사 ④ 지시형용사

07 neither ~ or, either ~ and는 알맞은 짝의 상관 접속사가 아니다.

08 ⓒ Not only A but also B는 B에 동사를 일치시키므로 are는 am이 되어야 한다. ⓓ neither A nor B는 B에 동사를 일치시키므로 is는 are가 되어야 한다.

09 ⑤ either A or B는 B에 수를 일치시킨다. Lindsay는 your friend의 동격이므로 were를 was로 써야 한다. ① are → is ④ are → am

10 '~인지 아닌지'는 whether 또는 if로 표현하는데 세 번째 단어가 부정어여야 하므로 not을 넣어 Whether or not으로 완성하면 된다. whether 뒤에는 바로 or not을 쓸 수 있지만 if 뒤에는 쓸 수 없다.

11 '나는 그것[종교]이 희망을 주기 때문에 사람들이 종교를 필요로 한다고 생각한다.'라는 의미가 되어야 자연스러우므로 빈칸에는 that이 알맞다.

12 not only A but also B = B as well as A: A뿐 아니라 B도

13 neither A nor B: A도 B도 ~ 아닌

14 if가 명사절을 이끌 때는 미래형 동사를 써야 한다.

21 UNIT 종속 접속사

1) when 2) while
3) as 4) since
5) after 6) before
7) until 8) as soon as
9) because 10) since
11) as 12) if
13) unless 14) though
15) although 16) even though
17) even if 18) so that
19) so 20) that
21) such 22) that
23) ~하기 때문에 24) ~하는 한편[반면]
25) ~하기 때문에 26) 명사
27) 부사 28) 명사
29) 부사

Level 1 Test
p. 128

A 1 until 2 Since
   3 because of 4 will attend
   5 waste 6 will visit

B 1 그는 내가 그 수수께끼를 풀 수 있도록 나를 도왔다.
   2 우리는 너무 늦게 일어나서 그 항공편을 놓쳤다.
   3 나는 민수가 언제 여기 도착할지 알고 싶다.
   4 네가 시내로 갈 때 차를 가져가지 마.

Level 2 Test
p. 129

01 ② 02 ②
03 ⑤ 04 ①
05 ⓐ will pass → passes 06 unless
07 Although the man apologized to his wife / she didn't forgive him
08 The machine was so complicated that I couldn't repair it.

≫ 해설

01 주어진 문장과 ②는 '~하면서'라는 의미로 동시 상황을 나타낸다. ① ⑤ ~하는 대로 ③ ~로서 ④ ~하기 때문에

02 although는 양보의 부사절을 이끌며, '비록 ~하지만'의 뜻이다. (비록 나는 기진맥진했지만 잠을 잘 수 없었다.)

03 '돈이 없기 때문에 돈을 빌려줄 수 없다'는 의미가 되어야 자연스러우므로 이유를 나타내는 since가 알맞다.

04 ⓐ ⓑ ~하는 동안 ⓒ ~이기는 하지만 ⓓ ⓔ 잠깐, 잠시(명사)

05 ⓐ 시간과 조건의 부사절에서는 현재 시제가 미래를 나타낸다.

06 if ~ not은 unless ~로 바꾸어 쓸 수 있다. (더 이상 질문이 없으시면 줌 회의를 끝내겠습니다.)

07 although(비록 ~일지라도)는 양보의 부사절을 이끌며 역접 관계의 but을 대신해서 쓰일 수 있다. (그 남자가 부인에게 사과했지만 그녀는 그를 용서하지 않았다.)

08 so ~ that...: 너무 ~해서 …하다

Level 3 Test
p. 130

01 ① 02 ②
03 ④ 04 ③
05 ③ 06 ①
07 ④ ⑤ 08 ①
09 ⓐ in order to → in order that 또는 so that ⓑ can → could
10 Shouldn't we wait until Jenny comes here?
11 Would you cut this sandwich in half for me so that I can share it with my friend?
12 While Daphne is shy, Roxy is energetic.
13 (1) too young to marry me
   (2) so young that you can't[cannot] marry me

≫ 해설

01 '~하기 때문에, ~함에 따라'의 뜻을 나타내는 as가 들어가야 한다.

02 ②는 '~하기 때문에'이고, 나머지는 모두 '~할 때'이다.

03 '그들이 마지막으로 연락한 지 몇 년이 지났다.'는 뜻이 되어야 하므로 as가 아니라 since가 알맞다.

04 전치사인 despite 다음에는 명사 또는 명사구만 나올 수 있다.

05 시간의 부사절에서는 미래를 표현할 때 현재 시제를 쓴다.

06 • so as to + 동사원형: ~하기 위해
   • so that ~: ~하기 위해

07 so ~ that...: 너무 ~해서 …하다 ④ so: 그래서(결과의 부사절을 이끄는 접속사) ⑤ too ~ to...: 너무 ~해서 …할 수 없다

08 though는 양보의 부사절을 이끌며, '비록 ~일지라도'의 뜻이다. (• 그는 비록 늦었지만 서두르지 않았다. • 그는 열심히 공부했지만 그 시험에 떨어졌다. • 비록 매우 춥긴 했지만 그는 외투를 입지 않았다.)

09 ⓐ I can ~ 문장을 이끌 때는 in order that 또는 so that을 쓴다. ⓑ 시제가 과거이므로 조동사도 과거로 일치시킨다.

10 시간의 부사절에서는 현재 시제가 미래를 대신하므로 will을 지우고 comes로 쓰면 된다.

11 so that + 주어 + can ~: ~하기 위해 / for me는 to부정사의 의미상 주어로, that절 이하에서는 I로 바꿀 수 있다.

12 '~하지만'이란 뜻의 등위 접속사 대신 쓸 수 있는, '그 사실에 비해서'라는 뜻의 단어는 while이다.

13 too + 형용사 + to + 동사원형 = so + 형용사 + that + 주어 + can't: 너무 ~해서 …할 수 없다

Review Test
p. 132

01 ① 02 ②
03 ① ④ ⑤ 04 ⑤
05 ⑤ 06 ①
07 ③

08 Not only she but also you are attractive.

09 (1) finishes (2) am

10 As

11 ⓐ will rise → rises ⓑ will come → comes

12 (1) whether 또는 if (2) that

13 Bob was so kind to me that it was hard to say goodbye.

14 so that you may survive

15 Since she studied very hard, she got good grades on her tests. / Although she studied very hard, she didn't get good grades on her tests. / Although she took a taxi, she was late for school. / Since she took a taxi, she wasn't late for school. 등

16 ⑤

17 saying no will be better not only for you but also for your friends

≫ 해설

01 ⓐ both A and B에는 복수 동사를 쓴다. (is → are) ⓑ either A or B는 B에 수를 일치시킨다. (knows → know)

02 • '네가 나를 도와줄 수 있는지'라는 의미가 되어야 하므로 if가 알맞다.
• neither A nor B: A와 B 둘 다 아닌
• either A or B: A와 B 둘 중 하나

03 though = although = even though: 비록 ~일지라도 (despite 와 in spite of 뒤에는 '주어+동사'가 올 수 없다.)

04 첫 번째 문장에는 while 또는 when이, 두 번째 문장에는 unless 또는 until이 적절하다.

05 ⑤에서 while은 '반면에'라는 뜻으로 역접의 의미를 지닌다. 주어진 문장과 나머지의 while은 '~하는 동안에, ~하면서, ~할 때'라는 뜻의 시간의 접속사이다. (집에서 Steve는 음악을 들으면서 숙제를 한다. ① 철이 뜨거울 때 때려라. ② 나는 피아노를 치는 동안에, 너는 따라서 노래할 수 있어. ③ 내가 멀리 있을 때, 내 배낭을 봐줘. ④ Leo는 아침을 먹으면서 신문을 읽는다. ⑤ 그녀의 남동생[오빠]은 좋아하지 않지만 그녀는 컴퓨터 게임을 좋아한다.)

06 명사 the fact를 이끌어주는 양보의 전치사 Despite 또는 In spite of가 알맞다. (그녀가 정직하다는 사실에도 불구하고 아무도 그녀를 믿지 않는다. 그건 상당히 슬픈 일이다.)

07 너무 바빠서 함께 할 수 없다는 내용이므로 「so+형용사+that+주어+can't+동사원형」(너무 ~해서 …할 수 없다) 구문을 쓰면 된다.

08 not only A but also B(A뿐 아니라 B도)는 B에 동사를 일치시킨다. 동사가 are이므로 B 자리에는 you가 와야 한다.

09 (1) 시간 부사절에서는 미래를 표현할 때 동사의 현재형을 쓴다.
(2) neither A nor B는 B에 동사를 일치시킨다.

10 첫 번째와 두 번째는 '~하기 때문에'의 뜻이고, 세 번째는 '~하면서, ~할 때'의 뜻이다. 이러한 뜻을 모두 갖는 접속사는 as이다.

11 시간과 조건의 부사절에서는 현재 시제가 미래를 대신한다.

12 (1) '~인지 아닌지'는 whether[if] ~ or not을 쓰므로 whether[if]가 알맞다. (나는 민수에게 그가 나를 좋아하는지 아닌지 물어볼 것이다.)
(2) 명사절을 이끄는 접속사 that이 알맞다. (내 생각은 우리가 오늘 저녁에 외식을 하는 것이다.)

13 「so+형용사/부사+that+주어+동사」 (너무 ~해서 …하다) 구문을 이용해 한 문장으로 쓸 수 있다.

14 in order to+동사원형 = so that+주어+may[can]: '~하기 위해' (다음 라운드로 살아남기 위해서는 너의 태도를 바꿔라.)

15 주어진 4개의 접속사 중 [보기]에 사용된 as를 제외한 3개를 이용해

어법에 맞는 문장을 만들면 된다. ([보기] 그녀는 매우 아팠기 때문에, 학교에 갈 수 없었다. [모범답안] 그녀는 열심히 공부했기 때문에 시험에서 좋은 점수를 받았다. / 그녀는 열심히 공부했지만 시험에서 좋은 점수를 받지 못했다. / 그녀는 택시를 탔지만 학교에 늦었다. / 그녀는 택시를 탔기 때문에 학교에 늦지 않았다. 등)

16 문맥상 '그들이 너의 진정한 친구들이라면 너는 이해받을 것이다'이므로 Unless가 아닌 If가 적절하다.

17 주어는 '아니라고 말하는 것'(saying no)이고 동사 will be가 온 후 '~을 위해' 전치사 for를 쓴 후 'A뿐만 아니라 B도' 의미인 not only ~ but also... 구문을 이용하여 but을 추가하면 된다.

[17~18]

> 사람들은 승낙이 항상 옳은 답은 아니라고 말한다. 이것은 또한 우정에도 적용된다. 만약 네가 항상 승낙한다면, 너는 너의 개인의 삶을 희생해야 하기 때문에 너의 우정은 위험에 처할 수도 있다. 너의 시간 중 일부는 너의 친구들을 위해 어떤 것들을 하는데 소비될 것이다. 네가 그럴 필요가 있을 때, 너의 친구들에게 아니라고 말하는 것을 두려워 말아라. 아니라고 말하고 당분간 불편한 것이 낫다. 네가 알겠다고 말하고 그것을 나중에 후회하기보다는 이번에 그것을 못하는 이유를 설명해라. 그들이 너의 진정한 친구들이라면 너는 이해받을 것이다. 결국 <u>아니라고 말하는 것은 너뿐만 아니라 너의 친구들을 위해서도 더 좋을 것이다.</u>

• 어휘 • apply to ~에 적용되다 | in danger 위험에 처한 | sacrifice 희생하다 | personal 개인의 | uncomfortable 불편한 | explain 설명하다 | rather than ~하기보다 | regret 후회하다 | in the end 결국

CHAPTER 11
가정법

UNIT 22 가정법 과거, 가정법 과거완료

1) 과거	2) 과거
3) 동사원형	4) had
5) p.p.	6) 과거
7) have	8) p.p.
9) 만일 ~라면, …일 텐데.	
10) 만일 ~였다면, …였을 텐데.	
11) 현재	12) 과거
13) were	14) were
15) but	16) without
15) but	16) without
17) had	18) been
19) had	20) but
21) without	

Level 1 Test
p. 136

A 1 would go   2 were 또는 was
   3 couldn't have booked

B 1 don't know / I'm not
   2 weren't[wasn't] / could get
   3 would have had / hadn't rained

C 1 were[was] / would be
   2 had been / would have gone
   3 would have been / hadn't come
   4 But for

Level 2 Test
p. 137

01 ④   02 ⑤
03 ③   04 ⑤
05 What would you do if you were me?
06 had gone / would have been[become]
07 am not / won't try on
08 had been more thoughtful

≫ 해설
01 가정법 과거 문장으로 주절에는 '조동사의 과거형+동사원형'이 와야 하고 내용상 ④가 적절하다.
02 주절에 yesterday가 나온 것으로 보아 과거의 상황이므로 가정법 과거완료가 와야 한다.
03 주어진 문장은 가정법 과거완료이며, As you didn't ask me, I didn't help you.로 바꿔 쓸 수 있다.
04 실현 불가능하거나 현재 사실의 반대 상황을 가정하므로 am을 were[was]로 써야 한다.
05 현재 사실의 반대를 가정하므로 가정법 과거의 형식에 맞게 쓰면 된다.
06 과거 사실의 반대를 가정하므로 if절에는 had+p.p.를 쓰고, 주절에는 would have+p.p. 형식으로 쓰면 된다.
07 가정법 과거(긍정)는 「As+주어+직설법 현재(부정)」로 전환할 수 있다.
08 should have+p.p.는 '~했어야 했는데 하지 않았다'의 의미로 과거의 사실을 후회하는 표현이다. 따라서 If절에는 가정법 과거완료가 들어가야 한다.

Level 3 Test
p. 138

01 ① ③   02 ④
03 ①   04 ② ⑤
05 ③   06 ③
07 ⑤   08 ③
09 If we had had more time, we would have gone to Central Park.
10 If there were[was] no Heaven / would there be no Hell
11 reserved → had reserved / would have → would have had
12 (A) make the same mistake again and again
    (B) If you listened carefully

≫ 해설
01 가정법 과거는 직설법 현재로 전환할 수 있으며 긍정은 부정, 부정은 긍정으로 바꾼다.

02 If it were not for ~는 '~이 없다면'이라는 표현으로, If it were not for water, nothing could live.로 재배열할 수 있다.
03 가정법 과거완료 문장으로, 직설법 과거 As Ella ate too much crab, she didn't enjoy the lobster.로 전환할 수 있다.
04 「But for[Without] ~, 가정법 과거」는 If it were not for ~ 또는 Were it not for ~로 전환한다.
05 If it had not been for ~ = Had it not been for ~ = Without ~ = But for ~로 전환할 수 있으며, 과거 사실에 대한 가정으로 주절에는 가정법 과거완료 형태가 와야 한다.
06 ⓑ 주절이 가정법 과거완료이므로 Had it not been for the rope로 써야 한다.
07 가정법 과거완료 주절이므로 would not have been으로 써야 한다. ④의 had had는 뒤의 had가 본동사로 쓰인 것으로 올바른 표현이다.
08 ③ Would it be로 보아 가정법 과거임을 알 수 있다. 따라서 bring은 brought이 되어야 한다. (→ Would it be okay if I brought a friend?) ① I wouldn't worry if I were you. ② Without air, nothing could live. ④ But for him, we would lose everything. ⑤ He would have more money if he didn't buy the clothes.
09 과거를 가정하는 상황으로 가정법 과거완료 구문을 이용한다.
10 현재에 대한 가정으로 가정법 과거를 사용하여 영작한다.
11 과거 사실에 대한 가정으로 가정법 과거완료를 사용해야 한다.
12 첫 번째 문장은 현재 사실이므로 현재 시제로 쓰고, 두 번째 문장은 현재 사실에 대한 가정이므로 가정법 과거 형태가 와야 한다.

UNIT 23   I wish 가정법, as if 가정법

1) 과거   2) had
3) p.p.   4) ~라면 좋을 텐데
5) 현재   6) ~였다면 좋을 텐데
7) 과거   8) 현재
9) 과거   10) 과거
11) had   12) p.p.
13) 마치 ~인 것처럼   14) 현재
15) 마치 ~였던 것처럼   16) 과거
17) 현재   18) 과거

Level 1 Test
p. 140

A 1 hadn't moved   2 had been
   3 were 또는 was

B 1 hadn't[had not] bought   2 had read

C 1 could understand   2 didn't live
   3 is / were[was]   4 talked / had witnessed

Level 2 Test
p. 141

01 ③   02 ③
03 ⑤   04 ④
05 (that) I didn't complete the course

06 I wish you cared more about me.
07 ⓐ met → had met
08 She behaves as if she were a successful businesswoman.

》》》해설

01 I wish 가정법 과거는 현재 사실에 대한 유감을 표현할 때 사용하므로 ③이 맞다.

02 I'm sorry 직설법 과거(부정)는 I wish 가정법 과거완료(긍정)로 전환할 수 있다.

03 현재 사실과 반대인 상황을 가정할 때는 as if[though] 가정법 과거를 쓴다.

04 as if 가정법 과거완료(긍정)는 In fact 직설법 과거(부정)로 전환할 수 있다.

05 I wish 가정법 과거완료(긍정)는 I am sorry 직설법 과거(부정)로 전환할 수 있다.

06 현재 사실과 반대되는 소망을 나타내는 I wish 가정법 과거를 쓴다.

07 과거 사실과 반대되는 가정이므로 as if[though] 가정법 과거완료로 써야 한다.

08 현재 사실과 반대의 상황을 가정하므로 as if 가정법 과거 구문을 사용해야 하며, 진행형을 사용하지 말라고 했으므로 behaves로 쓴다.

Level 3 Test

01 ④   02 ④
03 ③   04 ④
05 ⑤   06 ③
07 ④   08 ⑤
09 ④
10 (A) wish (B) past (C) have (D) had
11 were → had been / can't → couldn't
12 you had seen the fireworks
13 Think as though you were in my place.
14 ⓐ were → had been

》》》해설

01 과거의 사실에 대한 유감을 표현하므로 I wish I hadn't eaten too much last night.로 써야 한다.

02 I wish that Sue had been on my side back then.으로 영작할 수 있다. that이 주어졌으므로 써야 함에 유의한다.

03 ⓐ am → were[was] ⓓ has → had

04 과거의 일에 대한 유감을 나타내므로 I wish 가정법 과거완료로 써야 한다. had had에서 앞의 had는 조동사이고 뒤의 had는 본동사이다.

05 주절이 과거이고 그 전의 일을 가정하므로 as if[though] 가정법 과거완료로 써야 한다.

06 과거의 일에 대한 유감을 표현하므로 I wish (that) my dog had been able to speak (back) then.으로 영작할 수 있다.

07 '그녀는 나에게 모든 것을 알았던 것처럼 말했다'는 as if 가정법 과거완료 표현(과거 사실의 반대)이므로 직설법 과거(긍정 → 부정)로 전환할 수 있다.

08 현재 주위에 아무도 없는데 Dave가 누군가와 말하는 것처럼 보이므로 as if[though] 가정법 과거(긍정)로 써야 한다.

09 ④ I wish (that) 구문에는 가정법 문형을 쓰므로 pass를 passed 또는 had passed로 써야 한다. (→ I wish that you (had) passed

the exams.) ① I wish I had not done that. ② I wish I were happier. ③ I wish it had never happened. ⑤ I wish that you could speak Spanish.

10 과거 사실에 대한 유감을 표현하므로 (A) wish는 (B) past가, 이미 일어나 현재까지 영향을 미치는 상황으로 현재완료형의 (C) have가, 과거에 일어난 일을 wish(바라고) 있으므로 과거완료 형태의 (D) had가 적절하다.

11 주절이 과거이고 과거 사실에 대한 가정이므로 종속절에는 과거완료가 와야 하고, but 이하는 시제 일치에 맞도록 과거형이 와야 한다.

12 주어진 문장은 가정법 과거완료로 과거 사실에 대한 가정을 나타내므로 I wish 가정법 과거완료로 전환한다.

13 현재 사실의 반대를 가정하고 있으므로 as though 가정법 과거로 쓴다.

14 아버지가 젊었을 때는 과거이므로 as if 가정법 과거완료로 써야 한다.

Review Test

01 ⑤   02 ④
03 ②   04 ③
05 ④   06 ②
07 ④⑤   08 ②
09 ③
10 Had it not been for the life jacket
11 I would visit Nine Miles[Rick's Café, Dunn's River Falls] if I were in Jamaica now.
12 had seen / would have said / didn't see
13 (1) had / could give
   (2) don't have / can't give
14 if you had not put
15 (that) our city had succeeded
16 혜림: 직설법 과거
   규진: I wish (that) I hadn't deleted your folder.
17 ⓐ didn't see → hadn't seen
18 ①⑤
19 depressed / would help

》》》해설

01 과거 사실에 대한 가정으로 if it had not been for의 형태가 와야 한다.

02 가정법 과거완료는 if절에 had+p.p.가 온다.

03 ⓐ were → had been (또는 have eaten → eat) ⓒ would marry → would have married ⓕ would be lost → would have been lost

04 과거 사실에 대한 유감을 표현하므로 I wish 가정법 과거완료가 적절하다.

05 • 주절이 'would+동사원형'이므로 가정법 과거가 알맞다.
   • If절에 had+p.p.로 보아 가정법 과거완료 형태가 와야 한다.

06 I wish 가정법 과거 또는 과거완료를 쓰는데, 주어진 단어 중에 가정법 과거 동사(had)가 하나만 있으므로 ②가 적절하다.

07 ④ Were it not for → Had it not been for (또는 have died → die) ⑤ have → have had (또는 had 삭제)

08 현재 상황에 대한 가정으로 as if[though] 가정법 과거를 사용하여 He treats me as if[though] I were[was] a child[kid].로 영작할 수 있다.

09 현재 사실에 대한 가정으로 as if 가정법 과거로 쓰며, 빈칸에는 차례대로 as, if[though], had, is, enough가 들어간다.

10 주절이 가정법 과거완료인 것으로 보아 If it had not been for the life jacket인데, 8단어로 써야 하므로 Had it not been for ~ 구문으로 쓰면 된다.

11 질문이 가정법 과거이므로 대답도 가정법 과거 형식에 맞게 하면 된다.

12 과거 사실에 대한 가정으로 If절에는 가정법 과거완료가 오며, But 다음에는 직설법 과거가 와야 한다.

13 현재 사실에 대한 가정으로 첫 번째 문장은 가정법 과거의 긍정으로, 두 번째 문장은 직설법 현재의 부정으로 쓰면 된다.

14 가정법 과거완료의 if절은 「if+주어+had (not)+p.p.」이다.

15 과거에 이루지 못한 일에 대한 소망의 표현은 I wish 가정법 과거완료로 나타내며, 직설법이 부정이면 긍정으로 써야 한다.

16 I wish 가정법 과거완료(부정)는 과거 사실에 대한 유감을 표현하며, I'm sorry 직설법 과거(긍정)로 바꿀 수 있다.

17 내용상 과거의 일을 가정해야 하므로 as if 가정법 과거완료로 써야 한다.

18 ⓐ 말하는 순간의 반대의 가정을 하고 있으므로 가정법 과거 구문이 적절하다. 따라서 had felt를 felt로 고쳐야 한다. ⓔ 주어는 helping이므로 단수 동사인 is로 고쳐야 한다.

19 '당신이 우울하다면, 다른 사람들을 돕는 것은 당신을 그 우울증에서 나오도록 도울 것이다'가 글의 주된 내용으로 가정법 과거 문형에 맞게 빈칸을 완성하면 된다.

[18~19]

> Karl Menninger는 미국의 정신과 의사였다. 그는 한때 의료 보건에 대한 강의를 하며 청중들의 질문에 답한 적이 있다. 누군가 "만약 어떤 사람이 우울하다면 그 사람에게 어떻게 하라고 충고하시겠습니까?"라고 물었다. 대부분의 사람들은 그가 "당장 정신과 의사를 만나러 가세요."라고 말할 것이라고 생각했지만, 그는 그러지 않았다. 놀랍게도 Menninger 박사는 "집을 문단속하고, 철길을 건너고, 도움이 필요한 사람을 찾아 그 사람을 도우세요. 다른 사람의 걱정에 집중하는 것은 자신의 것을 잊는 데 도움이 됩니다."고 대답했다. Menninger 박사는 남을 돕는 것이 자신을 돕는 최선의 방법이라고 굳게 믿었다.

• 어휘 • lecture 강의 | medical health 의료 보건 | audience 청중 | depressed 우울한 | immediately 즉시 | to one's surprise 놀랍게도 | reply 대답하다 | focus on ~에 집중하다

CHAPTER 12
특수 구문

UNIT 24 강조, 생략

1) do	2) did	3) very
4) very	5) that	6) that[who]
7) 반복	8) appear	9) 목적
10) which[that]	11) 주	12) be
13) which[that] was		14) 주어
15) be	16) I was	17) 대
18) save	19) 강조	20) himself

Level 1 Test
p. 148

A 1 did deliver   2 It was Andy that[who]
   3 It was 30 minutes ago that

B 1 가주어-진주어 구문   2 강조 구문
   3 강조 구문   4 가주어-진주어 구문
   5 가주어-진주어 구문

Level 2 Test
p. 149

01 ①   02 ④
03 ③   04 ③
05 was Columbus that[who]
06 very
07 did stretch
08 ⓐ When is driven → When driven 또는 When it is driven
09 Perhaps love is like the ocean which[that] is full of conflict.

》》 해설

01 ①은 '하다'라는 뜻의 일반동사이고, [보기]와 나머지는 모두 본동사를 강조하는 조동사이다. (경제학자들은 감소하는 출생률에 대해 정말 걱정한다.)

02 ④ It is/was ~ that 강조 구문으로 동사는 강조할 수 없다. 동사는 조동사 do를 써서 강조한다. ② ③ that 대신 관계부사 when/where를 쓸 수 있다.

03 강조 구문으로 바꾸면 It was a peanut that I ate on Thursday. 가 된다. what은 선행사가 포함된 관계대명사로 강조 구문에 쓰일 수 없다.

04 목적격 관계대명사는 생략할 수 있다.

05 It is/was ~ that 강조 구문에서 It is/was와 that 사이에 강조하고자 하는 말을 넣는다. 사람일 때는 that 대신 who도 쓸 수 있다.

06 명사를 강조할 때는 명사 앞에 very를 쓴다. (그를 만날 생각만 해도 나는 행복해진다.)

07 강조의 do로 수·인칭 시제 변환을 하고, 그 뒤에 동사원형을 쓴다. (1800년대에 대초원은 눈이 볼 수 있는 만큼 멀리 뻗어 있었다.)

08 ⓐ 종속절에서 반복되는 '주어+be동사'는 생략 가능하다. 하지만 주어나 be동사 둘 중 하나만 생략할 수는 없다.

09 '주격 관계대명사+be동사'는 생략할 수 있다.

Level 3 Test
p. 150

01 ① ② ③　　　　　　　　02 ①
03 ⑤　　　　　　　　　　04 ⑤
05 ⑤　　　　　　　　　　06 ①
07 ②　　　　　　　　　　08 ④
09 I do believe you are teasing me
10 When told what to do, people do it.
11 It was / that
12 ⓐ When was it that you last visited mom?
13 but I forgot to

》》 해설

01 It is/was ~ that 사이에 강조하고자 하는 말을 넣고, '바로 ~이다' 로 해석한다. 강조하는 말이 사람이면 that 대신에 who를, 장소이면 where를, 시간이면 when을 쓸 수 있다.

02 ⓐ와 ⓔ는 강조적 용법이고, 나머지는 목적어로 쓰인 재귀적 용법이다.

03 ⑤의 do는 일반동사를 받는 대동사이고, 나머지는 강조의 do이다.

04 주어진 문장과 ⑤의 do는 강조의 조동사이다. 나머지는 의문문과 부정문에 사용된 조동사이다.

05 It ~ that 사이에 강조하는 because of jealousy를 넣어 표현해야 알맞다. (A: Jenny가 계속 나를 차갑게 대해. B: 그 애가 그러는 건 질투심 때문이야. 그 애는 네가 대회에서 우승한 것을 질투해.)

06 ①은 It이 가주어이고 that 이하가 진주어인 가주어-진주어 구문이다. 나머지는 모두 It~ that 강조 구문이다.

07 ① 반복되는 주어 ③ 대동사 ④ 주격 관계대명사+be동사 ⑤ 목적격 관계대명사는 생략할 수 있다. ② 재귀적 용법으로 사용된 재귀대명사는 생략할 수 없다.

08 ④ 동사 강조 do는 일반동사일 때 사용한다. 따라서 does를 없애고 be를 is로 써야 한다. (→ She thinks that he is wrong.) ① We did see some huge waves. ② Do not sit down on the bench. ③ You do look pretty in that dress. ⑤ I did find a good online shopping site.

09 동사를 강조하기 위해서 do가 필요하고 be는 주어가 you이므로 are 로 고치면 된다.

10 When people are told what to do, people do it.에서 종속절과 주절의 주어가 같으므로 people are가 생략된 형태이다.

11 It is/was ~ that 강조 구문을 이용한다. 강조하고자 하는 말을 It is/was와 that 사이에 놓고, '바로 ~이다'로 해석한다. (어린 Teresa 수녀에게 커다란 영향을 미친 것은 바로 그녀 가족의 관대함과 가난한 사람들에 대한 관심이었다.)

12 when을 강조하는 말로 의문문을 만들 때 when은 문장 앞으로 가고 의문문의 어순대로 'be동사+주어'(was it)의 순서로 쓴다.

13 대부정사 to를 쓰고 close를 생략해야 4단어로 문장을 완성할 수 있다.

1) 부사(구)　　2) 동사　　　　3) 주어
4) 부사(구)　　5) 주어　　　　6) 동사
7) 부정어(구)　8) be동사　　　9) 주어
10) 부정어(구)　11) 조동사　　12) 주어
13) 조동사　　14) 주어　　　15) So do I
16) 긍정　　　17) 조동사　　18) 주어
19) Neither am I　20) 부정　　21) 동사
22) 주어　　　23) Were I you

Level 1 Test
p. 152

A　1 Not only is she intelligent
　　2 Had he arrived here
　　3 On the stage danced the girls.

B　1 Here comes our commuter bus
　　2 Not a single word did she say
　　3 Hardly does he have　　4 어색한 곳 없음

Level 2 Test
p. 153

01 ①　　　　　　　　　　02 ①
03 ③　　　　　　　　　　04 ② ④
05 so do composers
06 Not only did I meet the actor
07 (A) either　(1) Me neither.　(2) Neither can I.
08 Never have I seen such a fast boy (before).

》》 해설

01 부정어 never를 강조하여 문장 첫머리로 보내면 「부정어(never)+조동사(have)+주어+p.p.」의 어순이 된다. never에 부정의 의미가 있으므로 haven't는 올 수 없다.

02 앞서 말한 것과 같은 상황을 표현할 때는 「So+be동사/조동사+주어」의 형태로 쓴다. 주어가 3인칭 단수(Ian)이므로 be동사는 is를 쓴다. (Jini는 재즈록에 관심을 갖고 있고, Ian 또한 그렇다.)

03 · 앞서 말한 문장에 조동사 can이 있으므로 동의할 때도 조동사 can 을 쓴다.
　· 앞 문장의 동사가 일반동사 lives이므로 3인칭 단수 주어 (Peter)에 맞는 does가 알맞다.
　· 앞의 never 부정문에 대한 동의가 되어야 하므로 neither가 알맞다.

04 ⓐ 장소 부사가 사용된 문장에서 주어가 대명사일 때는 도치하지 않는다. (goes she → she goes) ⓑ 도치된 문장의 순서는 올바르나 a few sheep이 복수(sheep의 복수형은 sheep)이므로 동사는 live 가 알맞다.

05 앞서 말한 것과 같은 상황을 표현할 때는 「So+be동사/조동사+주어」의 형태로 쓴다. 주어가 composers이므로 동사는 do를 쓴다. (작곡가들도 역시 그렇다)

06 부정어가 앞에 나가 주어와 동사가 도치될 때 과거 조동사 did가 나갔으므로 met는 동사원형 meet가 되어야 한다.

07 부정문에 대한 동의는 too 대신 either(또한, 역시)를 쓰고, not either는 neither와 바꿔 쓸 수 있다. Neither가 문장 앞에 나갈 때

는 '조동사+주어'의 순서로 쓴다.

08 현재완료 부정문에서 부정어(never)가 문장 앞에 나갈 때는 「조동사(have)+주어(I)+과거분사(seen)」의 순서가 알맞다.

Level 3 Test

p. 154

01 ② ④　　　　　　　　　02 ①
03 ④　　　　　　　　　　04 ⑤
05 ③　　　　　　　　　　06 ④
07 ② ④ ⑤　　　　　　　08 ④
09 Neither have I.
10 (1) can　(2) does　(3) am
11 he had → had he
12 Little did he realize the danger he was facing.
13 Were I rich

≫ 해설

01 ① had는 일반동사의 과거형이므로 대답에서 did를 써야 한다. ③ either → too ⑤ neither → either

02 「so+동사+주어」의 형태로 긍정의 진술을 부각시켜 '~또한 그러하다'의 뜻으로 쓴다.

03 앞의 상황과 같음을 나타낼 때는 「so+동사+주어」의 표현을 쓴다. ① do → does로 ② has I → do I ③ does → did ⑤ do → does

04 ⑤ 타동사가 나오면 도치할 수 없다. ① → There goes my weekend. ② did he stand → he stood ③ answered → answer ④ do I have → have I

05 부정어 never를 강조하여 문장 첫머리로 보내면 「부정어(never)+조동사(had)+주어+과거분사」의 어순이 된다. (나는 실제로 해보기 전에 스카이다이빙의 매력을 절대 이해 못했다.)

06 ④에서는 장소를 나타내는 there로 쓰였다. 나머지는 there가 유도 부사로 쓰여 주어와 동사가 도치되었다.

07 ⓐ 현재완료 문장이 도치될 때는 has/have가 주어 앞으로 간다.

08 ④ 부정어 도치 문장으로 본동사가 필요한데 visiting이 왔다. (→ Never will I visit this restaurant again.) ① There she goes again. ② There were no clouds in the sky. ③ Were I you, I would not agree. ⑤ Hardly is she aware of her performance.

09 「neither+동사+주어」는 '~도 또한 그렇지 않다'는 의미로 부정문에 대한 동의를 나타낸다. 시제가 현재완료이므로 조동사 have를 사용한다.

10 앞서 말한 것과 같은 상황을 표현할 때는 「So+be동사/조동사+주어」의 형태로 쓴다. (1)은 똑같이 can을 쓰고, (2)는 Peter가 3인칭 단수이므로 does를 쓰고, (3)은 주어가 I이므로 be동사 am이 알맞다.

11 부정어를 강조하여 문장 첫머리로 보내면 「부정어(no sooner)+조동사(had)+주어+과거분사」의 어순이 된다. (문을 열고 들어가자마자 그는 전화가 울리는 것을 들었다.)

12 부정어를 첫 단어로 써야 하므로 도치 구문으로 Little did he realize the danger로 시작하고, 마지막 단어를 현재분사로 써야 하므로 과거 진행형 he was facing으로 쓰고, 9단어로 써야 하므로 목적격 관계대명사를 사용하지 않으면 된다.

13 가정법 과거가 현재 사실의 반대이므로 과거 동사를 써야 하고, If I were rich에서 If가 생략되고 나면 주어와 동사를 도치시켜 Were I rich가 되어야 한다.

Review Test

p. 156

01 ①　　　　　　　　　　02 ⑤
03 ⑤　　　　　　　　　　04 ⑤
05 ④　　　　　　　　　　06 ② ③ ④
07 ③　　　　　　　　　　08 ②
09 ① ③
10 It was / that[who]
11 so does Robert
12 does
13 very
14 the largest city in Korea
15 Were I you, I wouldn't do that.
16 On the top of the hill stands an old castle.
17 Never have I thought that he told a lie.
18 ② ④ ⑤
19 could they move at all

≫ 해설

01 ①은 가주어-진주어 구문이고, 나머지는 It is/was ~ that 강조 구문이다.

02 ⓐ 장소 도치에는 did가 필요 없이 lived가 바로 와야 한다. (→ Around the building lived some homeless people.) ⓑ 조동사 does가 앞으로 나갔으므로 동사원형 help가 되어야 한다.

03 주어진 문장의 do는 강조의 조동사이다. ①과 ③은 의문문에 쓰이는 조동사, ②와 ④는 본동사, ⑤는 강조의 조동사이다. (그들은 정말 더 성숙해진다.)

04 「while+주어+be ~, 주어 …」에서 주어가 서로 같을 때 '주어+be동사' 생략이 가능하므로 ⑤는 talking이 되어야 한다. ③은 주어가 서로 달라서 그대로 쓴 경우이다.

05 조동사 did를 써서 동사를 강조하거나, 주어, 목적어, 부사(구)를 It was ~ that 사이에 넣는다. ① ⑤ He did break his right leg yesterday. ② It was he that broke his right leg yesterday. ③ It was yesterday that he broke his right leg.

06 장소 부사구(at the airport)를 강조하는 구문으로 가주어-진주어 구문이 아니다. that을 관계부사 where로 바꿔 쓸 수 있다.

07 동격 구문으로 '주격 관계대명사+be동사'를 생략할 수 있다.

08 ② 앞서 말한 것과 같은 상황을 표현할 때는 「so+be동사/조동사+주어」의 형태로 쓴다. 주어가 Ann이므로 동사는 has를 쓴다.

09 ⓑ 현재완료 문장에서 도치가 일어날 때 has/have가 주어 앞으로 간다. (→ Never has she eaten a taco before.)

10 It is ~ that[who] 강조 구문이다. 시제가 과거이므로 was를 써야 한다.

11 앞서 말한 것과 같은 상황을 표현할 때는 「so+be동사/조동사+주어」의 형태로 쓴다. Robert가 3인칭 단수이므로 조동사는 does를 쓴다. ([보기] 나는 키가 크고 내 여동생도 크다. → 나는 키가 크고 내 여동생도 그렇다. [문제] Julia는 시드니에 살고 Robert도 시드니에 산다. → Julia는 시드니에 살고 Robert도 그렇다.)

12 강조의 do를 써야 하는데 주어가 3인칭 단수이며 시제가 현재이므로 does를 쓴다.

13 명사를 강조할 때는 명사 앞에 very를 쓴다. (대륙 이동이란 바로 대륙들이 지구의 표면 위를 움직이는 것이다.)

14 콤마 뒤에 있는 which is를 없애면 두 개의 명사(구)가 나란히 연결되는 동격 구문이 된다. (한국에서 가장 큰 도시인 서울에는 고궁이 여러 개 있다.)

15 가정법에서 If가 생략되고 나면 도치가 일어나 '동사＋주어'의 어순이 된다.

16 장소 부사구 on the top of the hill을 문장 앞으로 보내고 '동사＋주어'의 순서로 적는다.

17 부정어(never)가 문장 앞으로 가면서 '조동사＋주어＋동사원형」의 어순이 된다. 주절은 '한 번도 ～한 적 없다'는 경험의 용법으로 현재완료를 쓰고, that절은 과거 사실에 대한 내용이므로 과거로 쓴다.

18 ⓑ stay는 형용사를 보어로 취하므로 close로 바르게 고쳤다. closely는 '가까이, 면밀히'라는 부사이다. ⓓ 부사구 Out of the shadows가 문장 맨 앞으로 이동하여 주어와 동사가 도치된 구문이다. 따라서 flying을 flew로 바르게 고쳤다. ⓔ disappear는 자동사로 수동태로 표현할 수 없으므로 바르게 고쳤다.

19 부정어구가 문장 맨 앞으로 이동하면 의문문 어순이 되므로 Hardly could they move at all.로 쓰면 된다.

[18~19]

> Lou는 심호흡을 했다. 그는 차갑고 어두운 동굴 안으로 걸어 들어가기 시작했다. 그 안에는 모든 것이 조용했다. 여기저기에 뼈가 바닥 위에 놓여 있었다. "우리는 더 깊이 들어가야 해."라고 Carmen이 말했다. "알아."라고 Lou가 말했다. "하지만 내 뒤에 바짝 머물러. 한 마디도 하지마." 그들은 동굴 속으로 더 깊이 걸어갔다. 곧 그들은 X 표시가 있는 바위에 다다랐다. 공기가 다르게 느껴졌다. 갑자기 이상한 울음이 어디선지 모르게 그들의 귀에 다가왔다. 그늘 밖으로 검은 형체가 날아갔다. 그것은 그들 옆을 빠르게 지나갔고 그림자 속으로 사라졌다. <u>그들은 거의 조금도 움직일 수가 없었다.</u>

• 어휘 • breath 호흡, 숨 | cave 동굴 | bone 뼈 | before long 곧 | out of nowhere 어디선지 모르게 | shadow 그림자 | figure 형체, 상 | not ～ at all 조금도 ～ 않다

MEMO

MEMO

내신 공략 중학영문법 3 문제풀이책